Zuzanna Dziuban (ed.)
The »Spectral Turn«

Memory Cultures | Volume 6

The series is edited by Aleida Assmann.

Zuzanna Dziuban (PhD) is a postdoctoral researcher at the University of Amsterdam and Freie University of Berlin. Her research focus is on memory studies, dead body studies, and the afterlives of the Holocaust.

ZUZANNA DZIUBAN (ED.)
The »Spectral Turn«
Jewish Ghosts in the Polish Post-Holocaust Imaginaire

[transcript]

Bibliographic information published by the Deutsche Nationalbibliothek
The Deutsche Nationalbibliothek lists this publication in the Deutsche Nationalbibliografie; detailed bibliographic data are available in the Internet at http://dnb.d-nb.de

© 2019 transcript Verlag, Bielefeld

All rights reserved. No part of this book may be reprinted or reproduced or utilized in any form or by any electronic, mechanical, or other means, now known or hereafter invented, including photocopying and recording, or in any information storage or retrieval system, without permission in writing from the publisher.

Cover concept: Kordula Röckenhaus, Bielefeld
Printed by Majuskel Medienproduktion GmbH, Wetzlar
Print-ISBN 978-3-8376-3629-1
PDF-ISBN 978-3-8394-3629-5
https://doi.org/10.14361/9783839436295

Content

Introduction: Haunting in the Land of the Untraumatized
Zuzanna Dziuban | 7

On Behalf of the Dead: Mediumistic Writing on the Holocaust in Polish Literature
Alina Molisak | 49

Scratch, Groove, the Imprint of (Non)presence: On the Spectrologies of the Holocaust
Aleksandra Ubertowska | 65

Sites That Haunt: Affects and Non-Sites of Memory
Roma Sendyka | 85

Healing by Haunting: On Jewish Ghosts, Symbolic Exorcism and Traumatic Surrealism
Magdalena Waligórska | 107

Of Ghosts' (In)ability to Haunt: ›Polish Dybbuks‹
Zuzanna Dziuban | 131

Not Your House, not Your Flat: Jewish Ghosts in Poland and the Stolen Jewish Properties
Konrad Matyjaszek | 185

Philosemitic Violence
Elżbieta Janicka and Tomasz Żukowski | 209

Authors | 263

Introduction: Haunting in the Land of the Untraumatized

ZUZANNA DZIUBAN

THE SUBSTANCE OF GHOSTS

Ghosts are made of ectoplasm; the ectoplasm is made of tears and coal dust. At least, so proclaims the narrator of Joanna Bator's novel *Dark, Almost Night* [*Ciemno, prawie noc*, 2012]. And ghosts permeate the Polish post-industrial city of Wałbrzych, where the novel's protagonist, Alicja Tabor, returns after a long voluntary exile. She engages with the town's violent present, defined by murder, sexual abuse, and religious and political fanaticism – and with its violent past, burdened with the World War, ethnic violence, the Holocaust, and the postwar redrawing of borders between Poland and Germany. Alicja encounters the ghosts of her long-dead relatives, of famous historical figures, of former German inhabitants of the town, as well as »Jewish ghosts« of victims of the Nazi concentration camps. The latter, red-eyed and almost invisible, emerge from forests and knock on the windows of Polish houses; the protagonist feeds them crumbs of bread strewn on a windowsill. The substance of ghosts populating Bator's book seems to render them homogeneous, yet they are anything but. Some are desired, some are seen as threatening, and others, such as the Jewish ghosts, remain virtually unsensed and unseen, relying on pity and care extended to them by the living. The ghosts' historical provenance, but even more so their ethnic, national, and religious differences, is what differentiates them from one another. The ›Jewishness‹ of Jewish ghosts establishes them as distinct from the other ghosts haunting Alicja, her former hometown, and, perhaps, Poland in its entirety.

In *Dark, Almost Night*, the Jewish ghosts play a marginal, if not ornamental, part. They act as lingering reminders of Nazi wartime crimes and the postwar resettlement of various minority groups – merely another layer of the town's troubled and troubling history. Even more, the ghosts of Holocaust victims are there to testify to Alicja's exceptional sensitivity, her ability to respond affectively and with altruistic care to a presence nobody else is able or willing to observe. Indeed, this care cuts against the grain of dominant sentiments shared by Wałbrzych residents, meticulously documented in the novel: their nationalism, xenophobia, persistent and omnipresent antisemitism, and fixation on Polish martyrdom and victimhood, and, thus, their exclusive attention to the »Polish ghost«. And Polish ghosts are in abundance, there are many to choose from; they are the dead conjured up by Polish Romantic poets, and the dead of more recent violent conflicts, of the Second World War, of the 1940 Katyń massacre, and of the failed Warsaw Uprising of 1944. These ghosts are entrenched in Poland's culture and imagination, their position secured by tradition and identity work structured around attentiveness to one's own dead.[1] To attend to the ghost of the Other is altogether different; a ›truth‹ that Alicja's attitude at once counters and reaffirms.

Alicja is far from alone in her encounters with the Jewish ghosts, however. In fact, such ghosts – in increasing numbers – roam a broad realm of Polish culture, literature, and theory. The figure started to emerge even before 1989, as interest awakened in the Jewish past in Poland, and proliferated after the Polish transition to a market economy and democracy in the 1990s; the past decade has witnessed a boom of narratives – artistic, literary, cinematic – featuring Jewish ghosts in their encounters with Poles, very much

---

1   On the position of ghosts in Polish culture in general, and the Romantic tradition in particular, see, for instance, Janion (2006). For an analysis of the ghosts of those who perished in the 1944 Uprising, see Napiórkowski (2014). The ghosts of Katyń appeared recently in the movie *Smoleńsk* (2016), a politically compromised thriller about the plane crash which in 2010 killed 96 leading Polish politicians, including the then president Lech Kaczynski, on their way to commemorate the seventieth anniversary of the Katyń massacre in Russia. The film casts the accident as a calculated attempt on the life of the Polish president, and aimed at a matyrological interpretation of his death.

alive and contemporary. Often, the ghostly presence structures the entire plot, unlike in *Dark, Almost Night*. This is the case, for instance, in Andrzej Bart's 2008 novel *Fabryka Muchołapek* [The Flytrap Factory], Tadeusz Słobodzianek's drama *Our Class* (2010 [2009]), Sylwia Chutnik's play *Muranooo* (2011), Igor Ostachowicz's novel *Noc Żywych Żydów* [Night of the Living Jews, 2012], and Marcin Wrona's movie *Demon* (2015). These Jewish ghosts are sensed and seen. They possess, fall in love, and tell their stories about ordinary life in prewar Poland – and sometimes about violent death in the Holocaust. In the near-total absence of Jewish communities in post-Holocaust Poland, the Jewish ghosts are gaining ground, becoming the subject of theoretical writing and a part of the cultural imaginaire.[2]

The *»Spectral Turn«: Jewish Ghosts in the Polish Post-Holocaust Imaginaire* is, at once, a demonstration and an interpretive exploration of this phenomenon. The book follows the figure of the Jewish ghost over various moments in recent Polish history and across realms of cultural production, popular imaginings, and theory. Establishing the aesthetic and affective politics of the ghostly as a subject of multiperspective and multidisciplinary inquiry, it asks about the position of Jewish ghosts in shifting cultural attitudes toward the Holocaust and the ›Polish-Jewish past‹ (and present), and about their role, which is as much representational and symbolic as it is political and ethical. As the volume spotlights the growing prominence of Jewish ghosts in Polish popular and academic culture and considers it against the background of present-day memory and identity work, it argues that the substance of ghosts is more dense and complex than tears, coal dust, and ectoplasm. Alicja did not get it right.

This recognition is informed not only by the close readings of Jewish ghosts collected in this volume, but also by other analyses of the »spectral turn« unfolding across geographies and cultures. Already in 2002, Robert Luckhurst addressed such a turn taking place in British literature or, better yet, in the genre of London Gothic. In 2004, in *Spectral America: Phantoms and the National Imaginary*, Jeffrey Weinstock proclaimed its advent in the United States. »Our contemporary moment is a haunted one« (Weinstock

---

2   Imaginaire is considered, after Charles Taylor, as an amorphous repertoire of images, stories, normative notions, and mechanisms of culture that underlie social life and organize experience and »the ways people imagine their social existence, how they fit together with others« (2004: 23).

2004b: 3), he wrote, commenting on a proliferation of ghostly figures and narratives of haunting in literature, cinema, art, and academia. The global and transcultural reach of the spectral turn was established some years later by Maria del Pilar Blanco and Esther Peeren. In *Popular Ghosts: The Haunted Spaces of Everyday Culture* (2010) and *Spectralities Reader: Ghosts and Haunting in Contemporary Cultural Theory* (2013a), they gathered articles evidencing its performative force around the globe as it cuts through scientific imagination, artistic practices, and routines from everyday life. Discarding traditional stances that cast ghosts as supernatural entities, projections of a troubled psyche, or merely signifiers of specific literary or filmic modes or genres, the spectral turn named the ubiquity of dispersed and polyvocal vocabularies of haunting permeating the present day. More important, it (re)established the figure of the ghost as a subject of critical study. Ghosts and haunting were to become influential and inter/transdisciplinary concepts, addressed not merely as (literally) ephemeral psychological or ontological epiphenomena – like the ›ectoplasm‹ floating around at the 19th-century spiritual seance – but *as ghosts* in all their complexity: representational, affective, and political. This is the conceptual trajectory we, too, follow in this volume.

The roots of this approach can be traced back to the publication of Jacques Derrida's *Specters of Marx: The State of Debt, the Work of Mourning and the New International* (1994 [1993]). It was there that Derrida radically reconceptualized the ghost (the specter) as a problem of the humanities, instantiating an important shift in its position in the field of theoretical reflection: from the margins to the center, or from a narrowly conceived generic marker to a theoretical idiom travelling through and between disciplines (Peeren 2014: 9). Suspending the ontological question of whether the ghost exists, Derrida established it as a deconstructive figure, as a figure of otherness and an agent of alterity moving between and destabilizing established dichotomies and ontological certainties. A transitional entity, located between life and death, present and absent, existent and non-existent, visible and invisible, material and immaterial, real and imagined, present and past, the ghost came to destabilize existent metaphysical and epistemological orders, orders of knowledge and power, and all instances of stability, sameness, homogeneity, and the self-same (Wolfreys 2002: 11). But Derrida also constructed the ghost as *real* and thoroughly political. Haunting, he wrote, »belongs to the structure of every hegemony« (1994 [1993]: 37). Intrinsic to social life itself, it rests upon and testifies to hegemony's inherent violence but also to its inherent incompleteness. Thus, ghosts and haunting pertain equally to epistemological and political planes – they speak to and about erasures, exclusions, and invisibilities inherent to every social order, and to the (after)effects of repressive configurations of power.

Following Derrida, and applying his abstract conceptualizations of haunting to a vast array of specific contextual and historical experiences of political/symbolic/economic violence – mostly those articulated through the medium of literature and art – scholars across the humanities and social sciences have reclaimed ghosts as consequential ›objects‹ of intellectual interest and investigation. In the fields of cultural and political theory, sociology, literary criticism, and memory studies, the spectral turn provided conceptual tools for theorizing the aftereffects of violence and repression, and a set of metaphors to expand the analytical scope of studies on the social, political, and cultural processes of exclusion, dispossession, and erasure. The ghosts, a metaphor of multiple valences, have been conceived as figures of displacement, as figurations of dispossessed subjects (Peeren 2014), or as symptoms of the »past gone awry« (Kriss 2013: 25). Focusing on the question of *why* and *how* ghosts operate, most studies have, therefore, not retained strong ties with Derridean readings of the specter in terms of the messianic, the past promise and the (im)possible future, and demanded that it speak and deliver a more or less clear and intelligible message. This is especially the case in the field of memory studies, the main bridgehead and most productive territory of the spectral turn, where, more often than not, the ghosts are of those who have disappeared or perished and, as such, sustain a complex relationship between the past and present, the living and the dead, that requires a slant attuned to the contextual and specific. They speak to and about what ›really‹ happened (and still happens). They are figures of particular (and peculiar) historicity and sociality, like the Jewish ghosts whose haunting of contemporary Poland this volume addresses.

Indeed, responding to the transcultural conviction that »only certain categories of the dead return to torment the living: those who were denied the rite of burial or died an unnatural, abnormal death, were criminals or outcasts, or suffered injustice in their lifetime« (Rand 1994: 167), memory research has entangled the subject of ghosts with the historical, social, and political. Transferred conceptually from the realm of individual to collective memory, ghosts have become thoroughly social (Gordon 2008 [1997]), communal

(Brogan 1998), and public (Bergland 2000), a means to address a broad array of experiences of political violence – colonization, racial and ethnic discrimination, dictatorship, state terror, war, social and cultural exclusion, forced disappearance – allowing their disturbing aftereffects to be traced in contemporary realities (Gordon 2008 [1997]; Assmann 2011, 2014; Brogan 1998; Blazan 2008; Etkind 2013; Schindel 2014; Bergland 2000). Critiquing existing structures of knowledge that remain blind to the continuous, if unobtrusive, agency of the past, the engagement with ghosts has exposed the very notion of linear and progressive history as contingent on, produced within, and sustaining specific relations of power. As the lingering traces of historically situated instances of violence, especially those that operate beneath the surface of received (dominant) narratives of the past, ghosts make visible the processes of erasure, repression, and marginalization that constitute a seemingly shared history. But, within this »unfinished business« model of haunting, they also demand redress: justice, proper burial, memory, ›truth‹, or healing.

And yet, it is precisely the particular historicity and sociality of ghosts that demands that each one be approached in its specificity – an intuition conveyed in Alicja's differentiation between the numerous ghosts haunting her Polish hometown and their varying abilities to threaten or console, to be seen by her and others. Accordingly, we ought to apply existing theoretical and analytical models with caution. Already in his pioneering article on the spectral turn, Luckhurst argues against the all-encompassing dynamics of the turn and the »generalizable economy of haunting« (2002: 534) and calls for attention to be paid to the particularity of ghosts. Similarly, the authors of *Spectralities Reader* (Del Pilar Blanco/Peeren 2013b) propose that spectral readings should be differentiated and multiplied, and that they acknowledge the contextual differences in the backgrounds of the ghosts they fathom so that the spectral turn may retain its explanatory force. Existing theoretical frameworks, they posit, can conceal rather than illuminate the complex reality of ghosts, especially when projected onto other empirical contexts.

There is, after all, an essential difference between ghosts that arrive to solve some unfinished business by telling their stories and those who seek bloody revenge. Reactions to the presence of ghosts can also vary dramatically: some ghosts are feared, others long awaited; some are intentionally summoned, others exorcised or chased away. If the specificity of ghosts demands new theoretical models, so too does the material reality of haunting.

Accounting for the generative loci of ghosts becomes the most sensitive response to the *how* and *why* of their presence. And it is precisely the fact that »not all ghosts are the same«, and that they »can have various functions, meanings, powers and effects, depending on their precise characteristics, context and name« (Peeren 2014: 12), that generates innovative theoretical framings, which in turn create the spectral turn, and not the other way around.³ This pertains also to the turn proclaimed in this volume: gathering divergent voices and analytical slants on Jewish ghosts in Poland, it argues that ghosts require readings resonant with, and giving justice to, their spatio-temporal, representational, and political specificity.

In this specificity rests the original contribution of this book to the broader landscape of contemporary theorizations of ghosts and haunting – in its attentiveness to a particular type of ghost, the Jewish ghost in post-Holocaust Poland, constructed through a situated theoretical lens. The way this task is undertaken varies across chapters, depending on the disciplinary and analytical positionality of the authors. Alina Molisak moves beyond or below dominant theorizations of ghosts and haunting to account for the particular cultural and religious traditions from which these ghosts emanate: a specific tapestry of Polish Romantic and Jewish tradition, translating into an aesthetic and ethical project of mediumship and mediumistic writing, of speaking with and on behalf of the dead. Aleksandra Ubertowska and Roma Sendyka locate their examination in the specificity of the Holocaust, and entangle ghosts with its troubled spatialities and materialities in Poland, and with questions

---

3   Interestingly, the metacritical distance to the language of »turns«, which I share with Peeren and del Pilar Bianco, is rendered operational, in their view, through the very figure of the ghost, whose uneasy ontological status and unsettling unpredictability mirror the destabilized structure of the strong humanistic paradigm. In this way, the ghost can provide a model for a differently constructed weak paradigmatic coup in humanistic reflection. »The ghost [...] could inaugurate an alternative logic of the turn as something not necessarily definitive or revolutionary in the sense of radically new. Instead of demanding a distancing, the twists and turns of haunting manifest as a layering, a palimpsestic thinking together, simultaneously, rather than thinking against or after. [...] The spectral turn may be read as a turn to the spectral, but also as the spectralization of the turn – its unmooring from defined points of departure, notions of linear progress, and fixed destinations.« (Del Pilar Blanco/Peeren 2013b: 32)

around the aesthetic and affective, posed from post-anthropocentric positions. The remaining chapters engage directly with the political particularity of Jewish ghosts and the role they have come to play in the Polish post-Holocaust imaginaire: Why do these ghosts appear (today)? What functions do they perform, and in whose interest? Whom do they haunt, why, and to what effect? What does their presence say about contemporary memory and identity work and about shifting cultural attitudes to the Holocaust? What do we stand to gain or lose from the unfolding of the spectral turn in contemporary Poland?

These questions are all the more pertinent in the Polish context, because those ghosts, indeed, differ considerably from other haunting figures running through the globalized spectral turn. Elsewhere, there is a straightforward link between the ghosts of minority groups – who use haunting to reclaim their collective past, rendered invisible by the dominant culture – and social and political critique. In Poland, by contrast, the ghosts belong to multiple groups laying claim to victimization, some of which themselves othered and victimized Jews. Thus the link between haunting and critique is troubled, if not reversed, in the case of the ghosts of Jews in Poland, who fell victim to German genocidal violence but were, too, subject to exclusion, discrimination, and violent dispossession by Poles. Against the field's conceptual neglect of, even blindness to, the experiences of anyone other than the victims, this book examines instances of haunting along collectivized, exclusionary lines, thus providing a passageway to (or a projection of) the obliterated experience of the Other. It is for this reason that, throughout the introduction, I use the terms Poles/Polish and Jews/Jewish. It is possible to resort to framings such as Polish Jews or Jewish and non-Jewish Poles, and, in this way, to evince the non-essentialist, civic definitions of national belonging. The terms ›Jews‹ and ›Poles‹, instead, give voice to dominant and deeply internalized exclusionary national self-definitions of non-Jewish Poles. As Henryk Grynberg bluntly puts it, not without irony, in *Monolog polsko-żydowski* [Polish-Jewish Monolog, 2003: 48], »In Poland, a Pole is not one who considers themselves a Pole, but one who is considered to be a Pole. Equally, a Jew is not someone who considers themselves a Jew, but who is considered a Jew. And under no circumstances can one be the one and the other.« The same logic, it seems, pertains to Jewish ghosts.

The otherness of Jewish ghosts, performatively established in *Dark, Almost Night*, along with many other works contributing to the spectral turn in

Poland, and interpretively unpacked in the chapters gathered in this volume, has its roots, of course, in the reality of the living, predating the Holocaust, shaping its aftermath, and cutting deep into the contemporary moment (Cała 1995 [1992], 2012; Michlic 2006; Banasiewicz-Ossowska 2007; Jeziorski 2009; Janicka/Żukowski 2016; Matyjaszek 2018). A growing body of research has exposed the scale and scope of prewar antisemitism, the complicity of Poles in the Holocaust, and the dynamics of anti-Jewish violence in its aftermath, all of which have contributed to a virtual absence of Jewish communities in contemporary Poland (Gross 2001 [2006], 2006; Engelking 2003, 2011; Grabowski 2004, 2013 [2011]; Tokarska-Bakir 2018; Engelking/Grabowski 2018; Żukowski 2018). The turbulent debates surrounding historical discoveries of the last decades that challenge established readings of the positionality of Poles vis-à-vis the Jewish minority and, more specifically, the Holocaust (Forecki 2010, 2018; Polonsky/Michlic 2004; Tokarska-Bakir 2004; Gross 2014; Janicka 2014-15), constitute a natural background for the readings of the Jewish ghosts in this volume. The book engages, too, with the interest in the history and culture of Jews in Poland that has been growing since 1989 (Gruber 2002; Meng 2011; Lehrer 2013; Lehrer/Meng 2015; Waligórska 2013), in tension but also in uneasy correspondence with the post-1989 surge of ethnonationalism. It is important to note the continued popularity and political legitimacy in Poland of nationalism, antisemitism, and violent and exclusionary cultural mechanisms, evidenced by the government enacting criminal sanctions for statements implying Polish participation in the Holocaust, by anti-refugee protesters burning an effigy of a Jew, and by many subtler everyday practices and discourses (Wiszniewicz 1997; Zgliczyński 2008; Cała 2012; Keff 2013; Forecki 2018).

The question about how the contemporary »haunted moment« figures in this complex cultural and political configuration underlies this book and constitutes a subject of dialog between the chapters. While all, in one way or another, address the historical dynamics of othering, discrimination, and violence that affected (and constructed) Jews in Poland, the authors differ in their readings of the substance, ›origins‹, and cultural and political work performed by the Jewish ghosts: Are they markers of intensified sensitivity of exceptional individuals such as Alicja in *Dark, Almost Night*? Do they signify a transformative readiness to embrace Jewish otherness and rework exclusionary constructions of ›Polishness‹? Are they figures of guilt and/or regret? Of traumatic memory? Or, conversely, do they speak to the haunting continuity of othering and violence – *as in life, so in death*?

The »Spectral Turn«: Jewish Ghosts in the Polish Post-Holocaust Imaginaire accounts for the many voices and understandings of the complex, evasive reality of ghosts in Poland. Moreover, this introduction, and indeed the rest of the book, is organized so as to reflect shifting trajectories in the production of, and interpretive involvement with, Jewish ghosts in Poland: from engagements with the representational, aesthetic, and affective politics of ghosts to their particular political positioning; from readings locating ghosts in the broader horizon of Holocaust art, literature, and theory to theorizations developed from within the empirical and material reality of haunting. This organization works along a specific analytical directionality – towards an understanding of ghosts that disentangles them from questions of *memory* and *trauma* and entangles them directly with questions of *order*, *power*, and *hegemony*. The next section examines the position of Jewish ghosts on the map of concepts and approaches constructing the Holocaust and its aftereffects as a source of ghosts – whether they haunt in Poland or elsewhere. I draw from a body of work that articulates the recent upsurge of Holocaust-related ghosts in the trauma-theoretical framework that constitutes a background for Polish readings of the Jewish ghosts through conceptual lenses of (post)memory and trauma. From there, working closely with contributions by Konrad Matyjaszek, Elżbieta Janicka and Tomasz Żukowski, and myself, I propose a different reading of Jewish ghosts, one attuned to power relations underlying and shaping the ghostly presence, and the structural continuity of those power relations through the present day.

GHOSTLY AFTERLIVES OF THE HOLOCAUST

The history of ghosts roaming literature, and their cultural role as a literary or narrative device is long. Introduced to cause surprise, fear, or doubt, to signal hesitation or incredulity, their presence has traditionally been associated with a set of reading and writing protocols and a cluster of thematic concerns distinctive to certain literary and filmic modes or genres: the gothic and neo-gothic, magic realism, and horror (Del Pilar Bianco 2012: 22). As figurations of the clash and/or of the blurring of boundaries between the real and the supernatural, the mimetic and imaginary, ghosts have been read as markers of – but have also been confined to – specific literary and representational traditions, often established as escapist, popular, ›low‹. It was a (re)theorization of ghosts through the broader problem of representation and representability, thinkability and unthinkability, and the ethical implications of the project of discursively and imaginatively framing the Holocaust, that led to the emergence of ghostly figures in Holocaust writing, to which it had remained, for a long time, largely immune.

After all, as the recent publication *The Fantastic in Holocaust Literature and Film* (Kerman/Browning 2015) reminds us, the »move away from the tradition of documentary realism that has so long dominated artistic responses to the Holocaust« (Wolfe 2015: 8) and the resulting attempt to embrace explicitly fictional strategies is a relatively new phenomenon. At first, this development drew fierce and discouraging criticism, and it still attracts some disapproval today. Nevertheless, over the last two or three decades, objections against figurative and imaginative engagements with the Holocaust – famously raised by Berel Lang and Elie Wiesel – have gradually lost their ability to »police generic and aesthetic boundaries within Holocaust literature«, as nicely phrased by Paul Eisenstein (2015: 85). It has become a prevalent strategy in Holocaust representation to break free, structurally and semantically, from the ›mimetic obligation‹. The multitude of Jewish ghosts that appears in contemporary Polish novels, films, and dramas finds its share of unreal, magical, and fantastic counterparts within the vast realm of international Holocaust cultural production. Let it suffice to mention W.G. Sebald's *Austerlitz* (2001), Anne Michaels's *Fugitive Pieces* (1997), Joseph Skibell's *Blessing on the Moon* (1997), David Grossman's *See Under: Love* (2002 [1986]), and Jonathan Safran Foer's *Everything is Illuminated* (2002).

The aesthetic turn towards supernatural codes and the experimentation with formal strategies and thematic motifs in antirealist fiction is, according to some scholars, dictated by the nature of the events to which they respond. Ghosts are complex articulations of the cultural and historical specificity of the realities with which they engage. In *A Fantastic Tale of Terror*, Kirsten Mahlke points out the structural correspondence between the »fantastic reality« of state terror in 1970s-1980s Argentina, responsible for the production of the ghostly figure of the disappeared, and the uncanniness inscribed in every effort to translate the experience into realistic representations (2012: 195-212). The fantastic narrative – conceptualized through Tzvetan Todorov's seminal work *The Fantastic* (1975 [1970]) – is, in Mahlke's view, better suited than any other representational mode to conveying the reality of long-lasting terror and the perpetuated lack of closure caused by enforced disappearance. Anne Hegerfeldt, making a clear connection between aesthetic recourse to the codes of the supernatural and the empirical realities of man-made violence, locates the experience of the Second World War, and specifically of the Holocaust, at the center of this phenomenon (2005: 56-61). After the Holocaust, Hegerfeldt claims, »reality itself has become incredible, inconceivable, fantastic«:

> In supernaturalizing cruel events, the texts express a stunned incredulity about the state of the world, implying that the idea of such things actually happening exceeds – or should exceed – the human imagination. [...] Therefore, far from denying the reality of such events, the fantastic tone conveys a heightened sense of despair over the fact that, tragically, they are only all too possible. (Hegerfeldt 2005: 61)

Although rarely acknowledged to date, the articulation of the »stunned incredulity about the state of the world«, in fact, predates fictionalized engagements with the Holocaust and permeates the corpus of survivors' testimonies, which often resort to the unreal and the ghostly as a way of conveying an immediate experiential and affective response to the war and the postwar reality. The language of haunting pervades many accounts in which Jewish survivors narrate their wartime fates as well as their encounters with destroyed homes and vacated ghettos, their estranged and de-realized sense of haunting (dis)continuity in the old urban spaces immediately after the Holocaust. These accounts give voice to the depth of alienation felt by the survivors, their intense loneliness, their despair in the face of the irreversibility of the damage, the sensation of »surrounding strangeness« accompanying visits to »cities without Jews« described by Yekhiel Kirshnbaum (1998: 261), the numbing »astonishment and horror« translated into the sense of sheer absurdity recounted by Jacob Pat (1947: 69). »Whenever you turn, there are memories and shadows of your relatives«, wrote Jakob Rosenberg (in Borzmińska 2007: 232). For Yakov Handshok, every square and every house was filled with »the terror of Jewish souls hovering in the air« (1998: 262-266).[4] The »spectralization of the real«, a term coined by Colin Davis (2007:

---

4   A set of ghostly metaphors is introduced in Natalia Aleksiun's article on Jewish survivors in Eastern Galicia in the immediate aftermath of the war, perhaps the

101), cogently frames the particular kind of attentiveness to reality induced by loss of homes, loss of loved ones, and shattering of whole communities and ways of life that rendered post-Holocaust landscapes as unreal and inhabited by the specters of an irreversibly vanished past.

This ghostly imagery finds a counterpart in another one, also derived from Holocaust testimonies, that depicts survivors themselves as ghosts, the living dead. In her contribution to this volume, Molisak writes of Jewish survivors as »hovering between life and death«, casting the post-Holocaust subjectivity as inherently marked and haunted by death – of others and of oneself. This condition is rooted in the paradoxical ontological status of those doomed to extermination yet living on, in the experience of the Holocaust as a passage through one's own death, so powerfully described by Jean Amery (1980 [1966]: 3). But haunting also speaks to the »radical difference« and »inaccessibility« of survivors' experiences (Molisak), which exceed our, and their, imagination; to the burden of carrying within them their own liminal experiences and the experiences of those who did not return; and to the ›impossible‹ status of the subject. This dual status of Holocaust survivors – doomed to being ghostly by the groundlessness of their own survival and simultaneously inhabited by the ghosts of others – found its way into the writings of Amery, Primo Levi, Elie Wiesel, Jorge Semprun, and also Henryk Grynberg and Hanna Krall (whose prose Molisak analyzes). Elsewhere, Alexandra Ubertowska introduced the notion of auto(tanato)graphy to capture the specificity of such auto›bio‹graphical writing, locating at its core the experience (or fiction) of one's death, which transforms the subject into a »specter, ghost, ›hologram‹ of the author-survivor« (2014: 76), who never (fully) returns from the camps, killing sites, forest, or hiding place. This mode of writing, too, predates contemporary imaginary engagements with the Holocaust; it articulates, moreover, the experience of its direct and immediate victims and conveys their despair, trauma, loss, and grief.

The translation of this mode of writing into imaginative framing of the Holocaust has taken place in the works of the second and third generation of descendants of Holocaust victims. Not experienced directly but rather mediated through inherited stories and images, through one's own sensitivities and affects, the trauma of the Holocaust has become the subject of

---

first to explicitly embrace ghosts in theorizing the experiences of those who survived the Holocaust (2013).

»postmemory«, as theorized by Marianne Hirsch (2008; 2012): a memory inherently vicarious, inventive, and diasporic, oscillating around the absent and inaccessible. Postmemory is articulated, first and foremost, on a personal level, in physical and imaginative acts of return performed by relatives of survivors to the sites of former Jewish life. Driven by a nostalgic longing for familial pasts and »desire for roots«, as is famously the case in Hirsch and Leo Spitzer's *Ghosts of Home: The Afterlife of Czernowitz in Jewish Memory* (2011), these ›returns‹, too, cast post-Holocaust landscapes as haunted (cf. Hirsch/Miller 2011; Ubertowska and Sendyka in this volume). In this case, it is not the arrival at the limits of imagination that the victims experienced, so much as the »haunting continuity« of irrevocably transformed ancestral hometowns, »emanating both seductive recollections of lost home and frightening reminders of persecution and displacement« (Hirsch/Spitzer 2010: xx), that populates post-Holocaust landscapes with ghosts; in this case, ghosts speak, too, of loss, grief, and transgenerational transmission of trauma.[5]

---

5 In her contribution to this volume, Sendyka reminds the reader about another ghostly dimension identified by Hirsch and Spitzer – the postmemorial returnees themselves figure as ghosts to the members of the local, non-Jewish population. In *Ghosts of Home*, Hirsch and Spitzer write that visitors »like us, searching for traces of this history, appeared like ghostly revenants or haunting reminders of a forgotten world: we unsettled the present by refusing to allow the past to disappear into oblivion« (2010: xx). In Sendyka's interpretation, this insight foregrounds the role of descendants and researchers (Hirsch and Spitzer are both), or perhaps anyone affected by the Holocaust, as »screens for spectral existence« carrying within themselves the ghosts of the dead. We are dealing here with a postmemorial reproduction of the dynamics described by Molisak (survivors haunted by the ghosts of those who did not survive), often theorized in the scholarship on the transgenerational transmission of trauma (cf., for instance, Schwab 2010). I place emphasis instead on the dynamics of othering and belonging conveyed by the quote. The postmemorial returnees position themselves against non-Jewish residents of the town who refuse to remember its Jewish past. In my contribution to this volume, without referring to *Ghosts of Home*, I expand on this idea, framing the figure of the living Jew returning to the hometown of her ancestors not so much, or not only, as a threat to actively embraced forgetting, but as a threatening Other willing to reclaim her misappropriated property – as a double of the figure of the Jewish ghost in Poland.

The literary and artistic incarnations of this postmemorial sensitivity, too, revolve around the notion that although the experience of the Holocaust remains unknowable, stories can imaginatively approximate and respond to the trauma it inflicted. In this vein, Anne Whitehead frames post-Holocaust literary encounters with the ghostly and the fantastic in the generic terms of »trauma fiction« (2004), thereby transgressing the *either/or* logic of the realist/antirealist debate around the problem of the (un)representability of the Holocaust.[6] For Whitehead, it is precisely the suspension between the real and imaginary introduced by ghost stories and fantastic occurrences that best speaks to the elusive nature of traumatic experience. Building upon the psychoanalytic insights of Cathy Caruth (1996) and Dominick LaCapra (1998, 2014 [2001]), she interprets the haunting quality of spatial and temporal disruptions pervading Sebald's *Austerlitz* or Michael's *Fugitive Pieces* as exemplary literary devices aimed at »mimicking […] forms and symptoms [of trauma]« (Whitehead 2004: 3).

Whitehead's reading offers a novel analytical response to the ever-increasing movement away from documentary realism and towards traumatic realism in fictionalized survivors' accounts and in works of the second and third generations. In *Magic Realism in Holocaust Literature: Troping the Traumatic Real*, Jenni Adams (2011) goes further, examining the emergence of a diverse and thoroughly international corpus of Holocaust literature, captured through the conceptual frame of magic realism. Defined broadly in terms of the coexistence of two incompatible or contradictory ontological codes – whereby the latter (magic) serves as an essential, though often subversive, counterpart of the former (real) – the magic realist mode of narration epitomizes, according to Adams, the problems faced when approaching the Holocaust in the »post-testimonial era«:

---

6   An in-depth and already classic investigation of the various facets of realism and antirealism in Holocaust studies is found in Michael Rothberg's *Traumatic Realism: The Demands of Holocaust Representation* (2000). In the same book, Rothberg proposes an original category of »traumatic realism« in reference to testimonial literature. Its transfer to the realm of postmemorial fiction is crucial for both Whitehead and Jenni Adams.

The very contradiction inherent in the magic realist ontological dynamics – the irruption of the unreal into a historically embedded and ontologically realist frame – necessarily problematizes issues of history, language, and reference. (Adams 2011: 21)

As such, it yields a particularly productive narrative and imaginary apparatus for the representatives of second or third generations struggling to come to terms with the traumatic experiences of Holocaust survivors – experiences which they themselves were obviously spared. From this perspective, the turn towards the unreal, the supernatural, and the magical, though traditionally associated with escapist trajectories in literature, facilitates in the novels of Foer, D.M. Thomas, and Andre Schwarz-Bart a critical narrative and dialogical self-positioning towards the »postmemorial other« (Adams 2011: 73). Imaginative investments – drawing from Jewish folk mythology, fairy tales, or the grotesque – mediate and negotiate encounters with the (inaccessible) reality of trauma.

Conceived as culturally and historically specific modes of Holocaust representation, both trauma fiction and magic realist Holocaust narratives, as conceptualized by Adams, share a common ›traumatic core‹ not only with the extensive body of Holocaust cinema – which for some time now has embraced the fantastic, magical, unreal, absurd, and grotesque as representational codes (cf. Elm/Kabalek/Köhne 2014; Kerman/Browning 2015) – but also with a broader corpus of contemporary literary works. In a recent publication, *Haunted Narratives: Life Writing in an Age of Trauma* (Rippl et al. 2013), the proliferation of trauma narratives permeated by »uncanny phenomena, personified or atmospheric« (Kriss 2013: 21) is ascribed, on the one hand, to the violent legacy of the 20th century, and, on the other, to the workings of the transgenerational transmission of trauma (cf. Fuchs 2010). This understanding of trauma as more than a purely individual psychological category – characteristic also of the above-mentioned readings by Hirsch, Whitehead, and Adams – allows the authors to establish an uneasy link between the aftereffects of political violence and their mediations in a range of cultural representations.

This trajectory resonates, in fact, with broader theoretical figurations of the Holocaust as a cultural and historical trauma that resists incorporation into the realm of perception and representation (cf., for instance, Caruth 1996; Felman/Laub 1992; LaCapra 1998; 2014 [2001]; Rothberg 2000). The discourse of loss, grief, and trauma, employed to articulate the complex experiences of Holocaust survivors and their immediate descendants, translates into redefinitions of the larger cultural landscape. Intimately entwined with the issues of thinkability, imaginability, and representation, this discourse gives voice to the shattering of a wider universe of meaning. It describes the »spectralization of the real« that undermines, or altogether destroys, existing modes of ordering the world and defies traditional attempts at narration and representation. But theorization of the Holocaust as a cultural and historical trauma also speaks to a deep crisis of confidence – on the existential, ethical, and political plane – in the validity and durability of any intransgressible frames of permissibility/impermissibility with respect to the human animal, which were so dramatically breached during the Second World War and the Holocaust. In this, the (often contested) diagnoses of the irrevocability of disturbance in the political, moral, symbolic, and aesthetic order(s) brought about by the Holocaust, cast the world after the Holocaust as inherently post-traumatic (LaCapra 2014 [2001]: 115). LaCapra, who casts this post-traumatic condition as a structural condition of contemporary culture and an ethical imperative, writes:

> In more metaphoric terms, one might suggest that the ghosts of the past – symptomatic revenants who have not been laid to rest because of disturbance in the symbolic order, a deficit in the ritual process, or a death so extreme in its unjustifiability or transgressiveness that in certain ways it exceeds existing modes (perhaps any possible mode) of mourning – roam the post-traumatic world and are not entirely ›owned‹ as ›one's own‹ by any individual or group. If they haunt a house (a nation, a group), they come to disturb all who live – perhaps even pass through – that house. How to come to terms with them affects different people or groups in significantly different ways. (LaCapra 2014 [2001]: 215)

Bridging cultural theory and the procession of literary, cinematic, and artistic ghosts and »uncanny phenomena«, LaCapra's metaphor entails a broadening of the impact of the Holocaust beyond survivors and their immediate descendants; the trauma is, as it were, democratized. In this way, the postmemorial paradigm expands to analytically cover a broader body of work and cultural production: across cultures, nations and groups, the trauma of the Holocaust and the disturbance or shattering of the symbolic order find articulation in the codes of the ghostly, the unreal, and the supernatural.

This assertion runs through several chapters collected in this volume. In her contribution, Ubertowska constructs a number of contemporary Polish novels populated with Jewish ghosts as instances of post-traumatic literature operating through a variety of spectrological tropes and motifs. Although Ubertowska focuses her analysis on another set of works, including the paintings of a Polish Jewish artist and Holocaust survivor and Jonasz Stern and Zygmunt Miłoszewski's literary thriller *Ziarno Prawdy* [The Grain of Truth, 2011], and employs Derridean conceptualizations of haunting (far removed from those proposed by LaCapra or Hirsch), the trauma-theoretical paradigm remains the underlying premise. It extends to the field of critical theory adopting a »spectral lens« on the Holocaust, to artistic practice struggling with and against intimate experiences of violence and dehumanization, and to recent Polish literature dealing with the persistence of antisemitic prejudices, unpacked by Ubertowska through notions of anachrony, seriality, materiality, and post-anthropocentric assemblage. Sendyka, too, characterizes the generalized trauma of the Holocaust as a syndrome whose effects are felt across national and cultural lines. Drawing from affect theory and the post-anthropocentric paradigm, she grounds her argument in what LaCapra frames as a »deficit in the ritual process«: the presence and affective resonance of human remains not naturalized by burial and active remembrance (at the former Nazi camps in Poland and in the cities destroyed during the war) inform a body of contemporary Polish literature and art, and translate into various scenarios of haunting and encounters with Jewish ghosts. It is only at the end of her chapter that she asks the reader to consider whether there is a difference between the postmemory of the descendants of the victims and that of their Polish counterparts.

This question is implied in LaCapra's framing of the post-Holocaust world as post-traumatic: the ghosts are not »owned«, he writes, but affect different groups or nations differently. This is perhaps best articulated in the recent scholarship on the ›German trauma‹ of the Holocaust and its ghostly afterlives. It rests on recourse to the concept of *Tätertrauma* – the trauma of the perpetrators (Giesen/Schneider 2004) – employed to convey the essential difference between the trauma of Nazism's victims and the psychological, cultural, and political effects of the Second World War on non-Jewish Germans, especially those effects that resulted from involvement in the extermination of Jews. In the words of Andreas Kraft, who traces its spectral after-effects in contemporary German fiction, the collective perpetrators' trauma differs from the victims' trauma insofar as it is not brought about by the existentially threatening experience of mortality: the perpetrator is [...] traumatized by their very deed, when in retrospect they realize that the act performed in an exercise of sovereign authority to exert power is, in reality, a crime. (2014: 154)

The shattering of the symbolic order lays bare the crime for what it really is and results in a »stunned incredulity« about oneself and the order that rendered the »deed« permissible and legitimate. And yet, argues Kraft, this has never been the experience of the immediate perpetrators of the Holocaust, who remain unable to see their deeds from the fundamentally altered cultural and political framework embraced by subsequent generations. Consequently, their descendants must also operate within a cultural universe haunted by the legacies and residues of National Socialism (and its configurations of power), which for decades were subjected to silencing and othering, and externalized by the demonizing of individual perpetrators. In this case, transgenerational transmission implies the inheritance of an excess of structural dynamics of violence one cannot and does not want to accommodate. The trauma of the perpetrators reverberates as a trauma that is not.[7]

---

7   In their classic work, *The Inability to Mourn: Principles of Collective Behavior* (1975 [1967]), psychoanalysts Alexander and Margarete Mitscherlich provide a different conceptualization of German trauma, locating it in the war defeat and Hitler's death, the loss of a strong structuring figure. Yet another interpretation is offered by Gabriele Schwab (2010), who adopts the theory of the transgenerational phantom proposed by Nicolas Abraham and Maria Torok (1986 [1976]); 1994 [1978]). Schwab writes about traumatic secrecy resulting from the German perpetrators' repression or denial of crimes, covering up of shame, disregarding their own inhumanity, and »emotional silencing of the Holocaust« (2010: 17). The ghostly economy of traumatic secrecy, she asserts, operates not only within familial frameworks but also at the level of the cultural unconscious; the encrypted trauma of the Holocaust, just like passed-down family secrets, lives on through phantoms haunting individuals, public life, and the practices of transgenerational writing. Here, paradoxically, it is the fact that the Holocaust has not shattered the symbolic order but remains the subject of repression that invests it with a traumatizing potential.

Magdalena Waligórska's contribution to this volume explores the distinctive ›Polish trauma‹ of the Holocaust. Ascribing the fantastic, uncanny, and grotesque in Polish cultural production to a collective trauma, she asserts that this trauma »is not that of Holocaust survivors, but one derived from what we could term a ›postmemory of witnesses‹, and is a specifically Polish one«. The forms this postmemory takes (as per Sendyka's rhetorical enquiry) are bound to reflect, therefore, the distinctive position occupied by Poles vis-à-vis the Holocaust, established here as that of witness or bystander (more on this below). Locating her reflection in the context of recent historical debates pertaining to the involvement of Poles in the genocidal violence and dispossession of the Jews, Waligórska acknowledges that the Polish postmemory of the Holocaust differs from the postmemory of the victims' descendants. The Jewish ghosts in Poland, she argues, speak of the shame and guilt embraced by (some) Poles after the 1989 transition, on the one hand, and, on the other, they articulate anxieties of the majority about the fate of properties misappropriated during the war (Grabowski/Libionka 2014; Leder 2014). But they also heal, absolve, and offer redemption, allowing those sentiments to be domesticated or put to rest. While the content of Polish postmemory is cast as contextual and specific, the structure through which it operates mirrors that of Jewish traumatic inheritance. Waligórska bases her argument on Hirsch's assertion, which establishes postmemory as a »structure of transmission« and not an »identity position« (Hirsch 2008: 114) – in other words, if descendants of victims inherit trauma from their ancestors, this can also take place in other transgenerational contexts.

But the indiscriminate transfer of the Holocaust-related notion of trauma and postmemory to other contexts, including post-Holocaust Germany and Poland, is a subject of growing concern and criticism. This resonates in Kraft's interpretation of *Tätertrauma* as uninheritable because of its deficiency. Gabriele Schwab, too, in her *Haunting Legacies: Violent Histories and Transgenerational Trauma*, expresses some unease about applying the trauma-theoretical framework to the legacy of perpetrators: »[…] there seems to be something almost obscene in discourse that looks at the effects of the war and the Holocaust on Germans in terms of trauma«, she notes (2010: 13). While Schwab manages to overcome her unease (redirecting the concept so as to address the defensive silencing of the Holocaust in German culture), this seems increasingly difficult for scholars working in the Polish context; Janicka is its most pronounced critic (Janicka 2014-15; cf.

Chmielewska 2016; Matyjaszek in this volume). The resistance against traumatic readings cuts, here, across epistemological, ethical, and political planes. In metatheoretical terms, it corresponds to broader objections against framing historical processes in a category of trauma that leads to their dehistorization and depoliticization: the magnetization of trauma by discourses of unrepresentability, unthinkability, and unimaginability relegates to the background the historical and contextual, the political and the social (cf. Bevernage 2012; Craps 2010).

But this resistance to talking about Polish trauma of the Holocaust also more narrowly reflects a growing body of research on the Polish realities of the Holocaust and its symbolic, cultural, and political ›effects‹ on Poles – findings that plead for critical revision of received concepts and theories, for attunement to their ability to conceal rather than to illuminate, to their capacity to exclude, marginalize, or invisibilize (and, thus, to produce a new set of ghosts). Janicka and Matyjaszek (who draws from Janicka in his contribution to this volume) base their criticism on the dominant conceptualizations of this trauma as a »trauma of the witness«. It is in these terms that Raul Hilberg's notion of bystandership, appurtenant to the victim-perpetrator-bystander triad (1992), was received in Poland. In recent years, also this figure of the passive, disengaged, indifferent witness/bystander (Błoński 2008 [1987]) has been denounced in light of research on dominant attitudes towards the Jews and wartime anti-Jewish violence, which cut deep into the postwar period in Poland (Gross 2014; Janicka 2014-15).

Yet, paradoxically, it was precisely the reality of postwar violence and the question of how antisemitism could have survived the Holocaust that gave rise to the first, highly influential interpretation of the Holocaust as a Polish trauma. This notion was introduced by Michael Steinlauf (1997; cf. Janicka/Steinlauf 2014-15) and testified to his struggle to accommodate the results of his research on the postwar responses to the Holocaust in Poland: the Holocaust was welcomed, cheered by some; it was blamed on the Jews; its outcomes, both material and social, appreciated; in its aftermath, people identified as Jews were still subjected to physical, symbolic, economic and structural violence; they were murdered, robbed, refused equal treatment by lower-level state administration, ostracized, and resented for being too visible in the higher echelons of power (Steinlauf 1997). This dynamic remained unchallenged and unchanged to the extent of effectively resisting the equalizing policies of the state socialist government, the first one to grant the Jews fully equal legal status in Poland and to officially combat antisemitism.[8] Building a false symmetry between two radically different experiences of the Holocaust, Steinlauf attributed this violence to »massive, traumatic exposure to death« resulting from »witnessing« the Holocaust and the shattering of the universe of meaning (1997: 53-61). If it was not acute traumatization by the Holocaust that drove Poles to exercise violence on a radically diminished Jewish minority, then what could it be? Of course, lack of traumatization could be the answer.

But Steinlauf's conceptualization took hold of the discursive realm of Holocaust studies in Poland as a legitimate framing of the experience and positionality of witness-bystanders. With time, its empirical grounding in early postwar violence wore off, bringing the notion closer to the theorizations of post-traumatic culture as structurally affected by the Holocaust or by the transgenerational transmission of trauma (cf. Bojarska 2007; Fabiszczak/Owiński 2013; Kowalczyk 2010; Ziębińska-Witek 2011). As the idea migrated, the factual contours and contents of the Polish experience of the Holocaust often could not bear the weight of trauma constructed as a disturbance in the symbolic order or as a structure of inheritance. The experience of the Holocaust lost its historical complexity and specificity. It is clear and ›commonsense‹ that the Poles were traumatized, but less clear what they were traumatized by. The Holocaust mutated into an empty signifier of ›trauma‹.

---

8   The last statement does not belong to Steinlauf's argumentative repertoire – in fact, he sees the imposition of state socialist rule as a major obstacle on the road to accountability for this dynamic of violence (due to state-imposed repression of the memory of the Holocaust and promotion of the Polish-struggle-and-martyrdom oriented politics of memory). But this was not necessarily the case: In the years immediately after the war, the newly established Polish government left ample room for the Jewish community to mourn and commemorate its loses (cf. Wóycicka (2013 [2009]). So when, by the late 1940s, the hegemonic narrative about the war was crystalizing – universalizing the experience of ethnic Poles and erasing the specificity of the Jewish war experience – it made political use of, and fed upon, the omnipresent popular antisemitism and the ubiquitous lack of empathy for the Jews. In the longer run, the state, viewed as alien and repressive by most Poles, also resorted to (ethno)nationalism and anti-Jewish sentiments to seek legitimacy.

Unpacking the trajectory of the concept from its inception to the present day, Matyjaszek demonstrates, therefore, that traumatic readings have the ability not only to occlude the complex reality of ghosts but also to invisibilize the continuity of cultural codes and the violent mechanism of culture that stood behind Polish involvement in the Holocaust and postwar violence, and that still reverberate in divergent realms of cultural (and knowledge) production. If the symbolic universe was not shattered, the dynamics of othering and violence, too, lives on. And it is exactly this troubling continuity – unacknowledged, silenced, often denied – and not traumatization by the Holocaust that might give rise to the ghosts haunting contemporary Poland.

FROM *POST-TRAUMATIC* TO *POST-HOLOCAUST*

The notion that haunting exposes lingering power structures, speaking to and about the effects of repressive configurations of power and exclusionary mechanisms of culture, rather than about memory and trauma, guides the Derridean reading of the specter. It has also found its way into theorizations of hegemony and normative violence proposed by Judith Butler – different from Derrida's reading but harmonizing with it nonetheless. In *Precarious Life: The Powers of Mourning and Violence* (2004; cf. 2000; 2010), Butler writes about the spectral excess that haunts cultural, and thus also epistemological and political, frames considered as »boundaries that constitute what will and what will not appear within public life, the limits of the publicly acknowledged field of appearance« (2004: xvii). Hegemony governs »what ›can‹ be heard, read, seen, felt, and known« (ibid: xx), and what will remain silent/silenced, invisible/invisibilized, unseen and unsensed, but it also fragments people into multiple identities and works through hierarchical structures that privilege some and dispossess others. In this reading, then, hegemony operates at the level of ontological claims that define what counts as reality, whose life is real and whose is not, and that sets the scene for differential valuation of human life, for exclusion and dehumanization; perhaps, the primary source of the spectral excess.

It is in these terms that Butler conceptualizes normative violence cutting through the cultural but also the political, material, and affective realms: dehumanization renders certain lives unnotable, unworthy, and unreal. It produces subjectivities and subject positions that hover outside ethically, affectively, and politically saturated frames of the thinkable and unthinkable, the permissible and impermissible. Such subjects, argues Butler, are essentially deconstituted and derealized. They are »neither alive nor dead«, they are »spectrally human« (2004: 33-34). This does not mean, however, that they altogether disappear; rather, their spectrality renders them excessive (from within the hegemonic order). As such, they are susceptible to physical, economic, structural, and symbolic violence, made thinkable, permissible, and legitimate, since harm inflicted upon a derealized life is not considered violence. In the hegemonic order, after all, this life is already established as unnotable and unworthy, as disposable (in both meanings of the term). In this way, the various wrongs and forms of violence inflicted upon those subjects merely deliver »the message of dehumanization that is already at work in the culture« (Butler 2004: 34).[9]

The dynamics of normative/conventional violence run through many, if not all, instances of political violence, and often underlie the everyday, seemingly mundane aspects of social life. It is a daily reality of dispossessed and expendable people and populations. (Butler locates it in the analytical

---

9   In Poland, Butler's *Precarious Life* has been employed previously in discussions of the afterlives of the Holocaust in Polish culture, specifically the notion (un)grievability, designating some lives as worthy and some as unworthy of grieving. It is also in these terms that Grzegorz Niziołek captures the affective and symbolic economy structuring responses to the Holocaust in Polish postwar theater, writing about a grief that was not: »Mourning must assume loss, yet Polish experiences testify rather to the existence of an excess of affects, difficult to discharge, securing the impossibility of perceiving the Holocaust in terms of loss [...]. [The Holocaust] did not unleash the feeling of loss and lack, but rather that of regained balance« (Niziołek 2013: 137). Here is yet another argument against considering the Polish response to the Holocaust as trauma. But Butler's conceptualization of the spectrally human could also shed new analytical light on postwar anti-Jewish violence by capturing the dynamics behind the survival of antisemitism in post-Holocaust Poland that troubled Steinlauf so much. Butler writes that, as »neither alive nor dead«, those who are unreal »have a strange way of remaining animated and need to be negated again (and again) [...], since they seem to live on, stubbornly, in this state of deadness«. She adds: »Violence renews itself in the face of this apparent inexhaustibility of its object.« (Butler 2004: 33)

context of the so-called war on terror and other wars waged by the USA but also of exclusions still suffered by queer people and those living with HIV/AIDS; many others could be added). Like Derridean haunting, it is a generalizable social phenomenon inherent to social life, not yet ready to part with abusive systems of power. This dynamic, with important contextual and structural differences, has shaped the experiences of colonization, of slavery, of racial, ethnic, and religious discrimination across various social and political contexts, of genocides, of wars, and of state terror, producing and enacting spectrality among the living – a generative ground for contemporary ghosts.

To view those ghosts through notions of memory (and trauma), of the troubling aftereffects of suffering endured in the past, of recovered knowledge about past violence and injustices, of access to marginalized and silenced experiences of the past, is, as I have shown, predominant in cultural theory and memory studies. Yet Butler's theorization of spectrality and normative violence suggests that there might be a more complex link between the hegemonic making (and undoing) of spectralized living and the procession of ghostly figures roaming literature, art, and theory. In this view, ghosts testify to the troubling continuity of othering and dehumanization still »at work in the culture«; it is not so much an *event* (or series of events) and its immediate (and mediated) experience that give rise to the ghosts but rather the ongoing presence of the frames that effectuated – and continue to effectuate – hierarchization, exclusion, dispossession. Those frames can, and often do, outlast the context of the event and outlive the spectral humans subjected to ›conventional‹ violence; they can also be summoned, time and again, (re)invented and put to work. Thus it is not the past that produces ghosts but the present, drawing from the (unreworked and unresolved) past. It might be that colonization, slavery, and the Holocaust are historically over and denounced, but they *live on* through repressive configurations of power and violent mechanisms of culture so long as those configurations have not been revoked or transformed (cf. also Trouillout 1995: 146-147). The spectral humans become stubbornly present ghosts.

This intuition resonates, too, in Gordon's theorizations of ghosts and haunting, notwithstanding her own insistence on framing haunting in terms of memory (2008 [1997]: 22). In a work that, in its own way, brought ghosts back to the field of the human and social sciences, *Ghostly Matters: Haunting and Sociological Imagination*, Gordon locates the ghost, again constructed as a social force, in the horizon of modernity and its forms of violence (slavery, torture, forced disappearance, capitalist exploitation). Haunting, of which the ghost is »empirical evidence« (Gordon 2008 [1997]: 8), is given many names in the book: it is an experiential modality, a particular mediation, memory and countermemory, a cultural experience, a »sensuous knowledge«, a structure of feeling. But what we also learn about ghosts is that they »hate new things« (ibid: xix), that they cling to the conditions that gave rise to them, that they are not of the past at all but of the present. Haunting, writes Gordon, »is one way in which abusive systems of power make themselves known and their impacts felt in the everyday, especially when they are supposedly over and done with (slavery, for instance) or when their oppressive nature is denied [...]« (ibid: xvi). She adds:

Ghosts are characteristically attached to the events, things, and places that produced them in the first place; by nature they are haunting reminders of lingering trouble. Ghosts hate new things precisely because once the conditions that call them up and keep them alive have been removed, their reason for being and their power to haunt are severely restricted. (Gordon 2008 [1997]: xix)

If it is not memory (and trauma) that produces ghosts but the unacknowledged or denied durability of cultural, political, and economic configurations, orders, and frames, then ghosts require a different set of readings – sometimes critical *re*readings of their existing and obdurate framings. This is the task I undertake in my contribution to this volume, which opens the section in which Jewish ghosts haunting contemporary Poland are reconfigured through notions of order, hegemony, and power, loosening links with the postmemorial paradigm. Following Gordon, but also engaging polemically with certain assertions underlying her conceptualization of ghosts and haunting, I ask what exactly it means for ghosts to haunt, and whether all ghosts are, in fact, invested with this ability. Are ghosts indeed the »empirical evidence« that haunting is taking place? Or, instead, can the »conditions that call them up and keep them alive« also restrict their power? This power is, in *Ghostly Matters*, associated with the ability to intervene in and refashion the hegemonic order within which the haunting unfolds. Observing that ghosts have varying capacities to haunt, I argue that their presence can just as well act as evidence of the order's strength and stability, and can even contribute to sustaining and perpetuating it. This, again, has much to do with the contextual specificity of ghosts, as well as with the positionality of the haunted towards the ghosts and their position inside or outside the order.

My analysis centers on a particular type of ghost – the figure of the dybbuk, a possessive spirit from Jewish mythology – in its various artistic, literary, and cinematic renditions in Poland since the late 1980s. I look, specifically, at Andrzej Wajda's 1988 staging of a classic of prewar Yiddish theatre, An-Sky's *Dybbuk*, at its 2003 reinterpretation by Krzysztof Warlikowski, and, finally, at Marcin Wrona's movie *Demon* (2015). My reading aims to challenge the firmly established framing of the dybbuk (as much by the authors themselves as by the critics of their work) as a figure of memory, in particular of Polish memory about Jews, and moreover memory cast as traumatic; a figure that bridges the impassable hiatus between presence and absence, present and past, living and dead, but also Self and Other.[10] Instead, returning to the meaning of the figure predating, and subversively challenging, its appropriated Polish readings through the notions of memory and trauma, I situate the dybbuk in the frame of a tale about a temporarily threatened but almost invariably restored order. In this frame, the question of power relations between the living and the ghosts becomes central, along with means to appraise the ghosts' transformative force: Do Polish dybbuks unveil or disavow, perpetuate or transform configurations and orders that called them into being? Has a dybbuk instantiating change arrived in Poland or is it still to come?

The interpretive direction closely binding the proliferation of Jewish ghosts in Poland with normative, hegemonic violence and with its unacknowledged and denied durability is even more pronounced in Matyjaszek's chapter. Although he does not refer to Butler but to Derrida, he traces the ghosts back to repressive ideologies that produced them and force them to reappear. Matyjaszek applies Derrida's notion of hegemony and spectrality to capture the dynamics of Polish national(ist) identity politics after the 1989 transition to a market economy – structured around capitalism,

---

10 The figure of the dybbuk runs, too, through Molisak's contribution to this volume. Her interpretation has a different directionality to mine and establishes the dybbuk as a figure of mediumistic writing performed by Polish Jewish authors, Krall and Grynberg, themselves survivors of the Holocaust. In this, it also differs from the conceptualizations constructing the dybbuk as a figure of Polish memory about Jews.

Catholicism, anti-communism, and ideologies of collective Polish victimhood – and the country's repositioning in the context of European memory culture centered on the Holocaust. The non-material, bodiless »non-subjects«, the Jewish ghosts, the ghosts of the victims of the Holocaust, are understood here, in line with Dylan Trigg's »phenomenology of ghosts« (2012), through material realities of haunting. But Matyjaszek also shifts attention to the question of the uses and usability of Jewish ghosts for contemporary Polish identity work. Ghosts, he writes, are not merely products of hegemonic violence, but are also conjured up to serve the needs of those whom they come to haunt. Moreover, the stakes are high, as the ghosts are »irreplaceable for legitimizing the haunted [hegemonic] groups in their hegemonic status«. In this reading, there is nothing transformative about Jewish ghosts. Instead, their presence casts Polish nationhood as haunted and traumatized, and thus becomes a source of various symbolic and political gains: the invisibilization of Polish involvement in the Holocaust and in wartime and postwar dispossession of the Jews, and the authorization of particular visions of Poland and Polishness. Disposability is the ghosts' defining feature.

But this disposability is cast, too, as historically and structurally grounded in the conditions producing the positionality of Jews vis-à-vis the Polish majority long before and during the Holocaust. Matyjaszek traces its origins to the dynamics of othering, exclusion, and antisemitic violence shaping Jewish life in Poland: the unequal access to rights, social resources, and spaces (universities, state administration, army); the direct and indirect discrimination; and, finally, Polish complicity in the Holocaust and violent dispossession of the Jews during and after the war. The violent mechanisms of culture that lay down conditions for the existence (and death) of the living are perpetuated through those that form the reality of the ghosts:

> The structural connection between the present appropriation of a non-corporeal ghost and the historical appropriation perpetrated on a Jewish victim of antisemitic repression *de facto* make the contemporary summoning of victims' ghosts an uncritical reenactment of mechanisms of violence present in former periods of Polish history, including the Holocaust itself.

Matyjaszek's interpretation speaks directly to the one proposed in the closing chapter of the volume. In a meticulous close reading of the 2008 documentary *Po-lin: Okruchy Pamięci* [Pol-lin: Scraps of Memory], Janicka and Żukowski unpack in detail how this »uncritical reenactment« is performed in a work cast, by filmmakers and reviewers alike, as a new, ›reconciliatory‹ take on the Jewish past in Poland. The acclaimed and repeatedly award-winning film, although created in the wake of historical revelations about wartime and postwar anti-Jewish violence, constructs a nostalgic account of prewar »Polish-Jewish coexistence«: contemporary Poles narrate their benevolent memories about the absent Jews, conjured up by archival footage from the 1930s. The film is populated with figurative ghosts; ghosts muted and trapped in the Polish narrative, which is selective, self-congratulatory, blind to its own violent mechanisms, and which reproduces, time and again, a hierarchical and discriminatory distribution of spaces and roles while rendering this discrimination invisible.

The conceptual lenses through which Janicka and Żukowski read *Po-lin* are »posthumous inclusion« and »philosemitic violence«, notions designed to convey the dynamics behind a broader set of discourses and practices from recent decades (cf. Janicka/Żukowski 2016). In the context of discussions about the Polish-Jewish past, these discourses and practices have attempted to reconfigure Polishness as liberal, (formerly) multicultural, and inclusive, and yet remain structurally unable to escape discriminatory frames, »sometimes despite the best intentions«. The posthumous inclusion, »which the living apply to the dead […], performed by the majority on the minority, by the group thus far excluding on the excluded group«, takes the form of philosemitic violence which casts Jewish ghosts – phantasmatized and exoticized, if not altogether invented – in roles designated by Poles. Objectifying the dead to the point where they become props for majority's identity work, we have ourselves presented and narrated back to us through the figure of the Jewish ghost.

It is in these terms that one could, in fact, reread Alicja's encounters with the Jewish ghosts in *Dark, Almost Night*. Those ghosts are summoned to differentiate Alicja from the xenophobic and nationalistic crowd, to testify to her exceptionality and empathy. This characterization is enhanced by the parallel drawn, perhaps unintentionally (which would render it even more striking), between the wartime past and the present day. The novel constructs the Jewish ghosts as victims of the Nazis, yet the relationship between Alicja and the spectral figures draws directly from the imagery of real ›encounters‹ between Poles and Jews in testimonials and historical scholarship. The contemporary setting of the novel serves as a mirror-image of past events. Then, as now, »tormented souls« knocked on the windows and doors of Polish houses, »asking for a glass of water, piece of bread, sheet of paper, and a pencil« (Bator 2012: 87-88). Then, as now, a few particularly sensitive and courageous individuals resisted omnipresent antisemitism and extended a helping hand to Jews, who, during the Holocaust, were hunted by the Nazis but also, as we know today, were denounced and murdered by the Poles. Only a few Poles provided the persecuted Jews with food or shelter, sometimes putting their own lives at risk. Their exceptional deeds are honored by the title of the Righteous Among the Nations.

Since the late 1960s, as a cultural and political construct, the category of the Righteous has played a central role in Polish narratives about the Holocaust structured around the notion of bystandership but also of the exceptional scale of altruism on the part of Polish helpers, which is evoked to invisibilize the scope of complicity of Poles in the genocidal violence against Jews (Tokarska-Bakir 2013; Forecki 2016, 2018). Appropriating the position of a Righteous for Alicja, the novel does not critically intervene in this narrative; instead, it uses the narrative to draw distinctions between Poles along political lines (far-right versus liberal) and also along class lines: Wałbrzych is a poor, provincial, post-industrial town of the type perhaps most affected by the 1989 transition; Alicja is a journalist from the capital and, thus, enjoys a higher symbolic status. The novel thus implicates and instrumentalizes the ability or inability to see the Jewish ghosts in the processes of social and cultural hierarchization; it accounts for divisions and antagonisms that cut through Polish society in the contemporary »haunted moment«. It is not a trauma of the Holocaust that produces Jewish ghosts in *Dark, Almost Night* but their objectifying disposability, the uncritical reenactment of the »mechanisms of violence present in former periods of Polish history« and spectrality between and among the living.[11]

---

11 The cultural work performed by Jewish ghosts in Bator's novel comes down to the elevating of the self-image through projected responsiveness to suffering, helplessness, vulnerability of the ghosts/the Jews. In the prose of Igor Ostachowicz (2012), Sylwia Chutnik (2014), and Andrzej Bart (2008), analyzed in other chapters of this book, Jewish ghosts, too, almost invariably rely on protection, ›hospitality‹, and care from the Poles. This translates into constraints imposed on

What insights, then, does the »spectral turn« provide into the Polish post-Holocaust imaginaire – a frame ordering what is heard, read, seen, felt, and known? Ghosts signal »lingering trouble«, argues Gordon, and thus cast the imaginaire as troubled by images, normative notions, and mechanisms of culture that render violence against the (ghostly) Other permissible and thinkable. It is in this sense that the eponymous notion of the post-Holocaust could be elevated to the level of a concept replacing those of the post-traumatic or postmemorial. The ›post‹ in LaCapra's theorization of post-traumatic culture speaks of a caesura imposed by an event that resists incorporation into the realm of perception and representation, of the shattering of the order beyond repair. But, perhaps more importantly, it speaks to continuity, to the force the experience of the event exerts on what comes afterwards, to the aftereffects, lingering traces, »haunting continuity« of trauma, rendered manifest through nightmares, flashbacks, and acting out. According to Hirsch, the ›post‹ in postmemory »signals more than a temporal delay and more than a location in an aftermath. Postmodern, for example, inscribes both a critical distance and a profound interrelation with the modern; postcolonial does not mean the end of the colonial but its troubling continuity.« (Hirsch 2008: 106) The ›post‹ does not, therefore, stand for an irreversible end but, instead, a tenacious presence of what could have been considered past but, in fact, continues to have tangible and intangible impact.

What the concept of post-Holocaust would convey, in turn, is a »troubling continuity« of longstanding, violent and violence-generating distinctions, of the dynamics of othering and exclusion not shattered by the Holocaust. But here, again, there is a lesson to be learned from the theorization of ghosts proposed by Gordon: unlike trauma, she writes, haunting is distinctive in that it unfailingly delivers a message that there is »something-to-be-done« (Gordon 2008: xvi).

Acknowledgements

The »Spectral Turn«: Jewish Ghosts in the Polish Post-Holocaust Imaginaire would never have seen the light of day if it were not for Aleida

---

their ability to haunt. Elsewhere, I consider the potential of some of those works as a critical practice (Dziuban 2014).

Assmann, the series editor as well as my guide and friend. I am deeply indebted to her for her insistence that the book should be written, in whatever way, and for many other things: her advice, warmth, and support extended when I needed it the most. It was Estela Schindel whose question acted as an incentive for me to trace Jewish ghosts in Poland and engage with their complex reality, and I am grateful for her company throughout this sometimes uneasy endeavor, as a friend and as an attentive reader. A sincere thanks goes to all authors who contributed to this volume, making the »turn« figuratively and literally possible. I am also grateful to Annika Linnemann at transcript for her patience, never once exhausted by the multitude of shameful and painful delays. A big thanks is extended, too, to Meabh Keane, Gilly Nadel, Sophie Oliver-Mahler, Miha Tavcar, and Sam Caleb, who provided their language skills correcting and editing different parts of the manuscript at various stages of its preparation, and to Robin Gill, a fellow translator of three of the chapters originally written in Polish. Kobi Kabalek, Łukasz Kozak, Ewa Stańczyk, Gudrun Rath, Elena Baltuta, Sergiu Sava, Agata Dziuban, Kirsten Mahlke, Natalia Judzińska, and Konrad Matyjaszek gave comments on various versions, drafts, ideas, all much appreciated. Finally, I am eternally grateful to Maurycy Zimmermann and Kobi Kabalek for always being there for me, in all possible ways. Without you two, I would most probably remain forever haunted.

Four of the chapters were previously published in German, Polish, or English, and I appreciate the permission to reprint them in this volume. Molisak's text first appeared as »Schreiben im Auftrag der Toten. Mediumistische Erzählstrategien in der polnischen Literatur« in Magdalena Marszałek and Alina Molisak (eds.), *Nach dem Vergessen. Rekurse auf den Holocaust in Ostmitteleuropa nach 1989*, Berlin: Kadmos (2010), pp. 181-196, and is reprinted with the permission of Kadmos Verlag. Ubertowska's text first appeared as »Rysa, dukt, odcisk (nie)obecności. O spektrologiach zagłady« in *Teksty drugie,* vol. 2, no. 158 (2016): 108-121, and is reprinted with the permission of *Teksty drugie*. Sendyka's text first appeared in *East European Politics and Societies and Cultures*, vol. 30, no. 4 (2016): 687-702, and is reprinted with the permission of SAGE Publications. Waligórska's text first appeared as »Healing by Haunting: Jewish Ghosts in Contemporary Polish Literature« in *Prooftexts: A Journal of Jewish Literary History*, vol. 34, no. 2 (2014): 207-231, and is reprinted with the permission of Indiana University Press. Janicka and Żukowski's text originally appeared as »Przemoc filosemicka« in *Studia Litteraria et Historica* 1 (2012): 1-39, and is reprinted with the permission of the authors.

LITERATURE

Abraham, Nicholas/Torok, Maria (1986 [1976]): The Wolf Man's Magic Word: The Cryptonomy, Minneapolis: The University of Minnesota Press.
Abraham, Nicholas/Torok, Maria (1994 [1978]): The Shell and the Kernel, Chicago and London: The University of Chicago Press.
Adams, Jenni (2011): Magic Realism in Holocaust Literature: Troping the Traumatic Real, London and New York: Palgrave Macmillan.
Aleksiun, Natalia (2013): »Returning from the Land of the Dead: Jews in Eastern Galicia in the Immediate Aftermath of the Holocaust.« In: Jewish History Quarterly 2/246, pp. 256-270.
Amery, Jean (1980 [1966]): At the Mind's Limits: Contemplations by a Survivor on Auschwitz and its Realities, Bloomington: Indiana University Press.
Assmann, Aleida (2011): »Ghosts of the Past.« In: East European Memory Studies 8, pp. 1-5.
Assmann, Aleida (2014): »Fotografie und Geister in der Gegenwartskunst: Treichel, Boltanski, Leibovitz.« In: Aleida Assmann/Karoline Jeftic/Frederike Wappler (eds.), Rendezvous mit dem Realem. Die Spur des Traumas in den Künsten, Bielefeld: transcript Verlag, pp. 167-190.
Banasiewicz-Ossowska, Ewa (2007): Między dwoma światami. Żydzi w polskiej kulturze ludowej, Wrocław: PTL.
Bart, Andrzej (2008): Fabryka Muchołapek, Warszawa: Wydawnictwo W.A.B.
Bator, Joanna (2012): Ciemno, prawie noc, Warszawa: Wydawnictwo W.A.B.
Bergland, Renee L. (2000): The National Uncanny: Indian Ghosts and American Subjects, Hanover and London: University Press of New England.
Blazan, Sladja (ed.) (2008): Ghost, Stories, Histories: Ghost Stories and Alternative Histories, New Castle: Cambridge Scholars Publishing.

Błoński, Jan (2008 [1987]): »Biedni Polacy patrzą na getto.« In: Jan Błoński, Biedni Polacy patrzą na getto, Kraków: Wydawnictwo Literackie, pp. 9-33.

Bojarska, Katarzyna (2007): »Obecność Zagłady w twórczości Polskich artystów.« (http://culture.pl/pl/artykul/obecnosc-zaglady-w-tworczosci-polskich-artystow).

Brogan, Kathleen (1998): Cultural Haunting: Ghosts and Ethnicity in Recent American Literature, Charlottesville and London: The University Press of Virginia.

Butler, Judith (2006): Precarious Life: The Powers of Mourning and Violence, London and New York: Verso.

Cała, Alina (1995 [1992]): The Image of the Jew in Polish Folk Culture, Jerusalem: Magnes Press.

Cała, Alina (2012): Żyd – wróg odwieczny? Antysemityzm w Polsce i jego źródła, Warszawa: Wydawnictwo Nisza.

Caruth, Cathy (1996): Unclaimed Experience: Trauma, Narrative and History, Baltimore and London: John Hopkins University Press.

Chmielewska, Katarzyna (2016): »Creating Trauma. Symmetries and Hostile Takeovers of (Jewish) Trauma.« Unpublished manuscript.

Chutnik, Sylwia (2011): Muranooo. Manuscript.

Craps, Stef (2010): »Wor(l)d of Grief: Traumatic Memory and Literary Witnessing in Cross-Cultural Perspective.« In: Textual Practice 24/1, pp. 51-68.

Davis, Colin (2007): Haunted Subjects: Deconstruction, Psychoanalysis, and the Return of the Dead, New York and Houndmills: Palgrave Macmillan.

Del Pilar Blanco, Maria (2012): Ghost-Watching American Modernity: Haunting, Landscape, and the Hemispheric Imagination, New York: Fordham University Press.

Del Pilar Blanco, Maria/Peeren, Esther (eds.) (2010): Popular Ghosts: The Haunted Spaces of Everyday Culture, London and New York: Continuum.

Del Pilar Blanco, Maria/Peeren, Esther (eds.) (2013a): The Spectralities Reader: Ghosts and Haunting in Contemporary Cultural Theory, London, New Delhi, New York and Sydney: Bloomsbury.

Del Pilar Blanco, Maria/Peeren, Esther (2013b): »The Spectral Turn/Introduction.« In: Maria del Pilar Blanco/Esther Peeren (eds.), The

Spectralities Reader: Ghosts and Haunting in Contemporary Cultural Theory, London, New Delhi, New York and Sydney: Bloomsbury, pp. 31-36.

Derrida, Jacques (1994 [1993]): Specters of Marx: The State of the Debt, The Work of Mourning and the New International, New York and London: Routledge.

Dziuban, Zuzanna (2014): »Memory as haunting«. In: Hagar: Studies in Culture, Polity and Identities 12 (Winter), pp. 111-135.

Eisenstein, Paul (2015): »The Summons of Freedom: Fantastic History in Jonathan Safran Foer's ›Everything is Illuminated.‹« In: Judith Kerman/John Edgar Browning (eds.), The Fantastic in Holocaust Literature and Film: Critical Perspectives, Jefferson: McFarland & Company, pp. 82-101.

Elm, Michael/Kabalek, Kobi/Köhne, Julia B. (eds.) (2014): The Horrors of Trauma in Cinema: Violence, Void, Visualization, Newcastle: Cambridge Scholars Publishing.

Engelking, Barbara (2003): ›Szanowny Panie gistapo.‹ Donosy do władz niemieckich w warszawie i okolicach w latach 1940-1941, Warszawa: Wydawnictwo IFiS PAN.

Engelking, Barbara (2011): Jest taki piękny słoneczny dzień... Losy Żydów szukających ratunku na wsi polskiej 1942-45, Warszawa: Stowarzyszenie Centrum Badań nad Zagładą Żydów.

Engelking, Barbara/Grabowski, Jan (eds.) (2011): Zarys krajobrazu. Wieś Polska wobec zagłady Żydów 1942-1945, Warszawa: Stowarzyszenie Centrum Badań nad Zagładą Żydów.

Engelking, Barbara/Grabowski, Jan (eds.) (2018): Dalej jest noc. Losy Żydów w wybranych powiatach okupowanej Polski, Warszawa: Stowarzyszenie Centrum Badań nad Zagładą Żydów.

Etkind, Alexander (2013): Warped Mourning: Stories of the Undead in the Land of the Unburied, Stanford: Stanford University Press.

Fabiszczak, Małgorzta/Owiński, Marcin (2013): Obóz – muzeum. Trauma we współczesnym wystawiennictwie, Kraków: Universitas.

Felman, Shoshana/Laub, Dori (1992): Testimony: Crises of Witnessing in Literature, Psychoanalysis, and History, New York and London: Routledge.

Foer, Jonathan Safran (2002): Everything is Illuminated, New York: HarperCollins.

Forecki, Piotr (2010): Od Shoah do Strachu: Spory o polsko-żydowską przeszłość i pamięć w debatach publicznych, Poznań: Wydawnictwo Poznańskie.
Forecki, Piotr (2016): Die Republik der Gerechten. In: Zeitgeschichte Online July 11 (https://zeitgeschichte-online.de/thema/die-republik-der-gerechten).
Forecki, Piotr (2018): Po Jedwabnem. Anatomia pamięci funkcjonalnej, Warszawa: Instytut Badań Literackich PAN.
Fuchs, Anne (2010): Phantoms of War in Contemporary German Literature, Films and Discourse: The Politics of Memory, London and New York: Palgrave Macmillan.
Giesen, Bernhard/Schneider, Christoph (eds.) (2004): Tätertrauma: nationale Erinnerung im öffentlichen Diskurs, Konstanz: UvK Verlag.
Gordon, Avery (2008 [1997]): Ghostly Matters: Haunting and the Sociological Imagination, Minneapolis: University of Minnesota Press.
Grabowski, Jan (2004): ›Ja tego Żyda znam!‹ Szantażowanie żydów w Warszawie 1939-1943, Warszawa: Wydawnictwo IFiS PAN.
Grabowski, Jan (2013 [2011]): Hunt for the Jews: Betrayal and Murder in Nazi Occupied Poland, Bloomington: Indiana University Press.
Grabowski, Jan/Libionka, Dariusz (eds.) (2014): Klucze i kasa. O mieniu żydowskim w Polsce pod okupacją niemiecką i we wczesnych latach powojennych 1939-1950, Warszawa: Stowarzyszenie Centrum Badań nad Zagładą Żydów.
Gross, Jan T. (2001 [2000]): Neighbors: The Destruction of the Jewish Community in Jedwabne. Princeton and New York: Princeton University Press.
Gross, Jan T. (2006): Fear: Anti-Semitism in Poland After Auschwitz: An Essay in Historical Interpretation, New York: Random House.
Gross, Jan T. (2014): »Sprawcy, ofiary i inni.« In: Zagłada Żydów. Studia i materiały 10, pp. 885-888.
Grossman, David (2002 [1986]): See Under: Love, New York: Picador.
Gruber, Ruth Ellen (2002): Virtually Jewish: Reinventing Jewish Culture in Europe, Berkley, Los Angeles, and London: University of California Press.
Grynberg, Henryk (2003): Monolog polsko-żydowski, Wołowiec: Czarne.
Handshtok, Yakov (1998): »In the Tracks of the Jewish Life that Disappeared.« In: Jack Kugelmass/Jonathan Boyarin (eds.), From a Ruined

Garden: The Memorial Books of Polish Jewry, Bloomington: Indiana University Press, pp. 262-266.

Hegerfeldt, Anne (2005): Lies that Tell the Truth: Magic Realism Seen Through Contemporary Fiction from Britain, Amsterdam and New York: Rodopi.

Hilberg, Raul (1992): Perpetrators, Victims, Bystanders: The Jewish Catastrophe, 1933-1945, New York: HarperCollins Publishers.

Hirsch, Marianne (2008): »The Generation of Postmemory.« In: Poetics Today 29/1, pp. 103-128.

Hirsch, Marianne (2012): The Generation of Postmemory: Writing and Visual Culture after the Holocaust, New York: Columbia University Press.

Hirsch, Marianne/Miller, Nancy (eds.) (2011): Rites of Return: Diaspora Poetics and the Politics of Memory, New York: Columbia University Press.

Hirsch, Marianne/Spitzer, Leo (2010): Ghosts of Home: The Afterlife of Czernowitz in Jewish Memory, Berkeley, Los Angeles, and London: University of California Press.

Janicka, Elżbieta (2014-15): »Pamięć przyswojona. Koncepcja polskiego doświadczenia zagłady Żydów jako traumy zbiorowej w świetle rewizji kategorii świadka.« In: Studia Litteraria et Historica 3/4, pp. 148-226.

Janicka, Elżbieta/Steinlauf, Michael (2014-15): »»To nie była Ameryka.«« In: Studia Litteraria et Historica 3/4, pp. 364- 480.

Janicka, Elżbieta/Żukowski, Tomasz (2016): Przemoc filosemicka? Nowe polskie narracje o Żydach po roku 2000, Warszawa: Instytut Badań Literackich PAN.

Janion, Maria (2006): Niesamowita słowiańszczyzna. Fantazmaty literatury, Kraków: Wydawnictwo Literackie.

Jeziorski, Ireneusz (2009): Od obcości do symulakrum. Obraz Żyda w Polsce XX wieku, Kraków: Nomos.

Keff, Bożena (2013): Antysemityzm. Niezamknięta Historia, Warszawa: Wydawnictwo Czarna Owca.

Kerman, Judith B./Browning, John Edgar (eds.) (2015): The Fantastic in Holocaust Literature and Film: Critical Perspectives, Jefferson: McFarland & Company.

Kirshnbaum, Yekhiel (1998): »The City Without Jews.« In: Jack Kugelmass/Jonathan Boyarin (eds.), From a Ruined Garden: The Memorial Books of Polish Jewry, Bloomington: Indiana University Press, pp. 254-262.

Kowalczyk, Izabela (2010): Podróż do przeszłości. Interpretacje najnowszej historii w polskiej sztuce krytycznej, Warszawa: Academica.

Kraft, Andreas (2014): »Gespensterische Botschaften an die Nachgeborenen: ›Cultural Haunting‹ in der neueren deutschen Literatur.« In: Aleida Assmann/Karoline Jeftic/Frederike Wappler (eds.), Rendezvous mit dem Realem. Die Spur des Traumas in den Künsten, Bielefeld: transkript Verlag, pp. 141-165.

Kriss, Tiina (2013): »Seeing Ghosts: Theorizing Haunting in Literary Texts.« In: Gabriele Rippl et al., Haunted Narratives: Life Writing in the Age of Trauma, Toronto, Buffalo, and London: University of Toronto Press, pp. 21-44.

Kugelmass, Jack/Boyarin, Jonathan (eds.) (1998): From a Ruined Garden: The Memorial Books of Polish Jewry, Bloomington: Indiana University Press.

LaCapra, Dominick (1998): History and Memory after Auschwitz, Ithaca and London: Cornell University Press.

LaCapra, Dominick (2014 [2001]): Writing History, Writing Trauma, Baltimore: John Hopkins University Press.

Leder, Andrzej (2014): Prześniona rewolucja. Ćwiczenia z logiki historycznej, Warszawa: Wydawnictwo Krytyki Politycznej.

Lehrer, Erica (2013): Jewish Poland Revisited: Heritage Tourism in Unquiet Places, Bloomington: Indiana.

Lehrer, Erica/Meng, Michael (eds.) (2015): Jewish Space in Contemporary Poland, Bloomington: Indiana University Press.

Luckhurst, Roger (2002): »The Contemporary London Gothic and the Limits of the Spectral Turn.« In: Textual Practice 16/3, pp. 527-546.

Mahlke, Kirsten (2012): »A Fantastic Tale of Terror.« In: Michael C. Frank (ed.), Literature and Terrorism: Comparative Perspectives, Amsterdam and New York: Rodopi, pp. 195-212.

Matyjaszek, Konrad (2018): Produkcja przestrzeni żydowskiej w dawnej i współczesnej Polsce, Kraków: Universitas.

Meng, Michael (2011): Shattered Spaces: Encountering Jewish Ruins in Postwar Germany and Poland, Cambridge and London: Harvard University Press.

Michaels, Anne (1997): Fugitive Pieces, London: Bloomsbury.

Michlic, Joanna Beata (2006): Poland's Threatening Other: The Image of the Jew from 1880 to the Present, Lincoln and London: University of Nebraska Press.

Mitscherlich, Alexander/Mitscherlich, Margarete (1975 [1967]): The Inability to Mourn: Principles of Collective Behavior, New York: Grove Press.

Napiórkowski, Marcin (2016): Powstanie umarłych. Historia Pamięci, 1944-2014, Warszawa: Wydawnictwo Krytyki Politycznej.

Niziołek, Grzegorz (2013): Polski teatr Zagłady, Warszawa: Wydawnictwo Krytyki Politycznej.

Ostachowicz, Igor (2012): Noc Żywych Żydów, Warszawa: Wydawnictwo W.A.B.

Pat, Jacob (1947): Ashes and Fire: The Story of Poland's Jewry Under and After German Occupation, New York: International Universities Press.

Peeren, Esther (2014): The Spectral Metaphor: Living Ghosts and the Agency of Invisibility, New York: Palgrave Macmillan.

Polonsky, Antony/Michlic, Joanna (eds.) (2004): The Neighbors Respond: The Controversies over the Jedwabne Massacre in Poland, Princeton and Oxford: Princeton University Press.

Randt, Nicholas T. (1994): »Secrets and Posterity: The Theory of the Transgenerational Phantom. Editor's Note.« In: Nicholas Abraham/Maria Torok, The Shell and the Kernel, Chicago and London: The University of Chicago Press, pp. 165-169.

Rippl, Gabriele et al. (eds.) (2013): Haunted Narratives: Life Writing in the Age of Trauma, Toronto, Buffalo, and London: University of Toronto Press.

Rothberg, Michael (2000): Traumatic Realism: The Demands of Holocaust Representation, Minneapolis and London: University of Minnesota Press.

Schindel, Estela (2014): »Ghosts and Compañeros: Haunting Stories and the Quest for Justice around Argentina's Former Terror Sites.« In: Rethinking History 18/2, pp. 244-264.

Schwab, Gabriele (2010): Haunting Legacies: Violent Histories and Transgenerational Trauma, New York: Columbia University Press.

Sebald, W.G. (2001 [2001]): Austerlitz, New York: Random House.

Skibell, Joseph (1997): A Blessing on the Moon, New York: Algonquin Books.

Słobodzianek, Tadeusz (2010 [2009]): Our Class, London: Oberon Books.

Steinlauf, Michael (1997): Bondage to the Dead: Poland and the Memory of the Holocaust, New York: Syracuse University Press.
Tokarska-Bakir, Joanna (2004): Rzeczy mgliste. Eseje i studia, Sejny: Fundacja Pogranicze.
Tokarska-Bakir, Joanna (2008): Legendy o krwi. Antropologia przesądu, Warszawa: Wydawnictwo W.A.B.
Tokarska-Bakir, Joanna (2013): The Unrighteous Righteous and the Righteous Unrighteous. In: Dapim 24/1, pp. 11-63.
Tokarska-Bakir, Joanna (2018): Pod klątwą. Społeczny portret pogrom kieleckiego, Warszawa: Wydawnictwo Czarna Owca.
Taylor, Charles (2004): Modern Social Imaginaires, Durham and London: Duke University Press.
Tzvetan, Todorov (1975 [1979]): The Fantastic: A Structural Approach to a Literary Genre, Ithaca: Cornell University Press.
Ubertowska, Aleksandra (2014): Holokaust. Auto(tanato)grafie, Warszawa: Instytut Badań Literackich PAN.
Waligórska, Magdalena (2013): Klezmer's Afterlife: An Ethnography of the Jewish Music Revival in Poland and Germany, Oxford and New York: Oxford University Press.
Weinstock, Jeffrey (ed.) (2004a): Spectral America: Phantoms and the National Imagination, Madison: The University of Wisconsin Press.
Weinstock, Jeffrey (2004b): »Introduction: The Spectral Turn.« In: Jeffrey Weinstock (ed.), Spectral America: Phantoms and the National Imagination, Madison: The University of Wisconsin Press, pp. 3-17.
Whitehead, Anne (2004): Trauma Fiction, Edinburgh: Edinburgh University Press.
Wiszniewicz, Joanna (1997): »Antisemitism without Jews and Philosemitism without Jews: Towards a New Jewish and Polish Memory.« In: East European Jewish Affairs 27/2, pp. 68-69.
Wolfe, Gary K. (2015): »Introduction: Fantasy as Testimony.« In: Judith Kerman/John Edgar Browning (eds.), The Fantastic in Holocaust Literature and Film: Critical Perspectives, Jefferson: McFarland & Company, pp. 7-12.
Wolfreys, Julian (2002): Victorian Hauntings: Spectrality, Gothic, the Uncanny and Literature, New York and Houndmills: Palgrave Macmillan.
Wóycicka, Zofia (2013 [2009]): Arrested Mourning: Memory of the Nazi Camps in Poland, 1944-1950, Frankfurt am Main: Peter Lang.

Ziębińska-Witek, Anna (2011): Historia w muzeach. Studium ekspozycji Holokaustu, Lublin: Wydawnictwo Uniwersytetu Marii Curie-Skłodowskiej.

Zgliczyński, Stefan (2008): Antysemityzm po polsku, Warszawa: Książka i Prasa.

Żukowski, Tomasz (2018): Wielki retusz. Jak zapomnieliśmy, że Polacy zabijali Żydów, Warszawa: Wielka Litera.

On Behalf of the Dead: Mediumistic Writing on the Holocaust in Polish Literature

ALINA MOLISAK

In various cultures where a formula exists for summoning the dead, mediation plays an essential role. There is a specific kind of medium, marked out or burdened with the role of intermediary. In Judaism, the special role of the cemetery, known not only as *beit kvaroth* (home of graves), but also euphemistically as *beit ha'hayim* (home of life), indicates the importance, in this cultural tradition, of the space given to the deceased, whose spirits, according to legend, float for eternity over it. The Central European areas where the Holocaust was perpetrated tend to be seen as a symbolic cemetery of all the murdered and burned – hence the Jewish spirits repeatedly appearing, indeed being emphasized, in art. Slavoj Žižek writes that, through funeral rituals, »the dead are inscribed in the text of symbolic tradition, they are assured that, in spite of their death, they will ›continue to live‹ in the memory of the community« (1991: 23). The inability to bury victims of the Holocaust, and therefore the fact that »they cannot find their proper place in the text of tradition« (ibid.), forces those who come after to seek other ways of dealing with their presence – sometimes by adopting the role of medium. This particular conception of mediation – the use of the living to articulate experiences undergone by those who perished – can be found in many postwar texts. However, I wish to demonstrate that this way of speaking about the Holocaust has been intensely present especially since the 1990s.

Contemporary Polish authors writing about the Holocaust use different narrative strategies. Hanna Krall is an attentive listener, reconstructing the fates of the protagonists, very often from scant fragments of information about their pasts. The work of Henryk Grynberg is, almost in its entirety, heavily entangled in autobiography, based on a single autobiographical voice, indeed the only one possible – grounded as it is in the author's own experiences. In the case of Marian Pankowski's novella *Była Żydówka, nie ma Żydówki* [There Was a Jewess, There Is No Jewess, 2008], we are dealing with a collage of sorts, with assembled fragments of utterances by both the author-narrator and the heroine he has created. The uniquely oneiric prose of Piotr Szewc in *Annihilation* (1999 [1987]), *Zmierzchy i poranki* [Sunsets and Dawns, 2000], and *Bociany nad powiatem* [Storks over the County, 2005], in turn, seeks to recreate the past by means of imagination and careful observation of fine-grained but significant material evidence, bearing witness to the presence of non-Polish inhabitants of the town in which the book is set.

I would describe the traditions from which these authors derive their work as a very specific Polish-Jewish tapestry. At the core of their writing about the Holocaust, especially in the works published in the late 1980s and thereafter, one can detect, on the one hand, the heritage of Polish Romanticism and, on the other, the cultural roots of Judaism. Here, I want to point out two similar phenomena originating from the Romantic tradition and Jewish beliefs, which are deeply entangled with the certainty that a world of ghosts exists, and that they are still present among the living and affecting their existence. The belief in dybbuks (the soul of a dead person that enters the body of a living person and directs that person's conduct) has a long history in Judaism. They are first mentioned in the seventeenth century, when their activities are described and the methods of exorcising them detailed (cf. Unterman 1991: 62-63). In a similar vein, the possibility of contact with the world of the dead, especially with those dead who have not found eternal peace, is addressed by the Polish Romantic poets. In both cases, it is the spirits who cannot find rest and relief after death, the tortured souls, that permeate the world of the living, and that can sometimes be helped by the deeds of the living. The motif of the presence of the dead in today's world, of the posthumous existence of those who perished in the Holocaust, is omnipresent in the prose of the authors whose writings I analyze. These souls, in various ways, demand concrete actions – they request memory and remembrance from us.

THE WRITER AS MEDIUM

Debates both within and outside Poland during the Romantic era about the role of the poet as one who allowed the visible world to come into contact with the spirits, inviting them to appear in dreams and in waking life, suggest that poets could be assigned the specific position of mediums. This conception of their role means that writers were mediators between the world of the living and the realm of the underworld, driven by an interest in the existence of various ghostly figures inhabiting the metaphysical realm and their impact on the earthly life. Poets, acting as sensitive mediums, have used this position to introduce into the literary or, more broadly, the cultural narrative space, the wandering spirits of those who experience no peace after death. Maria Janion, the most outstanding Polish scholar of the Romantic era, writes that »the Romantics constantly stormed the border of the greatest ineffability – the ineffability of death« (Janion 2007: 70). They wanted to engage in a conversation with the dead, »the most impossible of all that exist« (ibid.); they established the tradition of listening to ghosts, of a silent dialogue with their mute otherness. A similar strategy is adopted by the contemporary writers mentioned above, who seek the most appropriate forms to record that which is impossible to represent – the Holocaust.

The role of the narrator in the vast majority of Hanna Krall's stories evokes this attitude: the storyteller is someone who listens carefully to the living survivors and the murdered dead. She poses questions to all protagonists, regardless of their ontological status – aware, however, of the impossibility of receiving answers. At the same time, the narrator is a medium used by both the living and the dead to speak. In one of the stories, she hears, »Read it aloud. [...] Well, write, write.« (Krall 2005b [1995]: 174)

In Henryk Grynberg's predominantly autobiographical early work, the positionality of a subject speaking on behalf of the dead gains an increasingly definite shape, eventually leading to a claim of exclusivity as to who has the right to speak on behalf of the murdered, who has the right to be *the* Romantic poet endowed with a special mission, singled out and exceptional. In a lecture at the Spertus Institute of Jewish Studies in Chicago, the writer said of himself, »A stray between the generations, Poles and Jews, living and dead, I belong both here and there, or neither here nor there.« (Grynberg 2001: 48) Many Holocaust survivors reflect on their ontological status in a similar way.

Often, especially in his more recent texts, Grynberg has also emphasized the persistent presence of ghosts:

Poland is [...] peopled with ghosts – mostly Jewish (this time truly ›zażydzona‹ [lit. overjewed]), [with ghosts] that cannot really be removed. [...] Ashes cannot be gathered – neither from the soil nor from the psyche, nor from history. (Grynberg 2003: 41)

The distinctive narrator created by Piotr Szewc, an artist who could be described as a representative of the so-called »second generation« of Holocaust writers,[1] resorts to yet another set of methods. A hunter for the past, a seeker of the bygone, he assumes the role of medium in relation to the space of the town, to houses, to objects. From the stories revealed by these objects, he reconstructs the world that existed before the Holocaust. A walk through the contemporary space serves as an excuse for telling stories about old times. As he photographs the town, the narrator focuses on details, tiny details, and makes manifest that he is, indeed, aware of non-memory: »Those few minor events [...] will vanish, [...] will not be salvaged.« (Szewc 1999 [1987]: 5) The reminders and exploration of »the past that isn't studied« (ibid.) also bring to mind issues of language and choice of medium, indicated by the narrator's reflections as well. The grasping of a particular subject or moment in time vanishes after all, along with the generalized naming. It enters the first stage of forgetting; it becomes impossible to remember. As the narrator makes efforts to capture the existence of the town, the »center of the world« for its inhabitants, the narrative »we« is conscious (as are the readers) of his limitations. The narrator's knowledge, even his most careful descriptions of gestures, smells, light and shadow, but also his awareness of future events (discreetly indicated by reference to the act of watching photographs being taken within the story's timeframe and then five decades afterwards), allow him merely to create »a world he could not quite imagine« (ibid: 13). The

---

1 Traditionally, the term »second generation« pertained to people born after the war to families of Holocaust survivors. Art Spiegelman's graphic novel *Maus* is perhaps the best-known example of art created by artists of this generation (cf. Young 1998). For the purposes of this chapter, I include Szewc's work in the category of »second generation« - writers born after the Second World War and engaging with the Holocaust.

suggestions, symbolic figures referencing the Holocaust, are signals to the reader, signs of this reconstruction, made possible by the mediumistic abilities of the narrating observer.

One of the most interesting texts published recently which takes up the issue of the Holocaust and memory is a prose piece by Marian Pankowski, *There Was a Jewess, There Is No Jewess* (2008). In this slim, very modest but precise book, the author chooses a similar perspective. In the first part of the novella, the author-narrator invokes the endurance of individual memory, recalling specific names and surnames from his prewar childhood. In subsequent parts, there is a recurrent trope of the »presence of those absent« (Pankowski 2008: 29), against which »the inhabitants of the Nowhere Land« (ibid: 66)[2] stand helpless – they look away, do not want to remember. This presence reminds them all too painfully not only of the fundamentally different Jewish fate during the Holocaust, but also of their own behavior at the time.

THE DEAD, GHOSTS, AND DYBBUKS

As in Romanticism, being singled out from the collective as a medium for ghosts that permeate present-day reality leaves a mark on the writer's entire life and makes an imprint on their creative biography. But it also allows them to occupy a special position – communion with the dead authorizes them to pass radical judgments against the living. The narrator in Henryk Grynberg's book, *Dziedzictwo* [Heritage, 1993], writes:

I felt a cold shiver standing face to face with evil, but I found in some of the eyes and words the warmth, which is necessary for me to live. I wrapped my father's bottle in a prayer shawl and I buried it together with dug up crumbs of my grandmother's home hearth. [...] I am unable to forgive. I do not want to. I do not feel empowered to do so. Let the murdered forgive, if they can. I am a weak man, and too much cannot be expected of me. And I don't think that God, who is justice, requires it. I think it is fair to condemn. Eternally. Without the statute of limitations. (1993: 45)

---

2   Nowhere Land, as Pankowski himself suggests, is Poland; this recalls Alfred Jarry's play *King Ubu*, which takes place »in Poland, that is, Nowhere«.

This bitter judgment was formulated by the author-narrator after his return from Poland, where he had been searching for his father's burial site. In meetings and conversations with the locals, recounted in a way that also captures the peculiarities of the language, he learns about the fate of his family and the circumstances of his father's death – he was murdered by local peasants. Grynberg's literary account was created in connection with Paweł Łoziński's documentary *Miejsce urodzenia* [Place of Birth, 1992], a film that captured the events of the writer's trip to Poland and explained the circumstances of his father's death.

In her deliberations on the Romantic era, Maria Janion evokes the opinion of Louis-Vincent Thomas, who universalizes the widespread belief that »the dead, if they are not separated from the living, drive them mad« (1980: 80). Janion adds, »We can say that the Romantics live in a state of madness induced by the constant presence of their dead« (2007: 70). I posit that those who are compelled by ghosts to convey the experience of those murdered in the Holocaust experience a similar »madness«. In Jewish tradition, the belief in the existence of dybbuks – the souls of the dead who cannot rest in peace – has a long history. Although dybbuks were traditionally considered to possess demonic features, there also exist approaches that construct dybbuks as damaged souls seeking redress for their grievances. The dybbuk may also be a soul shocked by a sudden and unnatural death, demanding spiritual support from the living and their assistance in settling scores with the world in which the deceased suffered exceptional evil (cf. Unterman 1991: 62-63).

Both cases – the Romantic impact of the dead on the living and the existence of dybbuks – bear some similarities. Both, I think, may be considered to underpin the narratives of Grynberg and Krall, as well as those of Szewc and Pankowski. Their literature is haunted by the dead – by the specters of those who suffered a sudden, unnatural death untamed by any ritual. Their constant presence accompanies the living; those who were deprived of a rite of passage disturb the symbolic order of the world, and, although they are seemingly absent and excluded, they exist and affect those who come after them.

But there is yet another way of understanding the existence of these visitors from »the other world:« it is often in these terms that one describes *survivors* of the Holocaust – in order to emphasize the hiatus in the history of humankind, the radical difference of their experience, its inaccessibility for us today. In Pankowski's story, the narrator emphasizes that he is accompanied by the real names of former schoolmates who, today, exist only in his memory as ghosts. In contrast, the protagonist of the story, Fajga Oberlander, comes from another place in a double sense: from the past of the Holocaust, when she visits her American »fellow-citizens–non-citizens« (Pankowski 2008: 13), but also from the peculiar »Nowhere Land« of Poland, forever marked – Poland, which is the primary place where the Holocaust unfolded.

In both Krall's and Grynberg's prose, the protagonists are recurrently cast as hovering between life and death, seen by their contemporaries as apparitions or ghosts. In an autobiographical text first published in 1979, titled *Życie osobiste* [Personal Life, 1989], Grynberg repeatedly emphasizes and enhances the constant presence of the murdered, whose insistence brings to mind phantoms, vampires or, indeed, dybbuks. They demand attention from the living, force them to think about the past, insist on being remembered. The presence of ghosts is felt particularly strongly during the biggest holiday, Yom Kippur, when the *Yizkor* prayer is recited. The word means »remember« or »recall«, in the imperative mood (Unterman 1991: 208). At this time, communion with the ghosts takes on the form of an almost physical co-presence: »they always arrive that day and circle over your head [...], the whole families, trains, cities become entangled in your hair« (Grynberg 1992: 134). The encounters with ghosts shape the entire existence of the protagonists of the narratives analyzed here, and not only in Grynberg's prose.

The ontological condition of the speaking subject, especially for Grynberg – in Krall's stories, it is rather the protagonists' condition – is a specific existence on the border between two worlds. Nevertheless, both authors define themselves to some extent as storytellers, as those who relate: they assume the position of representatives of the dead, of envoys of the spirit world, whose narration serves to keep the memory of individual existence alive. (Grynberg speaks of this more directly, without refined metaphors.) They also take upon themselves the duty to protect the dead against the living. What they protect the dead against is the contemporary »institutionalization of the past«, a phenomenon that renders individual memory absent or impossible. Pankowski acts in a similar manner, when he knowingly reveals the process by which a strongly typified female protagonist is created – a protagonist who, however, instead of framing the past and the story of her own survival in a way that would meet the expectations of her American listeners, offers a narrative which extends beyond the frame of known survivors' testimonies (cf. 2008: 10). Fajga's fragmentary account radically breaks with what her audience already knows about the fate of Jews during the war. This short dialogue is a good example of how the »tamed« narratives are questioned:

One night, it was cold, I slept in a car on a dead-end track... I was woken up in the morning by the train whistle and rumble of wheels. I was freezing. Where's my jacket? My jacket's gone! And with that, my ›journey‹ began.
Kupferman:
›It was probably a band of Poles prowling around the stations where the Germans packed the Jews into cattle trucks?‹
›No... there were no bands in the German presence. It was definitely this friendly, young Pole who advised me to find a ›warm wagon‹ for the night.‹ (Ibid: 22)

Since his debut with *Ekipa Antygona* [Antigone's Team, 1963], Grynberg has consistently followed an individual trail of a story told time and time again; his writing resembles the »descent into the depths of experience that seems to have no end« (Krawczyńska 2001: 172). Over the last twenty years, Grynberg's narrative has gradually moved beyond the autobiographical towards speaking on behalf of others, both victims and survivors, who, as a result of their trauma, cannot speak for themselves. This is clear in publications such as *Dzieci Syjonu* [Children of Zion, 1998 (1994)], a book which is simply an edited selection of documents, and in the story collection *Drohobych, Drohobych* (2002 [1997]), where each text is endorsed with an appropriate dedication, and where the writer assumes the position of mediator, of the one who speaks-in-the-name-of, who records other people's voices. In such cases, Grynberg employs a third-person narration or creates a protagonist not framed through autobiographical descriptions. Sometimes he introduces a female form in the narrative, as in the story »Escape from Boryslaw«, told by and from the perspective of a woman, a Holocaust survivor, who recounts the occupation, the time of her death, and her own rebirth, which she experienced thanks to postwar emigration to Israel (2002 [1997]: 49-72). A similar strategy, that of giving voice to survivors, especially to women, finds its way into many other stories, including »A Hungarian Sketch, »A Pact with God«, and »A Family Sketch« (Grynberg 2002 [1997]). This is where the difference lies – here emerges a writer who becomes an intermediary, a medium, who shares his talents with others so that they, too, have the opportunity to bear witness to the existence of those who perished, the dead who are still remembered by their relatives.

The suggestive poetic prose of Piotr Szewc can be read as an instance of memory construction, that is, primarily as a work of imagination. As the text indicates, this kind of memory becomes possible through repeatedly undertaken engagements with the traces of the »shadow«:

> You would have to get close, lean over, and perhaps in the sand and in the dried mud you would be able to glimpse the outline of the shadow, right next to a clearly stamped bootprint, maybe the toes of the one who, without doubt, had wandered here, would have grasped the thick air like a handrail, maybe some hope of salvation would smolder. (Szewc 2000: 90)

This is the kind of memory work that Szewc advances towards the ghosts (shadows) that, since the Holocaust, continuously accompany us in Poland.

From the very beginning of her creative work, Krall assumes the position of a listener, a reporter, creating a particular distance within the third-person narrative, entwining Jewish, Polish, and German destinies. In her prose miniatures, she frequently returns to the traditional Jewish motif of the dybbuk and extrapolates the figure in post-Holocaust times, most directly in the text titled »The Dybbuk« (2005a [1995]). In this story, the protagonist initially tries to break free from the ghost inhabiting him – it is the spirit of his brother, who was killed in the ghetto and whom he did not even know. The story tells of the symptoms of dybbuk possession and of attempts at exorcism. In the end, the protagonist resolves the ethical dilemma by accepting life with the dybbuk; he wants to safeguard the memory of the existence of another in order to preserve his own identity.[3] The prose piece *To ty jesteś Daniel* [So You Are Daniel, 2001], partially a diary, partially a collage of various notes, addresses the phenomenon of a substitute life, lived on behalf of someone who was killed. The barely sketched story of Szulim is split into two parts.

---

3   Commenting on Krzysztof Warlikowski's play *The Dybbuk* (which premiered in Wroclaw in 2003), which was based on both the classic (1919) drama by Szymon An-sky and on her own modern short story, Krall emphasized that »An-ski discusses an innocent time. We, in our time, know that the dybbuk cannot be chased away. It is our memory. Without our dybbuks we would be worse and more stupid.« (Krall/Warlikowski/Cieślak 2003).

He leaves his Eastern European shtetl, goes to Florence, gets married and has a daughter. After his internment in Auschwitz, Szulim starts a new life and marries another woman. When he announces to his second wife that their daughter will be named after the first, who died in the Holocaust, she, terrified, bears a son. History repeats itself in the next generation, as his son's wife bears Szulim a grandson, scared by her husband's deep conviction of the need to give the child the name of his murdered half-sister. Szulim's son is the protagonist who most firmly believes in the posthumous life, convinced that he will meet his sister, and that grey-haired Sissel will be waiting for him and will recognize her brother.

The memory of the past is not only hidden in the body but also, apparently, very much stuck in thought patterns, sometimes even subconsciously passed on to successive generations. It is in this vein that we can read the diagnosis proposed by Pankowski, conveyed in authorial comments accompanying the collage prose – his strong words on the Polish othering of the Jews, who were always alien and estranged, and on the inheritance of the memory of the past, including the shamefully concealed and antisemitic past. Not only the memory of those who perished but also the patterns of hate speech and xenophobic attitudes are passed on to subsequent generations, and (as Pankowski's narrator believes) not much has changed, in this respect, in the country on the Vistula River. The Polish space inherited by coming generations is populated as much by the ghosts of murdered Jews as by specters of antisemitism.

An interesting difference between Grynberg's and Krall's prose is that, for Grynberg, it is survivors who communicate with Jewish ghosts, that is, those who, like the narrator himself, live on the border between the two worlds. For Krall, the presence of ghosts is experienced quite broadly; the metaphysical perspective is extended onto all of contemporary reality. She writes that the Polish residents of the town »entrust their trouble [...] to Our Lady of Leżajsk [...] and the tzaddik« (1995: 24); they apparently believe in the constant spiritual presence of the Jewish Tzadik Elimelech, famous for his ability to overpower demons. The tenants of postwar blocks built over the former Warsaw ghetto cannot cope with the ghosts haunting their houses, and only a prayer recited by the rabbi »frees« them of this tiring, alien presence (Krall 1998). Many of the characters in Krall's prose speak directly about »bearing within« other people, about experiencing their ghostly presence. In the story »Hamlet«, after becoming the executor of a friend's will, the narrator takes upon herself the task of reconstructing the fate of Adam, a pianist and the friend's partner: »She left me your papers and your spirit in her will. Could I refuse?« (2005c [1995]: 198). In the course of studying the fate of the pianist, she even dialogues with the ghost: »Do you intend to interfere with my writing?« (ibid). The omnipresence of ghosts and spirits particularly affects the space of dreams, of the subconscious, but it also permeates descriptions of the real world: »Two buildings are part of the property above which hover the spirits of bankers, artists and philosophers.« (Krall 2005c [1995]: 170)

TWO WORLDS

A certain similarity between Krall's and Szewc's prose is to be found in their aforementioned awareness of the coexistence of worlds – the past and the present – and in the way they construct narration, which could be described as probabilistic. The narrators convey multivariable events – it could have been this way, it could have been otherwise; they lay before us alternative scenarios of the life that has been prematurely wiped out. A peculiar uncertainty, indicated by the narrator, also permeates the stories heard by Krall. Uncertainty accompanies Szewc's narrator too, when he delves into the »pluperfect time«: »All the events we witness are certain and obvious but the presence – the existence – of the Hasidim is and was uncertain.« (1999 [1987]: 74) The task at hand remains to search for opportunities to reconstruct the destroyed world, to explore the »mystery of traces«, which, despite all of the uncertainty, might coexist with the awareness of being that – according to Emmanuel Lévinas – »although it exists, it does not exist entirely, it remains suspended and can begin again any time« (1979 [1961]: 230).

This probabilistic nature of narration is emphasized by the use of grammatical tenses. For instance, in Krall's story »Prawnuk« [The Great Grandson, 2017 (1991)], the reconstruction of the past is framed in the future tense (»It will be so...«). Szewc writes in the present tense, focusing on the recording of elements of the represented world, but sometimes delves into probabilistic divagations and speculates about the intentions or planned activities of his protagonists: »Maybe he's returning home. Or maybe he's going to his office« (1999 [1987]: 8). »It's only logical to assume that it carries grain« (ibid: 4). »It could be this way. It could happen« (Ibid: 16). Interestingly,

Krall sometimes draws attention to a particular detail, an object, but she mainly listens to other people's stories; as a voice of the second generation, Szewc is already deprived of this opportunity. For him, objects, buildings, lichens on the walls of houses become the medium of the story. In the novel *Sunsets and Dawns* (2003), as we encounter a space organized around the market square pump, the traders' stalls, shops full of secrets, and a world of deformed, degraded objects (voices from the attic!), we experience an elusive and flickering world, one that is nevertheless framed by a recurrent motif of the rhythm of time, of duration, of arresting ›in the frame‹. We learn most about this duration, however, from the smokestacks – they have been peering at past events for a long time now and will also be privy to those that will be seen in the future by the walls of the houses. The expectation of impending disaster is clear – small signals, a »splinter, a gap« of being (Szewc 2000: 83), a shade that cannot creep close enough, a woman, Salome, who after many years »rather heard the train rolling on the tracks than felt and remembered what had left on it forever, taking also her, and if not her, then part of her world [...]« (ibid: 33).

While the storytellers in Krall's or Grynberg's prose possess fragmentary knowledge, Szewc's narrator has at his disposal merely temporary associations, »selected glimpses« (1999 [1987]: 81), which are nevertheless subject to abstraction or forgetfulness. At the same time, in concordance with the intentions of the older writers, he repeatedly emphasizes the purpose and meaning of storytelling: »To save, but how? For whom? Before it is irrevocably lost, before it sinks into non-being, into eternal oblivion. [...] What can be saved before it is fulfilled?« (Ibid: 100)

It is different for Pankowski – here, the author-narrator, who has at his disposal an arsenal of real, remembered figures, prefers to construct a protagonist, Fajga. We learn about her fate from two different sources: her own account and that of the author-narrator, to whom Fajga turns in a moment where she is having trouble conveying her own memories: »It's better when the author says what comes next... I couldn't« (2008: 48). Led by the narrator, Fajga comes to tell yet another story to the Polish reader: that of Polish wartime antisemitism. It is no coincidence that, from the very beginning, when she tells her experience of hiding, of fighting for survival, she recurrently refers to a particular space – a »szopa« [barn] (ibid: 21). For the residents of the North American Azojville,[4] the phenomenon seems quite incomprehensible at first, indeed someone asks: »What is a ›szopa‹?« (Ibid.) The szopa, in Pankowski's text, is to some extent reminiscent of the barn from the famous book by Jan Tomasz Gross, *Sąsiedzi* [Neighbors, 2001 (2000)], about the pogrom in Jedwabne.[5] Here, it also becomes a ghastly symbol of the dangers that Jews faced during the Holocaust – not only from Nazis or Nazi collaborators, but from ordinary people. In Fajga's story, it is the children who prove to be cruel, »playing the Jews« (ibid: 46), in the framework of a spectacle controlled by the adults, without any compassion towards their neighbors, mandated by their religion.

TWO TRADITIONS

What connects these authors, whose literary achievements in the last twenty years have provided ways to write about the Holocaust in Poland? I posit that it is their faith in the medium of literature, combined with their awareness of its limitations. They convey an undisguised helplessness in the face of the words used to describe the past, openly address their inadequacy, and call into question traditional ways of narrating the Holocaust. Their language, so often subjected to doubt, draws its strength, as I have attempted to show, from an equal observance of at least two traditions – Polish Romanticism and Central European Judaism. Also typical is a specific mode of irony, at least for Krall and Pankowski.

Two of these authors, Pankowski and Grynberg (especially in more recently published texts), tend towards combining literary creation with direct diagnoses of the present. Both draw attention to the fundamental difference of the Jewish fate during the Holocaust, when being Jewish meant a death sentence, being excluded from the human race. Both also emphasize the

---

4 I note the irony present even in such a detail as the invented name of the town – azoj + ville. Azoj in Yiddish means, among other things, like so, something like. Semantically, therefore, an interesting play on words follows – these are the American descendants of Eastern European Jews who lived in the U.S. »apparently-town«, something that might resemble a kind of fake, simulated shtetl.

5 It was there that in July 1941 over 340 Jewish Poles had been brutally murdered by their non-Jewish compatriots, the vast majority of them burned alive in a barn.

problem Poles have with noticing this difference of fate, the vexed tendency of Polish memory to focus exclusively on its own suffering, and the still widespread reluctance to bring to light disgraceful behaviors directed towards the Others. Pankowski does so in a short chapter titled »O starzeniu się wydarzeń i o Żydach odartych z człowieczeństwa« [The Aging of the Events and Jews Stripped of Humanity] and in the »Epilogue«, where he speaks on behalf of the community living in the European »Nowhere Land«, a community jealous of the »precedence in the history of the suffering of nations«, a community unwilling to recall the Others (2008: 66). It may well be that the community's very ignorance of its own unwillingness to remember is what burdens these writers with this topic, so uncomfortable for a self-aware debate. Since we »cannot comprehend the enormity of the wrongs committed against Jews« (Pankowski 2008: 66), all we might demand is that writers, on behalf of both the dead and the living, write more fragile words, search for ways to clarify the world of both the present and the past, in which Polish and Jewish histories were so entangled.

The fact that Pankowski and Grynberg, who have lived in exile for decades, still write in Polish suggests that this is an informed choice – to exist, the word must be read. But is it not the case that all four authors, in writing about the Holocaust, to some extent, in different ways, »calm« the Polish (reader's) conscience? Are we not dealing here with a »delegated« memory of sorts, a memory more comfortable for the community than the debates, exposing frailties, that erupted after the historic publication of Jan Tomasz Gross's books? Or is it rather about compulsion, a pressure exerted by the presence of »Jewish ghosts« in contemporary Poland, and about the role these ghosts play in shaping our contemporary identity? What can be seen with certainty is the need of successive generations (Pankowski was born in 1919, Szewc in 1961) to examine the subject of the Holocaust, of that which is rationally incomprehensible, impossible to capture, disturbing.

Translated from Polish by Robin Gill and Zuzanna Dziuban

Literature

Grynberg, Grynberg (1963): Ekipa Antygona, Warszawa: Państwowy Instytut Wydawniczy.
Grynberg, Henryk (1989): Życie osobiste, Warszawa: Oficyna Wydawnicza Pokolenie.
Grynberg, Henryk (1992): Życie ideologiczne. Życie osobiste, Warszawa: Państwowy Instytut Wydawniczy.
Grynberg, Henryk (1993): Dziedzictwo, Londyn: Aneks.
Grynberg, Henryk (1994): Dzieci Syjonu, Warszawa: Wydawnictwo Wielka Litera.
Grynberg, Henryk (2001): »Bohaterstwo dzieci Holocaustu.« In: Res Publica Nowa 8, pp. 45-49.
Grynberg, Henryk (2002 [1997]): Drohobycz, Drohobycz, and Other Stories, New York: Penguin Books.
Grynberg, Henryk (2003): Monolog polsko-żydowski, Wołowiec: Czarne.
Janion, Maria (2007): Niesamowita Słowiańszczyzna, Kraków: Wydawnictwo Literackie.
Krall, Hanna (1991): »Prawnuk.« In: Hanna Krall, Fantom bólu. Reportaże wszystkie, Kraków: Wydawnictwo Literackie, pp. 695-703.
Krall, Hanna (1995): Dowody na istnienie, Kraków: Wydawnictwo a5.
Krall, Hanna (2001): To ty jesteś Daniel, Kraków: Wydawnictwo a5.
Krall, Hanna/Warlikowski, Krzysztof/Cieślak, Jan (2003): »›Bez dybuków będziemy gorsi i głupsi‹. Rozmowa z Hanną Krall i Krzysztofem Warlikowskim.« In: Rzeczpospolita no 232 (https://archiwum.rp.pl/artykul/458642-Bez-dybukow-bedziemy-gorsi-i-glupsi.html).
Krall, Hanna (2005a [1995]): »The Dybbuk.« In: Hanna Krall, The Woman from Hamburg and Other Stories, New York: Other Press, pp. 137-154.
Krall, Hanna (2005b [1995]): »The Tree.« In: Hanna Krall, The Woman from Hamburg and Other Stories, New York: Other Press, pp. 167-184.
Krall, Hanna (2005c [1995]): »Hamlet.« In: Hanna Krall, The Woman from Hamburg and Other Stories, New York: Other Press, pp. 195-247.
Krawczyńska, Dorota (2001): »Twarzą w twarz, maską w maskę, w potrzasku.« O *Racoonie* Henryka Grynberga. In: Teksty Drugie 6, pp. 165-175.
Lévinas, Emmanuel (1979 [1961]), Totality and Infinity: An Essay of Exteriority, Dordrecht, Boston and London: Kleuwer Academic Publishers.

Pankowski, Marian (2008): Była Żydówka, nie ma Żydówki, Warszawa: Wydawnictwo Krytyki Politycznej.

Szewc, Piotr (1999 [1987]): Annihilation, Normal: Dalkey Archive Press.

Szewc, Piotr (2000): Zmierzchy i poranki, Kraków: Wydawnictwo Literackie.

Szewc, Piotr (2005): Bociany nad powiatem, Kraków: Wydawnictwo Literackie.

Thomas, Luis-Vincent (1980): La Cadavre: De la biologie à l'anthropologie, Paris: Ed. Complexe.

Unterman, Alan (1991): Dictionary of Jewish Lore and Legend, London: Thames and Hudson.

Young, James E. (1998): »The Holocaust as Vicarious Past: Art. Spiegelman's *Maus* and the Afterimages of History.« In: Critical Inquiry 24/3, pp. 666-699.

Žižek, Slavoj (1991): Looking Awry: An Introduction to Jacques Lacan through Popular Culture, Cambridge and London: The MIT Press.

Scratch, Groove, the Imprint of (Non)presence
On the Spectrologies of the Holocaust

ALEKSANDRA UBERTOWSKA

>»The future can only be of ghosts.«
> JACQUES DERRIDA (1994 [1993]: 45)

>»From the back with a bang slammed the heavy door to the old synagogue, as if all the spirits had flown out to see what had happened.«
> ZYGMUNT MIŁOSZEWSKI (2011: 17)

Spectrological scholarship devoted to post-traumatic literature, especially writings on the Holocaust, develops most frequently a conceptual trajectory which manifests itself in a fairly obvious way. It is an interpretive trope gravitating toward the description of Jewish ghosts, specters, the »living dead«, returning from the dead to obtain a proper burial, to request the closure of the symbolic »cryptic« syntagm initiated behind the walls of the Warsaw ghetto, in Jedwabne, or at the deportation camps in Transnistria.[1] This

---

1   Przemysław Czapliński introduced the concept of »retrograde catastrophe« to mark the place of the genocide of the Jews in Polish culture, explaining its formulation thusly: »Is it possible that a fire which broke out long ago is only now beginning to subsume buildings? Or that an earthquake that happened at one time

approach validates the literary matter of the analyzed texts. Spectral sceneries, poetic images, conventions determining the condition of the world presented are very frequent in the field of Holocaust literature. It suffices to quote some randomly selected examples: *Cienie* [Shadows, 2007] by Kornel Filipowicz, *Pensjonat* [The Pension, 2009] by Piotr Paziński, *Tamta strona* [The Other Side, 1984] by Bogdan Wojdowski, W.G. Sebald's collection of short stories *The Emigrants* (1996 [1992]), the poetry of Nelly Sachs and Jerzy Ficowski, and, finally, recent novels with a heavily exposed hauntological motive: Andrzej Bart's *Fabryka muchołapek* [The Flytrap Factory, 2008] and Igor Ostachowicz's *Noc żywych Żydów* [Night of the Living Jews, 2012]. All these works substantiate the view expressed by Colin Davis that »the history of Europe can be understood as the failed endeavor to rid itself of its ghosts. But [...] we are not yet ready to give up on our dead.« (2007: 8).

However, the impact of hauntology also manifests itself in the fields of criticism and cultural theory. The spectral mode of interpretation has established an individual methodology within Holocaust studies and is practiced by representatives of various research orientations. Marianne Hirsch locates it at the heart of aesthetic sensibility, articulated through the conceptual frame of »postmemory«, relating it also to personal experience, as evidenced by the publication of the famous autobiographical book *Ghosts of Home: The Afterlife of Czernovitz in Jewish Memory* (Hirsh/Spitzer 2010). This book could be seen as a paradigmatic example of how hauntology aids the study of postmemorial literature, especially in relation to the space as an anchor of memorial operations. In *Ghosts of Home*, this principle predominates: virtual maps of former streets and squares are projected onto the real topography of contemporary Ukrainian cities; the protagonists of Hirsch's narrative inhabit multiple temporal dimensions, exceeding the limits of the conventional

---

is destroying the town today? Yes, I think that such a fire and such an earthquake are possible – once unobserved, and thus unreal, and real only when they are finally noticed. This is a retrograde catastrophe. The witnesses did not see that it was happening, did not recognize its essence, did not consider any preventive measures for the future. When after time had passed their descendants regained the ability to see and understand, when they developed remedial measures, the catastrophe which had once occurred starts to happen again, spreading in all directions.« (2015: 37).

realities of fragmentary retrospective stories. The method practiced by Marianne Hirsch is used, to varying degrees, in many genres. The spectral analysis is carried out by Jakub Momro, who, in *Widmoontologie nowoczesności* [Spectroontologies of Modernity, 2015], interprets Elfriede Jelinek's novel *The Children of the Dead* (1998 [1996]); in similar vein, Sylwia Karolak undertakes a brief review of literary specters in a monographic issue of *Czas Kultury* (2013); and Elżbieta Janicka adopts the spectral lens in her photo-essay *Festung Warschau* (2012), devoted to the politics of memory evolving in the area of the former ghetto. James E. Young, too, employs multiple spectral terms in his book on postmodern Holocaust art: the »vicarious past«, »holograms«, »after-images« (the German translation of his book uses an even more evocative notion to define these representations: »Nach-Bilder« (2002 [2000]). For Young, spectrality is almost synonymous with postmodernism, with the art that comes *after* and parasitizes on modern forms of witnessing (or, conversely, on that of the avant-garde experiment).

One can nevertheless get the impression that the concept of Jewish ghosts, phantoms, understood as personal doubles of the Jewish residents who haunt the contemporary inhabitants of Zamość, Śródborów, Muranów, and of the spectral spaces of Jewish towns, is somewhat depleted interpretively and leaves the researcher, especially the literary scholar, little room for maneuver. At the same time, a significant discrepancy is marked here: »Jewish specters« appear to be well-embedded in the worlds represented in the post-memorial novels of Szewc, Paziński, and Ostachowicz, but the attempt at an interpretation (or discursive framing) of these figures reveals intellectual limitations and entanglement of the authors in ambiguous aporias. Specters, ghosts, and Jewish zombies are figures that seem to be as terrifying as they are ludicrous, affording a slightly perverse amusement as they avert, mediate and locate the experience of the »uncanny« within the frame of a soothing convention. It is hard to avoid the impression that those figures are epistemologically tamed, and, in aesthetic terms, ambiguously balance on the verge of kitsch.

ANACHRONIES OF THE SPECTER

In view of the above, it seems reasonable to revisit Jacques Derrida's hauntology, as outlined in the French philosopher's later books *Specters of*

Marx (1994 [1993]) and *Of Spirit* (1989 [1987]), and in his collection *The Truth in Painting* (1987 [1978]). Their re-reading will be accompanied here by a conceptualization that seeks in Derridean theory for pragmatic tools potentially helpful in analyses of post-traumatic literary texts and artworks. After all, Derrida is the founding father of the spectral theory as author of these works and, significantly, of *Fors* (1977 [1976]), where he introduces and interprets Nicolas Abraham and Maria Torok's *Cryptonimie* (albeit important in the present context, this text will not be addressed in this chapter) (cf. for instant Marzec 2012). The intellectual work dedicated to these writings confirms the validity of J. Hillis Miller's opinion, who, in an article rewritten recently for a Polish journal, declared that we are living in a »Derridean time« even after the death of the author of *Specters of Marx* (2014: 7). As a matter of fact, Derrida's philosophy captures not only the dynamics of contemporary intellectual configurations but also of those configurations that only begin to appear on the horizon of history.

In his books, the French philosopher formulates a very original concept of the specter, fairly distinct from vernacular presumptions about its condition. His thoughts on spectrality are structured around three thematic axes: the problems of time, series/seriality, and material form (of specters). Derrida situates spectrality within several overlapping orders, palimpsestic and circular, whose modifications in the broader discursive field lead to the effect of self-reversal. In this way, the very reflection on the specter becomes spectral, indeterminate, and incommensurate with itself.

In Derrida's view, the most significant trait of spectrality is anachrony, a temporal out-of-jointness in which temporalities overlap or take the form of an ontological »coalescence« of various temporal orders, as it were. Anachrony constitutes the essential condition of spectral thought, serves as its vantage point and permeates it from the very first sentence. After all, Derrida's book opens with a recall of »the specter of communism« in Marx's *Communist Manifesto*, which arrives from the future. Its contemplation takes the form of anticipation, marked by fear, but also by excitement. This also pertains to the prophesy of leftism, the leftist revolution, emerging on the horizon of contemporaneity (cf. Kuźniak 2014). Marx – or rather his »specter«, whose arrival is promised by Derrida – exists as a future present, located at the intersection of times whose relationship is unstable, oscillating ontologically. Therefore, the condition of the specter that looks at us without being seen, evinces a fundamental quality of existence, a »non-contemporaneity of present time with itself« (Derrida 1994 [1993]: 29), which translates into a warped, dislodged temporality. Its essence is expressed well by the Derridean formula »The future can only be of ghosts. And the past.« (Ibid: 45) The specter inhabits multiple temporal orders, entangling them and binding them together. The time of the specter is, therefore, »this time of the present [that] comes from the future to go toward the past« (ibid: 28), it is a movement in which (self)understanding is won through (re)recognition of events that, this time, manifest as ghostly. The procession of specters in which humans de-recognize themselves proceeds through ruptures, inconsistencies and differences, retracting or reinscribing an event in a new temporal code. History, in turn, is a »sticking together« of these temporal disjunctions, says Derrida.

Derrida's spectrology situates itself at the polar opposite of the phenomenon which we might call the anthropomorphization of ghosts. Inspired by Hamlet's »the thing«, in *Specters of Marx* Derrida radically depersonalizes the specter, casting it as »between something and someone« (1994 [1993]: 5), although a *persona* can at times serve as its form, or costume. Elsewhere, Derrida writes of the specter as sited between the person and their phantasm, as being something decidedly inhuman (posthuman?). He defines spectrality as »a structure of disappearing apparition« (ibid: 125), as the projection of phantoms on a screen which also turns out to be ghostly. This way of thinking can hardly be reconciled with the imagery of kind-hearted ghosts or zombies, which permeate contemporary Polish literature. Instead, it resembles the method of spectral analysis in physics, where the composition of a substance is determined on the basis of the colored »afterimage« of its heated sample, or where a star which no longer exists can be tracked down by its remaining light trace. It seems eligible, therefore, to assume that the spectral discourse serves, in Derrida's view, as a means of formulating radical (post)metaphysical statements: what he seems to be saying is that we see the world as it was or will be (and not as it *is* now); we are dealing with a thing of the »past« or of the »future« and its ghostly ambiguous, disturbing traces.

Speaking of specters in Derridean terms always involves thinking in terms of the series, of *seriality*. Spectrality takes the form of a chain of specters attached to other (internal) specters: »I am haunted by myself who am (haunted by myself who am haunted by myself who am … and so forth)«, writes the narrator in Derrida's essay (1994 [1993]: 166). A series is a structure of self-implication of successive spectral signifiers. The specters, therefore, appear in the field of language, the domain of doublings, of tonal and semantic oppositions, of graphic duplications, such as quotation marks or attributive expressions effectuating multiplication, dissemination of concepts (»the truth of truth«, »the trace of a trace«, »the specter of a specter«). What they bring to mind is a mirror image or a probing, an insistent search for the essence of a concept. As the philosopher says, »the oscillation of the genitive translates all by itself the malaise, the *Unheimlichkeit* of the thing« (Derrida 1987 [1978]: 372), creating its ghostly or, in this context, more intrinsic reflection. It creates an abyssness of discourse, so desired in Derridean spectral analysis, in which, thanks to an infinitely referential structure of *mise en abyme*, the specter emerges as an »empty« negative, the double of a noble (Hegelian) spirit (cf. Baran 1995).

It is for this reason that, in Derrida's view, rewriting, translation, borrowing, stylization, and a predilection for citations are linguistic and literary equivalents of spectrality. After all, the sentence opening *Specters of Marx* is a kind of quote of a quote, a transposition of a formula that was invoked many times in multiple contexts, both affirmative and contesting, and is therefore suspended in the network of readings, which blur the clarity of the source text but at the same time make its existence inalienable (cf. Kofman 2000).

The last condition for the appearance of the specter, as articulated in Derrida's abyssal, cavernous »truth of truth«, is *materiality* – materiality expressed most fully in the images of things damaged or deformed (therefore, quite literally, »former« things). Their distinctive status rests upon the fact that they are »separated from the subject«, sunk in their reistic condition. This trait of spectrality is elaborated on in Derrida's interpretation of the worn-out, abandoned shoes immortalized in the paintings of Vincent van Gogh. Wear, deterioration and abandonment appear in things that materialize the most expressive quality of thingness: porosity and uselessness, while at the same time carrying a »sticky« memory of a relation to a human being, a nostalgic reference to someone who has left a trace of their presence in the materiality of the shoes. The materiality of a thing is a parergon or cartouche of the specter, in a misty and aconceptual way problematizing its liminality. In other words, materiality is a supplement of spectrality that goes beyond its ontological boundaries, because, for the spirit to exist it must penetrate its own creation and take on a material form. Without the material imprint or an outline of the discourse, the specter would be inaudible, as is the case with the singularity of literature that has not been captured within the order of an institution.[2]

The discourse on spectrality developed by Derrida in *The Truth in Painting* seems most inspiring for a scholar looking at Holocaust representations. From the point of view developed in this chapter, the post-traumatic specters emerge as material traces of the »void« (the absence, emptiness), as a material scratch, an imprint of presence, of a breath or movement. Their existence resembles that of phantom pain, and this metaphor – employed by Ruth Ellen Gruber in relation to the absence of Jews in Central and Eastern Europe (2002) – very well reflects the inalienability of the body and the porosity of matter. Such a condition also locates the (post)metaphysical discourse on the (non)presence of the specter within the chiasmatic junction of categories concave/convex, interior/border, simulacrum/original, adherence/separation (the specter being situated at the center of their continuous exchange). Derrida considers van Gogh's shoes as an allegory of representation: they retain the quality of mediation and, at the same time, of irremovable materiality, but are also seen as the most perfect materialization of spectrology. After all, Derrida writes that »it's a question of knowing whether the shoes in question are haunted by some ghost or are ghosting/returning [la revenance] itself« (1987 [1978]: 258). Within the horizon of spectral analysis human subjectivity disappears; we might say that it »dissolves« in the intense materiality of an imprint.

Through their status of being abandoned and because of their ownerlessness the shoes evoke the language of economy, whose words pertain to appropriation, dispossession, plunder, and mass robbery of the property of victims of extermination camps. The most powerful, multivalent symbol of these practices, deeply ingrained in contemporary cultural imagery, is the heap of shoes displayed in the museum at the former camp of Auschwitz-Birkenau. The shoes, which once belonged to the victims of the camp, remain poignant but also exposed to destruction, disturbing in their indefinite status as material relics and museum exhibits. In his polemic engagement with the interpretations of van Gogh's paintings proposed by Martin Heidegger and Meyer Schapiro, Derrida tries to establish the identity of the »owner« of the shoes, assign them to a specific location or space (rural or urban), and guess

---

2   I am referring here to the idea developed by Derrida in the interview *The Strange Institution Called Literature* (Derrida/Attridge 1992).

their gender. The point is not to determine any bourgeois property rights but to locate the focal point of the spectrological narrative at the heart of the act of violence, of the spectacle of mass destruction, which has left a tangible yet ambiguous trace.

> But an army of ghosts are demanding their shoes. Ghosts up in arms, an immense tide of deportees searching for their names. If you want to go to this theatre, here's the road of affect: the bottomless memory of dispossession, an expropriation, a despoilment. And there are tons of shoes piled up there, pairs mixed and lost. (Derrida 1987 [1978]: 329-331)

For Derrida, we could repeat, the discourse of the specter unfolds in a field structured around the philosophical problems of 1) anachrony, 2) translation, and 3) materiality. It is a field of forces which exert an impact on one another, form »hauntological« junctions, undergo unforeseeable transformations. The morbid nature of the specter thus emerges as dislocated, filtered through a variety of prisms, from unexpected inconsistencies, ruptures of philosophical or literary discourse. Derrida's specter is ahistorical, inhuman, and therefore posthuman indeed. It can also be unpredictably ominous. The specter represents the level of epistemological meta-knowledge, performing a role comparable to that of an archaeological dig or medical X-ray image, which exposes the hidden dimension of things in one flash. The cluster of information it carries, however, shimmers, fades, and »personates« other messages or speaking styles.

EXPOSURE AND MIMICRY

In the novel *Ziarno prawdy* [A Grain of Truth, 2011], Zygmunt Miłoszewski finds an unexpected way to develop spectral tropes, forefronting the motifs of theatricality, the bodily macabre, and multilevel mimicry. They are employed in the book to mask the uncanniness (*Unheimlichkeit*) of evil constructed here as revenge and/or pogrom violence. The act and theme of displaying/showcasing is of pivotal importance: the plot evolves and revolves around a scene, reiterated throughout the book, in which a butchered body, subjected to elaborate tortures, is theatrically exposed in an initially indecipherable, flagitious ritual.

Without a doubt, the *Grain of Truth* does not belong to the literary canon; it lacks finesse and a complex formal organization. However, these weaknesses are counterbalanced by Miłoszewski's piercing look at the reality of contemporary provincial Poland through the prism of an important anthropological problem which has animated public debates in the country for several decades: that of attitudes towards the Other, of infamous historical episodes marked by violence against others, minorities, strangers. And it is exactly the generic classification of the book that can be considered its main asset: as a popular thriller, Miłoszewski's book remains on the margins of the dominant public discourse about Polish antisemitism and evades appropriation by »normative poetics«, leaving the author enough room to experiment with the trope of a »Jewish ghost«. Miłoszewski's novel skillfully avoids the traps of literary spectrology. Instead, by resorting to the style of sarcastic rationalism, the author manages to abstain from the tone of false sublimity so often employed in contemporary postmemorial Holocaust literature.

In the novel, Derridean specters take the form of meanings that reveal themselves in the shifting levels of the structure. Albeit to some extent narratively transparent, Miłoszewski's text has an interesting, tangled composition reminiscent of a Chinese box story. Similar themes or tropes, essentially spectral in nature, reappear time and again at various levels of the narrative: the (alleged) presence of ghosts, frenetic images of bloodshed and »living flesh«. They permeate the depictions of the world presented in the novel, the memoirs and archival documents quoted, and the very symbolic matrix of these repetitions, and are epitomized by Karol de Prevot's (in)famous painting in the Sandomierz Cathedral, which is dedicated to blood libel.[3]

The ghost is the character seen in the recording of the street camera (the figure of the alleged murderer), but also the narrator of morbid monologues, whose identity remains undisclosed for a long time. It is unclear whether these monologues are the retrospective thoughts of the Jewish doctor Wajsbrot or the feverish thoughts of the killer who feigned his own death. In any case, the narrator speaks from the abyss, from the world of the dead, or

---

3 In the postscript to the book, Miłoszewski quotes as his main source of inspiration Joanna Tokarska-Bakir's famous book on ›blood libel‹, *Legendy o krwi. Antropologia przesądu* (2008), and the disturbing persistence of the myth in Poland.

from within a »mortuary fiction«, his condition being that of the specter, the ghost, the voice of the dead.

> Everything is hidden in the graves, and what remains is somehow very distant and veiled with sentiments that cannot be fathomed. Such a force of grief and bitterness, such a desire for destruction, simply the wish for revenge. To occupy his thoughts he repeats in his head, over and over, ad nauseam, all elements of the plan, it seems that there can be no error, but this does not lessen the fear, the tension does not disappear. He wants to run, but the plan does not include escape, he must wait. This waiting is terrible – the sounds are too loud, the lights too bright, the colors too vivid. The ticking of the clock on the wall is annoying like the chimes from the town hall, every second makes him furious. (Miłoszewski 2011: 112-113)

The »Jewish themes« already emerge in the first sequences of the novel. The trope of Jewish vengeance, visited upon the residents of »the ecclesial town with an antisemitic past«, is carefully staged and framed through the presence of a mysterious Hasid (a phantom or visitor from »the other side«), captured by a street camera at the crime scene; the presence of a characteristic prop (a *chalef* knife traditionally used for ritual slaughter); and, finally, the presence of a posed corpse (pointing to the motif of blood). Successive crimes appear to represent variants of ritual slaughter and related antisemitic prejudices.

Almost from the outset, the investigation revolves around a presumed »ethnic« motive for the offences, suggesting that the series of violent crimes is a perverse realization of the Christian myth of ›blood libel‹ (perverse because performed by a ghost, a Jewish avenger). This interpretation gradually replaces the prosecutors' rational hypotheses, diverting them from their initial (correct) guess of who could be the murderer. The clue to the crime (or rather the most probable hypothesis) is in fact provided at the beginning of the investigation. And yet, despite the fact that rational thinking prompts him to dispute ›blood libel‹ as a motive, the protagonist, prosecutor Teodor Szacki, falls for it and surrenders to the strength of the antisemitic myth.

In Miłoszewski's book the Derridan anachrony and the coalescence of various temporal orders take on a gloomy, depressive character. There seems to be no escape from the clash between the antisemitic performatives and the rational discourse of Enlightenment. The existing symbolic order determines the dynamics of this dispute. The staging of the ›blood libel‹ within its frame constitutes not merely one dimension in the Chinese box story but a sinister matrix of the spectral *mise en abyme*. Prosecutor Szacki cannot waive its power; all he can do is helplessly witness the performative force of the irrational narrative as it takes effect.

The theme of Jewish vengeance turns out to be a clever staging. But to what end? The symbolic excess and the abundance of overlying meanings are deposited like folds obstructing the smooth surface of reality, deferring the moment of unveiling the truth (i.e. the knowledge of how trivial the murderer's motives were). Spectrality thus emerges as a strategy of mimicry, of convoluted theatrics, superimposed on the theater of social life in which everyone plays specific, preassigned roles. Szacki and Elżbieta Budnik, the victim, embody the spirit of modernity, of modern rationalism and the ideal of tolerance of the Other; Jerzy Szyller personifies ›enlightened‹ nationalism and the economic, neoliberal social philosophy; the inhabitants of Sandomierz represent xenophobic prejudices. Spectrality, as conceptualized in the previous section, makes this distribution of roles visible, while at the same time exposing the fragility and persistence of the affective economy structuring ethnic identity constructs.

But what has happened to the Jewish ghosts, to the *Hasidim* so suggestively present in the first chapters of the book? The spectrality related to the Jewish death has, apparently, been located at other levels of the text. In Miłoszewski's perverse novel, the Jewish »spirit« emerges as real, carnal, irritating, devoid of taste and good manners, causing embarrassment. It is embodied in the figure of another policeman, Inspector Leon Wilczur, the son of Doctor Wajsbrot. The specter is, therefore, present from the beginning of the story. It accompanies the main protagonist like a shadowy double.

In a way, Wilczur exhausts the Derridan definition of the specter: morbid, strange, almost abjectual, he evades capture within existing frames of reality. Even the narrator perceives him as a personification of demonic negativity (»there was something in him that repulses«; his statements »were always marked by negativity« (Miłoszewski 2011: 43). Ultimately, as a character who plays with the eponymous concept of truth, Wilczur effectively undermines the epistemological approach of the narrator.

›How to explain this to you …‹, Wilczur mused, his face acquiring a ghastly, corpselike expression. In the dim light of the pizzeria, behind the veil of cigarette smoke, it looked like a clumsily animated mummy. ›People put up with him just because Budnik chose him. They think that he is a freak, but he has the right to be one, and if this woman stands at his side, he cannot be that bad. (Miłoszewski 2011: 46)

›He adored her, but there was something dirty in this adoration‹, Wilczur seeped his poison, ›something possessive, sticky, I would say.‹ (Ibid.)

The relationship between Wilczur and the concept of truth is deep, it is essential. The very title of the novel, albeit sarcastically ambiguous, suggests that truth is granular in nature, that it consists of discrete clusters (of matter? of meanings? of information?), is idiosyncratic, uneven, wryly curved, and resembles the Cartesian-Kantian *logos* dismantled by the deconstructionists (cf. Burzyńska 2006: 416). In the novel, similar aesthetic categories and registers characterize Wilczur; descriptions of his figure emphasize deformity, ataxia, roughness, crushedness, as though he was constantly falling out with a convention.

However, the most important dimension of spectrality is created by the subtexts, which inevitably direct the reading and situate the murders in a concrete historical context. The images of bloodshed, desecrated bodies and deformed, hardly recognizable corpses that circulate in the novel evoke associations with the mechanisms of pogrom violence and its cruel, atavistic, xenophobic reflex; with the role invariably played by the symbolic order in setting off ferocity against the Other. Topographic convergences underpin this interpretive frame: Kielce, the local metropolis, is mentioned repeatedly, Sandomierz being merely its small-scale reflection. In a similar vein, the violent injuries and the scale of deformation of the bodies evoke Julia Pirotte's historical photographs of victims of the 1946 Kielce pogrom. The link between those two levels – the level of the fictional crime story and that of the historical crime, in which Poles played the role of perpetrators – remains vague, tangled and multidirectional. And yet we may risk the hypothesis that the fictional crime in Miłoszewski's novel constitutes a distant reflection, an »afterimage« of the violent past, a specter projected on a screen which, in line with Derrida's formula, »also turns out to be ghostly«. The multilevel work of the specter carries here a veiled historical message, creating an effect of »truth« in which the events emerge, albeit distorted, sublimated, and temporally disjointed.

Space plays a pivotal role in this process: specific narrative sequences unfold through disclosure of successive spatial figures carrying deep symbolic meaning. Cellars, corridors, abandoned buildings, ruins, archives and cemeteries are elements of the imaginary topography, but they are also (all too) readable figures of the collective unconscious and memory (Assmann 2003 [1999]). Fragmentary memories, props of uncertain use and destiny, and suddenly interrupted stories about a Polish-Jewish coexistence have been deposited in these abandoned places. The explosion induced by the killer, which in the most literal sense shakes the foundations of Sandomierz, effectuates a symbolic transfer of layers of collective forgetting, initiates tectonic movements of memory dominated by amnesia and Judeophobic prejudices.

In a similar way, Miłoszewski mixes orders, destabilizes stable relationships and neat categorizations, sometimes in a way that is difficult to digest. In the fictional world of the novel, the boundaries between the categories of hiding/chasing, perpetrator/victim, surface/depth, superstition/enlightened discourse, and private/public are subject to blurring and displacement. Those destabilized orders fuse in a violent entanglement that enhances the orders' affective power when it becomes clear that Grzegorz Budnik, a local activist fighting against xenophobia and the killer, directed his vengeance against both his unfaithful wife and the antisemitic community. The merging of these two affective orders, whose meaning is not specified in the novel, evokes a vague premonition of »great terror«, to borrow Marcin Zaremba's term (2012). The reasons and motives for the hideous crimes remain incomprehensible, which sets in motion the spectral chain, the Derridean series of places and people haunted by ghosts.

As mentioned above, the presence of specters and hauntings in *Grain of Truth* establishes a layer of meaning that eclipses the »essence« of things. The »real corpse« (a prop from a detective story) emerges almost as a substitute, reiterating the pogrom of 1946 and masking the inability to work out the truth about its circumstances and consequences. Compensative »truths« (i.e. elaborate stagings of the crimes) and a language of substitution obscure the most acute dimension of ghastliness: the realization that Jews will never return to Sandomierz, not even as specters or ghosts. From a spectrological perspective, the real value of Miłoszewski's book lies in its deployment of the figure of radical disillusion: the reader must be confronted with the story about (Jewish) ghosts in order to experience the overwhelming sense of loss of the Other and the – perhaps even more grievous – loss of a soothing belief in the possibility of its recovery.

TRANS-SPECIES SUBSTITUTIONS: JONASZ STERN'S BONES AND FISHBONES

Derridean spectrology problematizes the nature of the specter and casts it as non-anthropomorphic, ahistorical, inhuman, and therefore essentially posthuman. This diagnosis is confirmed by a spectral analysis of the paintings of the Polish-Jewish artist Jonasz Stern, who is associated with the Kraków Group. In his works, the spectrological trope transpires as a binding agent, cutting across and linking together his biography, artworks and their meta-artistic discourse.

During Nazi occupation, Stern lived in the Lviv ghetto. This period is documented in a series of expressionist linocuts devoted to the exceptionally traumatic events in the history of the ghetto community (such as the ›hunt for the children‹). During the early stages of deportation, the artist managed to escape from a train carrying the Jewish residents of Lviv to the Bełżec extermination camp. In the final phase of the ghetto, however, he was recaptured and taken to the site of mass executions in a gorge in the Janowski forest. Stern survived the execution: when night fell, he escaped from under the pile of corpses and crawled naked to a nearby field.[4] He hid in the house of a Ukrainian peasant until the end of the war and went on to live in Hungary under the false name of a dead friend (cf. Zientara 2012; Markowska 1998; Stulecie 2005).

All these experiences meant that in his postwar artistic work Stern had to measure up against his own specter, against the unfulfilled variant of his fate. In other words, Stern himself seemed an almost literal incarnation of the specter, a resurrected being inhabiting the borderline between life and death. The self-perception as a dead man accompanied the artist like a »sticky« doppelganger, outlining his personality, as it were, and at the same time pointing out his difference with and within himself. This condition does not translate into a simple division, a cleaving of the self between the »real« person and his mirror-image or spectral reflection; instead, it initiates a complex process of permanent instability, the loss of a homogeneous identity which will henceforth be constantly challenged and exposed to self-questioning.

---

4   Jacek Leociak writes extensively on this and other similar episodes of »getting out of the grave« and on the resulting phenomenon of »resurrection trauma« (2009).

This condition brings to mind the dilemmas of the narrator in Derrida's *The Truth in Painting*: »What is ›my ghost‹? What does the phrase ›the ghost of my other I‹ say? My other I, is that myself or an another I who says ›I‹? or a ›myself‹ which is itself only divided by the phantom of its double?« (1987 [1979]: 373)

Apart from the paradocumentary linocuts of the 1940s, in which the artist deployed traditional figurative poetics, it is rather difficult to immediately discern in his works any direct references to the borderline experience of living in the ghetto and going through the ghastly ›failed‹ execution (only the titles of some paintings or cycles suggest that such references exist: for instance, *Emaciation, A Pit*, or one of the last collages titled *Humiliation*). In the mature phase of his artistic life, Stern developed a characteristic, easily recognizable technique. From the mid-1950s, he created »assemblages«, sticking »foreign« objects such as crumpled fabric, nets, fish and animal bones, feathers, skins of fish and, later, photographs onto the surface of the canvas. The resulting reliefs have become a record of a long-lasting process of collating a sort of collection or archive of organic residues.[5] This collection remains partially obscure, framed through emptiness and futility; after all, the things that the artist so meticulously holds on to usually fall victim to removal or destruction.

The objects attached to the surface of the canvas challenge their two-dimensionality but also strike at the very concept of artistic representation, at the aesthetic rigors that constitute conventional reality. However, in Stern's work, this is not merely an avant-garde gesture aimed at deconstructing existing conventions of representation. The point is not to represent the Holocaust or create mimetic effects. The meaning of artistic activity has been conceived here differently, more radically: by using bones and fish skins, Stern constructs cosmogonic diagrams or maps of reality.[6] The titles of his compositions make this intention clear: there are countless »landscapes«, »sceneries« and »zones«. Stern derives his spectral cosmogony from the

---

5 In the article *Memory through Art*, Alicja Kuczyńska made an interesting observation, writing that a characteristic attribute of artistic inscriptions of the Holocaust is their emphasis on storing, on collecting, which replaces the imperative of recreating reality (2011 [2009]: 657).

6 It is worth recalling that the motif of fish and the bit played a significant role in Derrida's interpretation of Valerio Adami's images (cf. Derrida 1987 [1978]).

peripheries of the organic world, from the area where the distinction between the living and the dead reflects an unstable opposition. Whereas the Vitruvian Man by Leonardo da Vinci was a model of the cosmic era of optimistic humanism, Stern's *Landscape I* constitutes a »residuary« model of the universe, one constructed from the perspective of nothingness, of a mass grave or refuse bin. The specter, Derrida says, always comes from the earth, from something »humble, humid, humiliated« (1994 [1993]: 117). It is looked down upon as unpleasant, and is accepted reluctantly, with discomfort.

Bones appear to be a universal substance which comprises a plurality of meanings and uses. Its abjectual dimension is clearly present in waste and residues which cause feelings of disgust or distaste. As remains of dead beings which were not buried according to funeral rites they carry a connotation of mortuary and decay. Yet the context of Stern's biography brings in another set of meanings related to forensic investigation, to processes of evidence-gathering, and to the exploration of mass graves by archaeologists and forensic experts (cf. Sturdy Colls 2013 [2011]). Because of their durability and relative insusceptibility to decay, bones and organic debris come to serve as evidence in courts or emerge as relics of lost civilizations. Seen in this light, they cross the border of the inhuman and become important artefacts in the symbolic order of human civilization.

But why did Stern use bones of fish, birds and other animals, instead of human remains? What motives were behind this flight toward the non-human? Or could it be that the ontological break that exists in anthropocentric metaphysics, the cut, the typographic »slash«, the distinction between the human and the non-human/post-human was irrelevant for Stern and had no significance for his artistic imagination?

It can be assumed that, by replacing human remains with bones of animals and transforming them into ambiguous forms representing the borderline experience, Stern practiced in his art the principle of »trans-species substitution«. Appearing as if »in place of« or »in the name of« human remains, the bones of fish, birds and other animals represent the former and allow them to exist in the reality of a work of art. By revoking the distinction between human and non-human, by exposing its conventionality and embeddedness in the structures of power, Stern allows animal bones to serve as the »specter of the human« and, more generally, as a spectral allegory encompassing all species. With this strategy, bones gain the value of universalism, of semioticity; they are endowed with an extended subjectivity.

This is an essentially spectral operation: it reconstructs the absence; it summons phantoms from the world of the dead and embeds them in the materiality of the present. The representational dynamics of Stern's paintings unfolds through transitions and transformations; the Latourian »morphism« in his works replaces all neat boundaries and divisions. It is worth mentioning here that the term »assemblage« is employed not only in the field of art history, but also in contemporary environmental criticism. Rosi Braidotti writes about the »assemblages« of human and non-human actors (Braidotti 2013), and her conceptualization corresponds to the one that informs Bruno Latour's theory of »entanglement« of beings (Latour 2005). In Stern's compositions, the remains of animals (particularly fish) absorb memories of human death; what is human is united with its animal analogue. Here, too, the anthropocentric understanding of spectrality considered as a negative counterpart of human subjectivity, of consciousness and ethical sensitivities, becomes blurred (cf. Braidotti 2013). In Stern's *Red Noticeboards*, spectrality is positive, endowed with agency, with the power to dissolve and weaken the anthropocentric determinants of human dominance over non-human beings.

Writing is the realm where these »specio-morphisms« come into being. Bones stuck to canvases establish chaotic, asemantic systems (as in the abstract collages of the *Extermination* cycle from 1964), but sometimes they are also arranged in horizontal lines and form orderly, rhythmic strings, as if they were carrying a secret entry (*The Silence of Genres* from 1965 is one such example). This peculiar proto-writing seems more raw and primitive than pictograms, but at the same time it radicalizes the idea behind them.[7] In fact Stern's »letters« link two aspects of the sign, organically weaving together the signified and the signifier. The material properties of bones as convex signs also seem important here. Stern's bone is a crack, a letter, or a groove in a painting. Excessive in form, it protrudes from the surface and calls for attention.

To create a posthuman script seems a gesture more radical than abandoning the figurative in favor of the abstract. One could argue that Stern's three-dimensional reliefs replace Masaccio's Renaissance perspective; that the illusion of geometric spatial arrangement is displaced here by one organized

---

7   Eleonora Jedlińska interprets Stern's fish and bird »letters« differently, namely as »reflections of the image of Moses' Tablets of Law«, reading into them a quasi-theological message (2001: 121).

by material porosity, the rawness of proto-signs, and the calm stability of »what remains«. The language of bones turns out to be a net of meanings projected onto the desolate, post-catastrophic world. But it also becomes a Derridean »specter of a specter«, a spectral multiplication in which the retrospective converts into a prospective vision. In this context, Stern's technique could be read as a strategy of resistance against the necropolitical dimension of biopower, which saw its most extreme manifestation in the Nazi extermination camps. The language of waste turns out to be more durable than the memory of destruction. By materializing spectrality it transforms the narrative of the haunting Jewish specter into a message of indestructibility of life (in terms of supra-species).

Translated from Polish by Robin Gill and Zuzanna Dziuban

LITERATURE

Assmann, Aleida (2003 [1999]): Erinnerungsräume: Formen und Wandlungen des kulturellen Gedächtnisses, München: C.H. Beck.
Baran, Bogdan (1995): Filozofia ›końca filozofii‹: Dekonstrukcje Jacquesa Derridy, Warszawa: Spacja.
Braidotti, Rosi (2013): The Posthuman, Cambridge: Polity Press.
Burzyńska, Anna (2006): Anty-teoria literatury, Kraków: Universitas.
Czapliński, Przemysław (2015): »Katastrofa wsteczna.« In: Poznańskie Studia Polonistyczne, Seria Literacka 25/45, pp. 37-66.
Davis, Colin (2007): Haunted Subjects: Deconstruction, Psychoanalysis, and the Return of the Dead, New York and Houndmills: Palgrave Macmillan.
Derrida, Jacques (1977 [1976]): »Fors.« In: The Georgia Review 31/1, pp. 64-116.
Derrida, Jacques (1989 [1987]): Of Spirit: Heidegger and the Question, Chicago: University of Chicago Press.
Derrida, Jacques (1987 [1978]): The Truth in Painting, Chicago and London: The Chicago University Press.
Derrida, Jacques (1994 [1993]): Specters of Marx: The State of the Debt, The Work of Mourning and the New International, New York and London: Routledge.

Derrida, Jacques/Attridge, Derek (1992): »›This Strange Thing Called Literature‹: An Interview with Jacques Derrida.« In: Derek Attridge (ed.), Jacques Derrida: Acts of Literature, New York and London: Routledge, pp. 33-75.
Gruber, Ruth Ellen (2002): Virtually Jewish: Reinventing Jewish Culture in Europe, Berkley, Los Angeles and London: University of California Press.
Hirsch, Marianne/Spitzer, Leo (2010): Ghosts of Home: The Afterlife of Czernowitz in Jewish Memory, Berkeley, Los Angeles and London: University of California Press.
Janicka, Elżbieta (2012): Festung Warschau: Raport z oblężonego miasta, Warszawa: Wydawnictwo Krytyki Politycznej.
Jedlińska, Eleonora (2001): Sztuka po Holokauście, Łódź: Biblioteka Tygla Kultury.
Kalendarium (2005): Stulecie: Prace Jonasza Sterna (1904-1988) z lat 1930-1980, Sopot: Państwowa Galeria Sztuki.
Karolak, Sylwa (2013): »Widma (z) Zagłady.« In: Czas Kultury 2, pp. 118-125.
Kuczyńska, Alicja (2011 [2009]): »Pamięć poprzez sztukę.« In: Tomasz Majewski and Anna Zeidler-Janiszewska (eds.), Pamięć Shoah: Kulturowe reprezentacje i praktyki upamiętnienia, Łódź: Oficyna, pp. 683-686.
Kuźniarz, Bartosz (2014): »Człowieku, w twojej głowie straszy! Derrida o duchach późnego kapitalizmu.« In: Czas Kultury 5, pp. 58-67.
Latour, Bruno (2005): Reassembling the Social: An Introduction to Actor-Network-Theory, Oxford: Oxford University Press.
Leociak, Jacek (2009): Doświadczenie graniczne: Studia o dwudziestowiecznych formach reprezentacji, Warszawa IBL PAN.
Markowska, Alina (1998): Język Neuera: O twórczości Jonasza Sterna, Cieszyn: Wydawnictwo Uniwersytety Śląskiego w Cieszynie.
Marzec, Andrzej (2012): »Widma, zjawy i nawiedzone teksty – hauntologia Jacquesa Derridy, czyli o pośmiertnym życiu literatury.« In: Magdalena Gerbacik et al. (eds.), Wymiary powrotu w literaturze, Kraków: Wydawnictwo Libron, pp. 255-262.
Miller, Hillis J. (2014): »Jak czytać Derridów: indeksowanie 'moi et moi', Der und Der, mnie i mnie, tego i tamtego.« In: Czas Kultury 5, pp. 6-17.
Miłoszewski, Zygmunt (2014): Ziarno prawdy, Warszawa: WAB, Warszawa

Momro, Jakub (2014): Widmontologie nowoczesności. Genezy, Warszawa: Instytut Badań Literackich PAN.

Study Colls, Caroline (2013 [2012]): »Gone But Not Forgotten: Archaeological Approaches to the Landscape of the Former Extermination Camp at Treblinka, Poland.« In: Holocaust Studies and Materials 3, pp. 253-289.

Tokarska-Bakir, Joanna (2008): Legendy o krwi: Antropologia przesądu, Warszawa: Wydawnictwo WAB.

Young, James E. (2002): Nach-Bilder des Holocaust in zeitgenössischer-Kunst und Architektur, Hamburg: Hamburger Edition.

Zientara, Maria (2012): Holocaust Survivors: Artur Nacht-Smaborski, Erna Rosenstein, Jonasz Stern, Kraków: Muzeum Historyczne Miasta Krakowa.

Sites That Haunt: Affects and Non-Sites of Memory

ROMA SENDYKA

WHO KNOWS WHY

»Something isn't quite right,« wrote the British geographer Andrew Charlesworth in his report on his fieldwork at the site of the Płaszów concentration camp. Charlesworth took a group of students to the site in 1993. As they went from the camp itself towards the wartime residence of Commandant Amon Göth, Charlesworth noted that something »isn't quite right, but we don't know what it is that is wrong.« (2004: 293) »It's a strange place,« writes Beata Chomątowska, detailing common reactions to the Warsaw neighborhood of Muranów, the site during the war of the Warsaw Ghetto. »Even visitors from abroad notice that... Passing through it you feel like you're in a kind of dream. You don't know what you're going to find around the next corner.« What you end up doing, continues Chomątowska, is »circling around and around, trying to assemble a whole out of pieces that don't fit together.« (2012: 14) It is an idea often repeated: the recurring impression of things not fitting, of topographical conflict, of a disparity between the viewer and the scene appears frequently in the accounts of those who visit the places I have termed elsewhere »non-sites of memory« (Sendyka 2014 [2013]; 2013).[1] These abandoned, neglected locations, which nevertheless retain the

---

1   I define non-sites of memory as the localities of acts of genocide to which the past century has been witness (the chronological delimitation is made by the twentieth-century origins of the term, as well as by the reach of the »living memory«

right to commemoration, generate a particular kind of affective aura that eventually becomes their trademark. From amongst the many available testimonials on the topic of the uncanny non-site of memory I have selected two, written by different authors on different locations, that I wish to analyze in terms of the encounter with the aura of places that have been stripped of their »placeness« and »homeliness« (a quality described in German by the term *heimlich*) – of their potential habitability – and of their memory. What is it that »isn't quite right«? What is it that the visitor finds so unsettling, so *unheimlich*?[2]

Our first account is taken from a landscape architect, one of several people to propose projects to transform the feral terrain of the former concentration camp in Płaszów into a »place of memory«. The scene the author

---

connected with the presence of witnesses). They are scattered territories upon which people were killed in the Holocaust (Jews, Sinti and Roma) or other acts of ethnic cleansing (e.g. Bosnia, Wołyń [Volhynia]), or else territories of similarly motivated resettlements (e.g. Sudeten Germans). The basic indicator is lack of information (altogether or of proper, founded information), of material forms of commemoration (plaques, monuments, museums), and of reparations (and of any official designation of the scope of the territory in question). Non-sites of memory also have in common the past or continued presence of human remains (bodies of deceased persons) that have not been neutralized by funerary rites. These sites do not, meanwhile, share physical characteristics: they may be extensive or minute, urban or rural, though they are often characterized by some variety of physical disturbance to the organic order (human remains, plants, animals) and to the inorganic order (ruins, new construction). The victims who should be commemorated on such sites typically have a collective identity (usually ethnic) distinct from the society currently living in the area, whose self-conception is threatened by the occurrence of the non-site of memory. Such localities are transformed, manipulated, neglected, or contested in some other way (often devastated or littered), the resultant discouragement of memorialization leading to ethnically problematic revitalization that draws criticism.

2   In his well-known critique of Ernst Jentsch's use of the term, Freud focuses on Jentsch's attempt to link the uncanny with the new and unfamiliar; he does not explore the possibilities of topographical critique, in which the unheimlich would be the unhomely, the uninhabitable as un-homey (Freud 2003).

describes would have taken place around 2007, after the announcement of a local architectural study competition:

It's a cloudy, rainy day. Grassy, empty fields extend all around us. The shape of the terrain creates a kind of natural amphitheater, but it brims over with drops, furrows, and lumps. Fresh snow enhances the slightest disturbance of the surface. A girl walking with her parents strongly opposes the continuation of the walk. She clearly manifests a desire to return and to leave a place that – who knows why – she finds unsettling and strange. (Froczek-Brataniec 2010: 290)

Our second account is taken from the English version of *The Taste of Ashes*, American historian Marci Shore's report on her fieldwork in Poland, the Czech Republic, Slovakia, Hungary, and Russia, which she conducted in the late 1990s. Here Shore describes her reaction to a visit to Muranów. This fragment has not been included in the Polish translation of the book:

In the evenings I took walks through what had once been the ghetto, through a neighborhood called Muranów, which was now full of communist-era apartment blocks, wholly unexceptional. On the way home to my apartment on Piwna Street, I vomited into the bushes. I felt numbness and nausea, and I did not even want to escape it. On the contrary: I was looking for a way to enter the war. (2013: 144-145)[3]

The two accounts share one feature that is immediately obvious, having to do with the kind of reaction had by the authors to the experienced place. The protagonists of both narratives each perform a simple act belonging to the order of »free time«. But the pleasure that ought to accompany activities undertaken voluntarily is, in the above accounts, replaced by the exact opposite sensation. This sensation is termed »unsettling« and »strange« by the observer reconstructing events in the first quote, although the protagonist herself appears to pass this point over in silence (»who knows why« she manifests a »desire to return«). Similarly, in the second passage, the sudden leap from the act of the evening walk to the narrator's unexpected somatic

---

3   Marci Shore does not recall the reasons for cutting this passage out of the (more extensive) 2012 Polish version of the book. One may assume this was not an act of censorship or auto-censorship but a result of editorial work, however startling the omission.

reaction is left unanalyzed. Shore merely describes her body's reaction, naming not emotions, but rather physical sensations (»I felt numbness and nausea«). Both, then, are overtaken by sudden affective experiences while walking. Affective, and not emotional, since the event occurs in the realm of their bodies, in that pre-personal territory lying outside of conscious control. The state experienced cannot be named. It is unsemioticizeable, so physical that neither a personal lexicon nor a social compendium of emotions is able to provide the terminology to elucidate it,[4] instead requiring behaviorist techniques of narration. Affect as »unformed and unstructured« is – as Brian Massumi suggests – »not entirely containable in knowledge« (2002: 206), though it is analyzable in terms of the effects of affect. Affect works within a space that is prior to and separate from that territory mapped by consciousness.

Massumi's theory of affects, based on Deleuze's interpretation of Spinoza, is in this sense similar to Silvan Tomkins' classic take: Tomkins also distinguishes affect from the realm of conscious feelings and emotions elaborated according to a »cultural memory script«. If we were to try applying the language of Tomkins' theory to the reactions of both of the people described in the citations above – treating, for just a moment, at least, these accounts as documents rather than as artistic creations – we would find that we are dealing with one of the negative affects outlined by Tomkins. Perhaps it is merely a question of distress, brought about by exhaustion, bad weather, the temperature, the physical conditions of the walk, an oncoming illness. Perhaps there is fear involved: the emptiness and gloominess of Płaszów, and the bleak gray of the communist blocks makes things seem ominous and inspire a desire for immediate escape. Or perhaps shame plays a role: a physical reaction in which one looks away, experiences a momentary »cognitive shock«, a temporary »inability to think clearly« (Nathanson 2008: xviii). And finally, we might consider, too, the possibility of disgust. The latter two affects – shame and disgust – are, as Eve Kosofsky Sedgwick writes,

---

4   »Feeling«, as conceived by Gilles Deleuze and Felix Guattari, assumes evaluation, estimation, appraisal of a material that provides it with meaning, »resisting emotion«, and is belated in comparison with emotion; it has the character of a tool, and it is »introceptive«. »Affect« is exclusively the »moving body in itself«, a form of liberation, a burst of emotion comparable to an active weapon, a »projectile«. (Deleuze/Guattari 2004: 441).

commenting on Tomkins, distinct from the rest. They require that a line be drawn between them and their positive counterparts: only that which initially promised pleasure can provoke humiliation or repulsion. »[S]hame, as precarious hyperreflexivity of the surface of the body, can turn one inside out – or outside in.« (Sedgwick 1995: 22) Disgust in particular, which protects the organism from toxins by means of the physical reaction of vomiting, demarcates the internal and the external and emphasizes the discrepancy between these two orders.

None of the »testimonials of place« cited above give a clear answer to the nature of the catalyst of the affect. After all, there must be some sort of stimulus involved – so what is the trigger in this case? Marci Shore describes a somatic reaction suggesting disgust – but what brings this reaction about? Warsaw's lousy architecture? What happens occurs when she is already »on the way home«, so the geographical point of reference must instead be the walk's initial destination: the territories of the ghetto. Why are they »nauseating«, abject? Their »overgrowth«, their being covered in apartment blocks – is that it? Ellipses, things left unsaid, an absence of subsequent analysis – these strategies of Shore's narrative appear to suggest that the abandoned and uncontrollably self-revitalizing sites of tragedies, in concealing their past, act upon the beholder in the precognitive sphere. Something they contain within, something enabling the participant's interaction, provokes a potent somatic reaction, and the connection between subject and object, place and visitor occurs on a level that cannot be reached by words or by consciousness. The bodily spasm narrated in this text does have, however, its non-journalistic qualities, becoming a kind of figure or metaphor for the reaction to Warsaw's amnesia.

The report on Płaszów is more complex: as an eyewitness account it is contaminated by suggestions and suppositions surrounding the reasons for the reaction of the young girl, despite efforts to make it seem objective such as the use of third-person perspective. The experience of the walk on the vacated terrain of the former concentration camp involves the entire family. The choice of the paradigmatic subject to externalize the reaction is, of course, significant: the figure of the child is used here as a means by which to convince the reader of the genuine, unfiltered nature of the emotions, of their purity, untainted by reason. Of similarly romantic provenance is the scene's opening with its description of the landscape, whose ill-boding aura seems to resonate with the child medium. The narrator suggests different sources of uncanniness: an »emptiness«, the scale of the terrain, its wintery, snowy – thus monochromatic – shade, its strange »drops, furrows, and lumps«. The myriad incongruities with the usual urban nature walk – i.e., in a park – seem to generate a cognitive dissonance and a sense of foreboding and anxiety that result in the desire to escape. The more the excerpt stresses the total truth of the reaction of the child, the easier it becomes, of course, to suspect the reverse, namely, that the little girl may be reacting to the reactions of her parents. Their historical knowledge of the place (as a former concentration camp), strange features of their approach to it (why would we come here in the winter, why wouldn't we take the path, why would we come on such a bad day, etc.), tension, silences, hints, and even involuntary physical reactions to aesthetic codes (the horror film, the unromantic landscape) might all alter the behavior of the child.

The affective resonance explicitly suggested by the first excerpt figures, of course, as the basic framework for both accounts. After all, why were these scenes recorded? Is the point not for the reader to succumb to the same unease, to get those same goose bumps that you get when faced with the uncanny? We have now transitioned into the field of biological etiology, the study of animal behavior, and of central interest is, as Deleuze and Guattari suggest, the capacity of bodies to be moved by other bodies being moved (O'Brien 2005: 50).

In both cases, however, we are able to construct a similar plot summary: sites of abandoned memory are incongruous, since inherited aesthetic codes are not in effect, there is emptiness where we expect plenitude in the layout of the terrain, there is no fulfillment where we expect there to be, and there are anomalies in development (monolithic apartment blocks, gashes in the ground) and in nature (thickets) that produce an excess of stimuli that results in the breakdown of an erstwhile functional symbolic system. Even information (»this was a ghetto«) and awareness do not aid in the creation of a relationship to a place that resists being introduced into narrative memory: the visitor to the non-site of memory suddenly finds herself in a scene with a dual character, a place that both allures and repels. The viewer gets pulled into this strange and inhospitable site, devoid of markers and interpretive clues, undomesticated, not wholly charted, missing its instructions for use, even for the most basic maneuvers, such as how to navigate through. As a result of the impossibility of establishing contact between the visitor and the place, in the face of the fragility of the symbolic system (Kristeva 1982: 76), identity is placed in harm's way, and furthermore, by extension, life itself is put at risk by being exposed to an encounter with death. The response is cramping up, spasms, vomiting, affect.

These are sites that haunt. But the question remains: what is it exactly we're so scared of?

LIVE ON MY BEHALF!

These »places of destruction«, forgotten places of suffering, possess – as diagnosed by Georges Didi-Huberman in *Phasmes: essais sur l'apparition* – a kind of terrible coherence by virtue of »the power of that which, whether destroyed or effaced, nevertheless *had not changed*« (2007: 115). Here Didi-Huberman cites Lanzmann who tried to conceptualize the reasons for the shock he had felt:

The shock emerges not only from the ability to assign a geographic reality and even a precise topography to names – Bełżec, Sobibór, Chełmno, Treblinka, etc. – that have become legendary, but also from the perception that nothing has changed. (Lanzmann 1990: 313)

If Lanzmann and Didi-Huberman are right, this means that non-sites of memory are hosts to a sort of chronotic tremor. The past tense is present; that which has passed has not been permanently eliminated from the horizon of experiences. Ulrich Baer, in his book *Spectral Evidence* (2005 [2002])[5] – a title as hauntological as Didi-Huberman's *Phasmes* (1998)[6] – attempts to explain this temporal disjuncture in terms of the »tension« between »the landscapes' simultaneous invitation to project ourselves into them« and »the inalterable pastness of photography«. This tension, in turn, leads to a sense of »nonbelonging and trespass«. It is impossible to reconcile our attempts to see ourselves in a landscape conventionally enjoining us to establish a collective

---

5 »Spectral evidence« is a legal term for evidence, as admitted in the 1662 Salem witch trials, consisting in reports by witnesses on what was said to them in dreams and visions by the spirit of the accused witch.
6 Phasmes (Phasmida) are a species of stick insect, camouflaging creatures colloquially known as »ghost insects« in a variety of European languages.

identity through place with the feeling that there is no way to project ourselves into a given space, to domesticate it, to make it our own. The space is marked by a »haunting déjà-vu« – a lingering sense of recurrence, of importunate haunting (Baer 2005 [2002]: 78).

In answer to the question, then, of why we feel frightened by these »places that haunt«, I would like to propose two ideas. The first is taken from the recent novel *The Winter Vault,* by Anne Michaels (2009), in which Lucjan – a Polish Jew and one of the protagonists of this bittersweet post-Holocaust love story – describes, after having emigrated, his experience of the reconstruction of Warsaw. This experience is in many respects quite similar to Shore's in *The Taste of Ashes,* but for Lucjan, it leads to some very different conclusions.

Walking for the first time into the replica of the Old Town, said Lucjan, the rebuilt market square – it was humiliating. Your delirium made you ashamed – you knew it was a trick, a brainwashing, and yet you wanted it so badly. Memory was salivating through your brain. The hunger it tried to satisfy. It was dusk and the streetlamps miraculously came on and everything was just the same – the same signs for the shops, the same stonework and archways… I had to stop several times, the fit of strangeness was so intense. I squatted with my back against a wall. It was a brutality, a mockery – at first completely sickening, as if time could be turned back, as if even the truth of our misery could be taken away from us. And yet, the more you walked, the more your feelings changed, the nausea gradually diminished and you began to remember more and more. Childhood memories, memories of youth and love – I watched the faces of people around me, half mad with the confusion of feelings. There was defiance, too, of course, a huge song of pride bursting out of everyone, humiliation and pride at the same time. People danced in the street. They drank. At three in the morning the streets were still full of people, and I remember thinking that if we didn't all clear out, the ghosts wouldn't come back, and who was this all for if not for the ghosts? (Michaels 2009: 308-309)

The inhospitable world that ensues from the Holocaust is, as diagnosed by Bauman (2008), a haunted one. Unlike the heroine of *The Taste of Ashes,* Lucjan is able to overcome his nausea by filling in the breach that opens up between then and now with memories, ultimately by invoking spirits. It would be hard to count how many times the metaphor of haunting has informed statements about the experience, years after the fact, of places marked by the Holocaust. The installation *Writing on the Wall* (1991-1996) by American artist Shimon Attie transformed guesswork into visible reality by projecting photographs from the 1930s onto the facades of buildings in the once Jewish district of Scheunenviertel in Berlin. Attie himself characterized the work in terms of a virtual transporting of the past into the present, a kind of corrective to a certain social memory (2003: 74-83), while critics noted the particular flickering, spectral form of this dislocation and glimpsed in the installation the revelation that the city was possessed by the absence of the murdered and deported, a sort of homage to the Jewish souls, as James E. Young notes in *Sites Unseen* (2000: 64). And in *Picturing the Vanished*, Dora Apel calls Attie's works a kind of »spectral depiction« (2002: 48, 68), an intervention consisting in the supplementation of the German present with the apparitions of the victims whom the past has absorbed. Revealing the presence of souls, providing them with the minimal physicality of apparitions, is a strategy that is also familiar from Daniel Libeskind's widely debated Jewish Museum in Berlin. The Museum's basic premises consist in, first, the drawing of lines connecting the places formerly inhabited by Berlin Jews, and, second, the generation of a sense of spectrality in museum-goers: in the Holocaust Tower, that emptiest of emptinesses amongst the five so-called »Voids«, you can hear the sounds of the street, snippets of noise that make their way in from outside, but you can also hear the sounds produced by the visitors themselves, bizarrely multiplied and deformed, resulting in a potent impression of being surrounded by whispering spirits.[7] Another important soundscape is given in the »Memory Void«, the floor of which is covered in metal »fallen leaves«. Menashe Kadishman's installation is theoretically intended to be traversed, and yet very few visitors actually dare to set foot on the piles of faces crying out – doing so would result in the release of the horrifying, ghastly voices of these figures.

The spectral character of the past can thus be manifested by means of artistic interventions that rely on visual or audial supplementation of a reality scarred by absence. That supplementing, artificial, a priori, that »materialization of apparitions« can also take another form, mentioned in passing by

---

7 In her article ›*Let the Dead Bury the Living*‹: *Daniel Libeskind's Monumental Counterhistory* (2007 [2004]), Ewa Domańska interprets the sounds in the Tower as evidence of the indifference of the city to the tragedy. I would maintain that this is not the only, or even the primary, sound domain to act upon the visitor.

Marianne Hirsch and Leo Spitzer in *Ghost of Home: The Afterlife of Czernowitz* (2010), when they explain the title of their book. They write that the few visitors to Czernowitz toward the end of the twentieth century, in search of traces of Jewish life, were reminiscent of »ghostly revenants or haunting reminders of a forgotten world« (2010: xx). The possibility that researchers entering into the world of forgotten violence themselves become screens for a spectral existence introduces a line of interpretation of the hauntological threads of post-memory that is extreme but that can nonetheless not be ignored.

The very fact that artists employ strategies to generate the impression of haunted spaces contradicts the hypothesis that the powerful negative affective aura of abandoned places of violence comes from a primitive, irrational pre-modern fear of ghosts. Attie would seem to suggest that the return of the apparitions is a necessary act for the soothing of memory, a kind of existential act of justice in the guise of extending an existence brutally interrupted, at least in this vestigial form. The same intention of »existential redress« is clearly an influence in the decisions of the protagonist of the grotesque quasi-horror text of Igor Ostachowicz. In *Night of the Living Jews* (2012), a Warsaw cynic becomes, in spite of his pragmatic capitalist views, the »supervisor of the outings of teenage corpses« around town, funding their »shopping sprees« (2012: 119), providing them with the opportunity to dress up and enjoy the pleasures of consuming life, compensating the Warsaw zombies not so much for their wartime deaths as for the post-war monotony of all the years they have spent in the city's cellars. The ghosts haunting Muranów lurk, too, in Sylwia Chutnik's horror-comedy *Muranooo* (2012).[8] In this play, the author invokes one of Warsaw's urban legends:

I was watching a TV documentary which stated that the houses in Muranów are all haunted, some of my friends who live there say that somebody keeps walking around their kitchen at night. I thought to myself, oh, come on. The TV documentary tried to convince [the viewer] that the ghosts who lived there require no exorcist. One just

---

8   It premiered on May 12, 2012, in Teatr Dramatyczny (directed by Lilach Dekel-Avneri). I am grateful to the play's producer, Maria Niziołek, for making the script of the play available to me. The text was re-published in the form of a short story titled *Muranooo* in the collection *W krainie czarów* (Chutnik 2014).

needs to ask them to leave. When you are haunted, you should ask: what do you need, perhaps you want me to live your life for you? (Szymańska/Chutnik 2012)

Chutnik plays out a scenario suggested by Hirsch: life now, the life of those who enter onto the scene of the crime, becomes double: life lived for the living and life lived for the absent. At the end of the play the ghost of the boy from the buried cellar asks the other characters in the play, but also the audience, which, like the Grandmother's Grandchildren, trapped by a pile of rubble, is momentarily locked in a sort of black box:

I only have one request. Carry it out for me, please. As soon as they free you from my hiding place, and you can hear the cranes and the excavators working nearby, would you live my life for me, just a little bit? Live for me a little up there, where the sky is, where the air is. (Chutnik 2012)

To venture a hypothesis regarding what it is that frightens us about non-sites of memory, why we are scared of their uncanniness, I would like to suggest that the most important reason from amongst many other possibilities (forms of the Freudian »infantilism of the psychic life«, such as the primal atavism of the fear of open space, the threat perceived in places whose application is not apparent; cultural patterns of reactions to »calling forth spirits«, the aesthetically motivated aversion to incongruous places) hinges upon the possibility of a sort of possession: the surrender of the currently living body into the possession of apparitions. The rationalized version of this would be the acceptance of the call to symbolically continue the interrupted life from the past, resulting in the restriction of the claims of self-determination of the subject itself in favor of the non-living other. This hypothesis can be developed further. Let us now examine the fear, shame, and disgust that overwhelm the visitor that has strayed so carelessly onto the terrain of the non-site of memory.

PIECES OF BODIES

The first photograph in Andrzej Kramarz's series *A Piece of Land* (2009) shows a clearing in a forest near the village of Siekłówka, located just at the foot of the Bieszczady Mountains. Kramarz accompanies his photographs with audio, in this case a recording in which Józef Skiba recounts the murder of his family during the occupation and the circumstances under which their bodies were later recovered in the forest:

> There was this farmer and his son who went. They got to this place and turned to go in the forest. His son got to the place of the murders and said to him, ›Daddy, there's something here, the ground is soft here.‹ They poked the ground with a stick, and it wouldn't budge. We went there immediately and started digging, I recognized my brother-in-law, Jasiek, by his shoes.[9]

The last image of the series is an urban landscape very familiar to Krakovians, namely, a photograph of Zamoyski Street. The audio that accompanies it tells the story of the destruction of a German cannon ambushed on the dead-end Zamoyski Street by the attacking Soviet forces. The resulting scraps of metal were harvested immediately by enterprising locals, while the bodies of three deceased soldiers scattered about the street were left longer. Eyewitness Marian Jabłoński states: »I saw human pieces on the ground, a large spiral cord… I can't remember after how many days the bodies were cleared up.«

I cite these two accounts here because they reveal the extent to which the very recent aversion to decomposing bodies departs from wartime experience as well as the experience of the period immediately following the war (exhumations, bodies uncovered upon the clearing of rubble, the discovery of mass graves). This may be the reason that it is only now that the ghosts of Muranów are able to frighten us so effectively, for the next generation, distancing itself and placing itself under the protection of the analgesic side of a culture concealing decay, illness, and death, has definitively lost the unflappable calm achieved by the previous one in the face of the dead body. And if we experience discomfort, disturbance, and ultimately fear in non-sites of memory, this anxiety around »haunting« may in fact be merely a symptom of a larger anxiety. For there can be no ghosts on non-sites if there are no unburied (»ill-buried«) bodies:

---

9   I am grateful to Andrzej Kramarz for making this material available at andrzejkramarz.com/?page_id=2154 (accessed on May 22, 2016).

So what is it that's got grandma shaking like that? The ghosts, of course, the dead – she says they come to her while she's asleep and shake her by the arm and croon into her ear: ›muranooo, you remember me, muranooo.‹

And on and on, every night, for years. With the only hand she's got left she covers up her head, and she breaths hard. She thinks again back to when she was a little girl, and she got buried in the shelter up to the very top of her head, and she starts to suffocate under her blanket, because the bedding gets as heavy as rubble. So she drags herself up and sits on the bed. Her nightgown sticks to her back, and her panic rises, and she doesn't want to get unstuck.

After a while her sleepy lids fall over her aged eyes. That seemingly endless crooning slowly comes to its end. She just can't get those syllables out of her head: moo-rah-nooooo. Like a pang of conscience or some incomprehensible curse. It rumbles around in her head until morning, roars, commands, sows anxiety.

No one will believe her that they're the ghosts of Muranów that live in the concrete made of the rubble, ruined and destroyed and then ground back up into the bricks that they used. And they built up everywhere there is to live now in Muranów brick by brick.

And in every brick: bones. Ground-up corpses. In Warsaw!!! (Chutnik 2012)

The idea of Muranów being haunted is inspired by the fact that there was not time to clean up the debris around this evacuated zone in the Northern District of Poland's capital city. The work already begun by the Germans (Chomątowska 2012: 203),[10] continued in the form of spontaneous and illegal searches for building materials over the course of the first years after the war,[11] later taking on an organized, and even international character following the decision to rebuild the area following the plans of Bohdan Lachert. The architect had imagined a sort of commemoration of the material past of the rebuilt space by means of crushing the brick already on-site and mixing it with concrete in order to make the prefabricated element needed to erect the new constructions. »It happens often enough that the shovel hits upon decayed human bones. These are meticulously collected and placed into special containers, of which numerous can be found around Muranów«, wrote a

---

10   The man in charge of the demolition was SS Officer Hans Kammler, who in June 1944 reported that the razing of the territory had to be called off.
11   For more on the »bricklayer-looters«, see Chomątowska (2012: 136), as well as the chapter *Rubble Looter* in Engelking/Leociak (2009 [2001]).

contemporary reporter from *Życie Warszawy* (quoted in Chomątowska 2012: 203). In spite of these efforts, many people remain convinced to this day that not all the workers were so ›meticulous‹ amidst the rubble, though estimating the level of negligence is impossible, making it difficult, too, to determine to what extent this legend is empirically founded. Yet the stories abound – like the one about the housing built up where the Skra Stadium was once located, the territory then host to mass graves. »I Have Seven Thousand (Dead) Neighbors«, reads the title of a recent article from the Warsaw press (Szyller 2013). Warsaw thus, like many other places in the region, undermines Jean-Luc Nancy's seemingly commonsensical assertion in *Corpus* that »[t]wo bodies can't occupy the same place simultaneously« (2008 [1992]: 57).

The fear of the corpse can, of course, arise from multiple reasons: we are scared of contagion, plague; at its broadest, we fear death, and furthermore, the impenetrable future represented by the corpse. In cultures both ancient and contemporary, we find the belief that the body is evacuated by the soul, which travels to another dimension, and when this happens, the corpse is put at risk of inhabitation by another soul, which, not being at rest, as a zombie, as the living dead, may demand retribution, may pose a threat to the living. Funereal rites tend to be regulated by certain requirements of timeliness and introduce distinct forms of »closure«, »distance«, and »protection«. From the Assyrians, the Egyptians, and the Greeks up to now, some have believed, as Christine Quigley shows in her history of the corpse, that noncompliance with the steps to set up a symbolic and physical barrier between the living and the dead may result in the spirit of the dead rising and plaguing those around, reclaiming the right to a ritual of transition (2005: 16-19). This idea, so widespread and so resistant to the passage of time, situated at the very foundations of the relationship between the living and the dead, explains the events that take place during *Night of the Living Jews*, in which Chuda foretells early on the revenge of the dead for the neglect surrounding their fate and their bodies:

Evil can't be covered over with rubble and earth, suffering needs to be respected and reckoned with, and blood, if not removed in time, if allowed indifferently to soak into the ground, will mix with clay and come out in a horde of golems slow as tanks, and the broken bones and mistreated bodies will drape themselves in whatever rags they've not been robbed of, pitch themselves with a force beneath biology into two-legged specters who know only pain, and with that pain they will act, running askew from door to door all down our quiet apartments. (Ostachowicz 2012: 14)

Chuda's vision may actually be seen as the act that launches the plot of *Night*, although the official reason provided within the plot itself is the appearance of a talisman stolen by a corrupt Pole. She delivers her speech in a symbolic place, as well, on Anielewicz Street, near what was once Gęsia Street, one of the most important Jewish streets in Warsaw. This was the route taken by all funeral processions, which ended at the cemetery where the street ends.

A similar act of »calling forth spirits« takes place in a speech written by Sławomir Sierakowski and Kinga Dunin for the script for Yael Bartana's 2007 *Mary Koszmary* [Nightmares]: »This is a call, not to the dead but to the living. We want three million Jews to return to Poland to live with us again! We need you! We are asking you to return!« The events that follow, presented in Bartana's next work, 2009's *Mur i wieża* [Wall and Tower], make the viewer overlook that the leader of the Jewish Renaissance Movement in Poland (Ruch Odrodzenia Żydowskiego w Polsce) invited not young Zionists into the country, but rather – in accordance with the Polish Romantic tradition of coexistence with the dead – those Jews who had been killed. Scrawled across the National Stadium is the number 3,300,000, raising no other association than the number of Jewish victims from Poland. The call is heeded only in 2011's *Zamach* [The Assassination] when Ryfka addresses us directly.[12] »I am a ghost of return«, she says, »Ich bin da [I am here]«. The monologues of Chuda, the Grandmother, and Ryfka create a kind of catalogue of the wrongdoings on the part of the residents of the post-ghetto city,[13] including an absence of respect for the suffering, an unwillingness to hold accountable (the perpetrators of said suffering amidst the ancestors of the current inhabitants), indifference, noncompliance with funereal ritual, forgetting about the dead, and ultimately the confiscation of their property, »disinheritance«, and »removal from the now«. In the affective realm of non-sites of memory, then, on top of the primary affect of »fear of ghosts and

---

12 The address begins at minute 8:46 of the film.
13 I take this term from Jacek Leociak's, *Aryjskim tramwajem przez warszawskie getto, czyli hermeneutyka pustego miejsca* [Taking an Aryan Tram Through the Warsaw Ghetto, or the Hermeneutics of the Empty Space, 2001].

rotted corpses«, there appears another layer, closer to secondary, socially elaborated emotions: the fear of accountability, or the shame of neglect.

The appearance of affects built around »spirits« may be interpreted as a sign of a crucial change. As Monica Casper and Lisa Jean Moore write in *Missing Bodies: The Politics of Visibility*, the social sphere administers bodies, celebrating some, hiding others, in the case of dead bodies as in the case of living ones. The processes of »discovering« previously contested bodies are connected with the act of changing their status: they cease to be »absent« and begin to be »missing«: »Thus ›missing‹ is a kind of invisibility, one usually characterized by a high degree of emotion.« (Casprar/Moore 2009: 3) In other words, once we acknowledge that we »miss« certain bodies, we reveal an affective connection with them (Rafał Betlejewski's *Tęsknię za Tobą, Żydzie* [I Miss You, Jew], beginning in 2006, may be understood as an attempt to intervene in the name of calling for a longed-for shift). I would also like to read this notion backwards: if we reveal affective attitudes towards certain absent bodies (disgust, shame – not necessarily positive affects), then, too, they go from being neutral or of no interest to being »missing«. Here another reinterpretation of the fear of ghosts, this time positive, becomes possible, as Avery Gordon writes in *Ghostly Matters:*

To be haunted in the name of a will to heal is to allow the ghost to help you imagine what was lost that never even existed, really. That is its utopian grace: to encourage a steely sorrow laced with delight for what we lost that we never had; to long for the insight of that moment in which we recognize, as in Benjamin's profane illumination, that it could have been and can be otherwise. (2004 [1997]: 57)

That we are beguiled by the mourning pleasure of the illusion of the possibility of an alternative scenario is demonstrated by pop culture; an example of the fantasy can be found at the end of Juliusz Machulski's 2013 comedy *AmbaSSada,* in which an unscathed Warsaw is home to Hasidic Jews in fur hats practically dancing, to the tune of Klezmer music, into a restaurant that boasts stuffed goose neck amongst its offerings.

PHANTOM-SITES

Aleida Assmann sees the body as a medium of memory. The body as zone of affective operations participates in the stabilization of recollections, serves as a kind of (ambivalent) precognitive stimulus (ensuring »authenticity« or its opposite, in which case it serves as a »motor of falsification«). »When a memory lodged in the body is completely cut off from consciousness, we speak of trauma«, Assmann writes (1999: 111), repeating a well-known psychoanalytical hypothesis. But when applied to the Płaszów or the Muranów case, this idea is opened up to another possible reading. The recollection of suffering and death is after all lodged in a body that is now dead: the events immediately preceding death were »anchored in neurons«. And their ties to consciousness have been permanently severed, consciousness having been destroyed in the act of the murder. Such trauma, deprived of a conscious subject, deprived even of a biological body, which gradually succumbs to decomposition, destroying all of the body's biochemical records that might act as anchor, would seem to rise in the air like a kind of spectral parasite seeking somewhere to settle. It is perhaps precisely this type of presentiment that allows for the easy supposition in non-sites of memory that »something is off«: that there is a phantom roving up above them, taking on a very physical form in the experience of some locals, approaching the observer, rising several feet above the ground, bluish-gold »lighted clouds« with human forms, as was the case in Kozie Górki, at the site of the mass grave near Niepołomice.[14]

Here phantoms and places form a coalition of sorts. As Assmann writes in her book:

Biographical and cultural memory cannot be [...] stored in places; they can set in motion and support the processes of remembering only in conjunction with other media of memory. Wherever all possibilities for transmission have been blocked, there arise phantom-sites, which become an arena for the free play of the imagination or for the return of expelled significations. (Ibid: 112)

---

14 Needless to say, scholars attribute the phenomenon of spontaneous combustion to the volatilization of the gases arising from the decomposition of the organic components of shallowly buried bodies (cf. Żychowska 2007).

This idea is contingent, of course, upon the assumption that the materiality of contested non-sites of memory does not generate any opportunities for the formation of »media of memory«, that their »spectrality« is merely metaphorical, having to do with the work of the imagination around that which has been postponed. In other words, when on these territories we are faced with a lack of »ruins«, »monuments«, or other form of legible »landscape«, we find no media of memory available to us – and plants, watercourses, or soil cannot be accounted as such. Proponents of a non-anthropocentric humanities would argue otherwise. Following the principles of geologists, geographers, and chemists, in fact, the corpse – in other words, the »medium of the inaccessible trauma of victims placed in mass graves« – decomposes, »contaminating« (or to use a word with no negative connotation: saturating) the environment with ions, bacteria, and chemical compounds, which enter into the water and the air, even – if infrequently – producing luminous aerial phenomena in the form of spontaneous combustion (the clouds at Kozie Górki) and possibly influencing the state of the organisms that absorb them, as well as causing changes in the chemical makeup of plants (incidents of discoloration), and perhaps, too, the psychic state of people and animals. Thus at the cellular level, in a way that has not yet been fully understood (cf. Żychowski 2008), the terrain of non-sites of memory is occupied by extra-cognitive processes and somatic connections.

***

In his introduction to Deleuze and Guattari's *Thousand Plateaus,* Brian Massumi gives the following definition of »affect« in his dictionary of ideas explaining the decisions he made as a translator:

AFFECT/AFFECTION. Neither word denotes a personal feeling (*sentiment* in Deleuze and Guattari). *L'affect* (Spinoza's *affectus*) is an ability to affect and be affected. It is a prepersonal intensity corresponding to the passage from one experiential state of the body to another and implying an augmentation or diminution in that body's capacity to act. *L'affection* (Spinoza's *affectio*) is each such state considered as an encounter between the affected body and a second, affecting, body (with body taken in its broadest possible sense to include ›mental‹ or ideal bodies). (2004: xvii)

I would argue that the dead bodies from non-sites of memory follow in a particular way but with uncommon precision Massumi's definition: they are bodies taken in the »broadest possible sense«, able to transition »from one experiential state of the body to another«, and furthermore, they are »affecting« bodies. In a metaphorical or even totally literal (molecular) way they influence the state of visitors to contested territories of historical violence. This is how »affective resonance« occurs, this »effect of the affect«: through the body's spasms when it feels exposed to an encounter that will alter its »functioning capacity«. The ultimate, extreme way of responding in the form of undertaking a »new functioning« would be the making available of the body as medium of memory for the body from the past – a response not so much to the enjoinment of »live my life!«, but rather to that of »remember with my memory«, or »experience my trauma«. In this way there arises a totally new problem, unremarked until now: while the post-memory of the victims has been debated at some length, what do we know about the different forms taken by the post-memory of the witnesses, of the bystanders?

Literature

Apel, Dora (2002): Memory Effects: The Holocaust and the Art of Secondary Witnessing, New Brunswick and New York: Rutgers University Press.
Assmann, Aleida (1999): Erinnerungsräume: Formen und Wandlungen des kulturellen Gedächtnisses, München: C.H. Beck.
Attie, Shimon (2003): »The Writing on the Wall, Berlin, 1992-1993: Projections in Berlin's Jewish Quarter.« In: Art Journal 3, pp. 74-83.
Baer, Ulrich (2005 [2002]): Spectral Evidence: The Photography of Trauma, Cambridge: MIT Press.
Bartana, Yael (2007): Mary, koszmary (http://artmuseum.pl/pl/filmoteka/praca/bartana-yael-mary-koszmary2).
Bartana, Yael (2009): Mur i wieża (http://artmuseum.pl/pl/filmoteka/praca/bartana-yael-mur-i-wieza).
Bauman, Zygmunt (2008): »The Haunted World.« In: Krystyna Oleksy/Jolanta Ambrosewicz-Jacobs (eds.), Remembrance, Awareness, Responsibility, Oświęcim: Auschwitz-Birkenau State Museum, pp. 271-279.

Casper, Monica/Moore, Lisa Jane (2009): Missing Bodies: The Politics of Visibility, New York: New York University Press.

Charlesworth, Andrew (2004): »A Corner of a Foreign Field that Is Forever Spielberg's: The Moral Landscapes of the Site of the Former KL Plaszow, Krakow, Poland.« In: Cultural Geographies 11, pp. 291-312.

Chomątowska, Beata (2012): Stacja Muranów, Czarne: Wołowiec.

Chutnik, Sylwia (2014): »Muranooo.« In: Sylwia Chutnik, W krainie czarów, Kraków: Znak, pp. 177-211.

Deleuze, Gilles/Guattari, Felix (2004 [1980]): Thousand plateaus, London: Continuum.

Didi-Huberman, Georges (2007): »The Site, Despite Everything.« In: Stuart Liebman (ed.), Claude Lanzmann's Shoah: Key Essays, Oxford: Oxford University Press, pp. 113-124.

Domańska, Ewa (2007 [2004]): »›Let the Dead Bury the Living‹: Daniel Libeskind's Monumental Counterhistory.« In: Edward Wang and Franz L. Fillafer (eds.), History of Historiography Reconsidered, New York: Berghahn Books, pp. 437-454.

Engelking, Barbara/Leociak, Jacek (eds.) (2009 [2001]) The Warsaw Ghetto: A Guide to a Perished City, New Haven: Yale University Press.

Forczek-Brataniec, Urszula (2010): »Interpretacja krajobrazu jako źródło koncepcji projektowej. Rozważania na podstawie pracy konkursowej na zagospodarowanie terenu dawnego Obozu KL Płaszów.« In: Architecture: Technical Transactions, pp. 289-297.

Freud, Sigmund (2003 [1919]): »The Uncanny.« In: Sigmund Freud, The Uncanny, London and New York: Penguin Books, pp. 121-161.

Gordon, Avery (2004 [1997]): Ghostly Matters: Haunting and the Sociological Imagination, Minneapolis: University of Minnesota Press.

Hirsch, Marianne/Spitzer, Leo (2010): Ghosts of Home: The Afterlife of Czernowitz in Jewish Memory, Berkeley and Los Angeles: University of California Press.

Kosofsky Sedgwick, Eve (1995): »Shame in the Cybernetic Fold: Reading Silvan Tomkins.« In: Eve Kosofsky Sedgwick et al. (eds.), Shame and Its Sisters: A Silvan Tomkins Reader, Durham: Duke University Press, pp. 1-28.

Kristeva, Julia (1982): Powers of Horror: An Essay on Abjection, New York: Columbia University Press.

Lanzmann, Claude (1990): »J'ai enqueté en Pologne.« In: Michel Deguy (ed.), Au sujet de Shoah, le film de Claude Lanzmann, Paris: Belin, pp. 211-217.
Leociak, Jacek (2001): »Aryjskim tramwajem przez warszawskie getto, czyli hermeneutyka pustego miejsca.« In: Lidia Burska and Marek Zaleski, Maski współczesności. O literaturze i kulturze w XX wieku, Warszawa: IBL, pp. 75-87.
Massumi, Brian (2002): Parables for the Virtual: Movement, Affect, Sensatio, Durham: Duke University Press.
Massumi, Brian (2004): »Notes on the Translation and Acknowledgments.« In: Gilles Deleuze and Felix Guattari, Thousand plateaus, London: Continuum.
Michaels, Anne (2009): The Winter Vault, New York: Random House.
Nancy, Jean-Luc (2008 [1992]): Corpus, New York: Fordham University Press.
Nathanson, Donald L. (2008): »Prologue.« In: Silvan S. Tomkins, Affect Imagery Consciousness: The Positive Affect, Vol. 1, New York: Springer, pp. xi-xxvi.
O'Brien, Ruth (2005): Bodies in Revolt: Gender, Disability, and a Workplace Ethic of Care, New York: Routledge.
Ostachowicz, Igor (2012): Noc żywych Żydów, Warszawa: Wydawnictwo W.A.B.
Quigley, Christine (2005): The Corpse: A History, Jefferson and London: McFarland Publishing.
Sendyka, Roma (2014 [2013]): »Prism – Understanding a Non-site of Memory (Non-lieu de Memoire).« In: John W. Boyer and Berthold Molden (eds.), EuTropes. The Paradox of European Empire, Chicago: University of Chicago Press.
Sendyka, Roma (2013): »Robinson w nie-miejscach pamięci.« In: Konteksty 2, pp. 98-104.
Shore, Marci (2013): The Taste of Ashes: The Afterlife of Totalitarianism in Eastern Europe, New York: Crown.
Szyller, Donat (2013): »Osiedle stoi na masowym grobie.« In: Gazeta Wyborcza December 12 (http://warszawa.wyborcza.pl/warszawa/1,34889, 15123096,Osiedle_stoi_na_masowym_grobie___Mam_7_tysiecy_sasiadow_.html).

Szymańska, Izabela/Chutnik, Sylwia (2012): »O duchach Muranowa«. In: Gazeta Wyborcza, May 10 (http://wyborcza.pl/1,75410,11683080,Sylwia_Chutnik_o_duchach_Muranowa.html).

Young, James E. (2000): At Memory's Edge: After-Images of the Holocaust in Contemporary Art and Architecture, New Haven: Yale University Press.

Żychowska, Marzena (2007): »Cmentarze zagrożeniem dla środowiska« (http://www.up.krakow.pl/konspekt/11/zychowska.html).

Żychowski, Józef (2008): Wpływ masowych grobów z I i II wojny światowej na środowisko przyrodnicze, Kraków: Wydawnictwo Naukowe Akademii Pedagogicznej.

Healing by Haunting

On Jewish Ghosts, Symbolic Exorcism
and Traumatic Surrealism

MAGDALENA WALIGÓRSKA

>»What's a ghost? Unfinished business, that's what.«
SALMAN RUSHDIE (1989: 129)

»Ghosts are political.«
MICHAEL MAYERFELD BELL (1997: 832)

Mary Koszmary [*Nightmares*, 2007] by the Israeli artist Yael Bartana is a short but powerful film. Opening her Polish trilogy, which also includes *Wall and Tower* (2009) and *Assassination* (2011), *Nightmares* depicts a speech by the charismatic leader of a fictitious Jewish Renaissance Movement in Poland. Addressing the empty bleachers in the eerie Decennial Stadium in Warsaw, the young activist calls for the return of 3.3 million Jews to Poland. His impassioned appeal is both an address to the absent – a lost world of Jews who are missing in today's mono-ethnic, Catholic Poland – and a summoning of ghosts who might heal the Polish soul.

Jews! Fellow countrymen! People!
    You think that the old woman who still sleeps under Rivke's quilt doesn't want to see you? That she has forgotten about you? You're wrong. She dreams about you every night. Dreams and trembles with fear. Since the night you were gone and her mother reached for your quilt, she has had nightmares. Bad dreams. Only you can

chase them away. Let the three million Jews that Poland has missed stand by her bed and lay your hands on that old quilt. Thin as a sheet, with the down long gone. I'm telling you, lay your hands on her and tell her: ›We're giving this quilt to you. What do we need it for? There's no longer any down in it, only pain.‹ Heal our wounds, and you'll heal yours. And we'll be together again.[1]

Rivke's quilt is a symbol of Jewish suffering and the Polish guilty conscience, but is also a tool that may enable reconciliation and give rise to a real Jewish return. The »Manifesto« of the Jewish Renaissance Movement in Poland (JRMiP), published in 2010 when Bartana was working on the third part of her trilogy, articulates a utopian wish for a mass Jewish (re-)migration to Poland and, at the same time, plays with the notion of Jewish spirits who haunt their former neighbors.

We do not plan an invasion. This will be more of a return of ghosts of the neighbors haunting you in your dreams – the neighbors you never expected to see again or those you have never had the chance to meet. (2010)

Bartana's art project, which was selected to represent Poland at the 2011 Venice Biennale, has been both very successful and highly controversial (cf. Lehrer/Waligórska 2013). Apart from the political implications the manifesto of the JRMiP has taken on in Poland and Israel, Bartana's filmic vision has become symptomatic of a more wide-ranging phenomenon in contemporary Polish popular culture – a fascination with the motif of the Jewish return.

This chapter focuses on one aspect of this imagined Jewish »homecoming« to Poland, namely a spate of new literary narratives about Jewish ghosts. Uncanny Jewish figures are not entirely new to Polish literature; Jews have been portrayed with some regularity in recent years both by Jewish and non-Jewish authors in Poland as bearers of mystical powers and individuals endowed with a particular spirituality.[2] Well known, for example, are Hanna

---

1   The video is available under http://www.artmuseum.pl/filmoteka/?l=0&id=200.
2   For more on the figure of the Jew in Polish literature see: Maria Janion, *Do Europy tak, ale razem z naszymi umarymi* (2000); Maria Janion, *Bohater, spisek, śmierć* (2009); Bożena Keff, *Postać z cieniem. Portrety Żydówek w polskiej literaturze* (2001); Elvira Grözinger, *Die schöne Jüdin: Klischees, Mythen und*

Krall's short story *Dybbuk* (2005 [1995]), about an American Jew possessed by the spirit of his brother who perished in the Holocaust, or Paweł Huelle's *Who Was David Weiser?* (1991 [1987]), about a Jewish boy endowed with supernatural powers, who eventually mysteriously disappears. But a new crop of authors employ the motif of Jewish ghosts in a novel way, staging them as protagonists of *Polish* history who return both to haunt Poles and to assist them in dealing with their shameful past of anti-Jewish violence.

Five contemporary literary works that rely on the topos of the Jewish ghost stand out in particular: Sylwia Chutnik's short stories *Kieszonkowy atlas kobiet* [Pocket Atlas of Women, 2008], her play *Muranooo* (2012), Andrzej Bart's *Fabryka muchołapek* [The Flytrap Factory, 2008], Tadeusz Słobodzianek's drama *Our Class* (2009 [2008]) and Igor Ostachowicz's *Noc żywych Żydów* [Night of the Living Jews, 2012]. Examining the ways such current Polish prose engages with the Polish-Jewish past, I will illustrate how this new topos of the Jew as incorporeal – yet related to real historical events, such as the Warsaw ghetto uprising or the Jedwabne pogrom[3] – suggests the emergence of a paradigm of memory, in which the medium of the fantastic is employed to deal with a collective trauma. In this case, however, the trauma is not that of Holocaust survivors, but one derived from what we could term a »postmemory of witnesses«, and is a specifically Polish one. If the concept of »postmemory« has been adopted in the first place to describe the experience of the »second generation«, or children of Holocaust survivors, Hirsch's theory of transgenerational transmission of trauma also concerns a more universal transfer between the generation of »those who witnessed cultural or collective trauma« and their descendants (2008: 106). Hirsch distinguishes between »familial postmemory«, transmitted by »stories, images and behaviors« passed on within a family and »affiliative postmemory«, which is »more broadly available to other contemporaries«

Vorurteile über Juden in der Literatur (2003); Bożena Shallcross, *The Holocaust Object in Polish and Polish–Jewish Culture* (2011).

3   Jedwabne is a town in north-eastern Poland and the site of a 1941 pogrom performed on the local Jewish community by the Polish inhabitants. The case became known after Jan Tomasz Gross's publication of *Neighbours* (2001 [2000]) and became shorthand for Polish wartime atrocities against Jews. The heated debate that followed Gross's publication was a milestone in the process of bringing Poland's complicity in anti-Jewish violence to light.

(ibid: 114). Given that Hirsch's category of »postmemory« should not be understood as »an identity position but a general structure of transmission« (ibid.), it is possible to use this category to investigate the way images and narratives of trauma become transmitted not only among the descendants of victims, but also to children of bystanders, and even to perpetrators of the Holocaust.

Analyzing how the figure of the ghost provides a vehicle for »countervoluntary memory«, Zuzanna Dziuban argues that the emergence of the highly ambivalent metaphor of the Jewish ghost in the Polish literary landscape is symptomatic of an acute crisis (2014). Indeed, the motifs of haunting in contemporary Polish prose indicate in the first place an anxiety about inhabiting formerly Jewish spaces or sites of the Holocaust. This unease, most poignantly expressed in Chutnik's *Muranooo* and Ostachowicz's *Night of the Living Jews*, points to a transgenerational transmission of memory about Poland's Jewish past that can be related to the recent historical debates about Polish complicity in the dispossession and killing of Jews during and in the aftermath of the Second World War.[4] Focusing in particular on two recurrent topoi – that of traumatic history encoded in urban spaces, and the motif of restorative justice – this essay analyses how the ghost story becomes not only a vehicle for expressing some of the central anxieties concerning the memory of Polish-Jewish past, but also a redemptive genre that offers narrative closure.[5]

---

4   The most important recent historiographical publications that addressed the issue of Polish complicity in anti-Jewish violence include Jan T. Gross's *Neighbours* (2001 [2000]); *Fear* (2006), as well as a wealth of other publications, such as Barbara Engelking's *Szanowny Panie Gistapo: Donosy do władz niemieckich w Warszawie i okolicach w latach 1940-1941* (2003) and her *Jest taki piękny słoneczny dzień: Losy Żydów szukających ratunku na wsi polskiej 1942-1945* (2011); Jan Grabowski's *Hunt for the Jews: Betrayal and Murder in German-Occupied Poland* (2013 [2011]); Joanna Tokarska-Bakir's *Okrzyki pogromowe* (Wołowiec: Wydawnictwo Czarne, 2012) and *Pod klątwą: Społeczny portret pogrom kieleckiego* (Warszawa 2018); Mirosław Tryczyk, *Miasta Śmierci: Sąsiedzkie pogromy Żydów* (2015).

5   Noël Carroll defines »narrative closure« as »the phenomenological feeling of finality that is generated when all the questions saliently posed by the narrative are answered« (2007: 1).

SPACES CONTAMINATED WITH HISTORY

It is a hot summer day in Muranów, Warsaw. The district, literally rebuilt from rubble on top of the levelled wartime Jewish ghetto, is today a residential district of neat streets lined with dull socialist blocks of flats. Life in the district is monotonous and predictable until, one day, residents start hearing a mysterious scratching sound from their cellars.

Night of the Living Jews by Igor Ostachowicz is perhaps the most controversial Polish novel dealing with the Holocaust since Jerzy Kosiński's *The Painted Bird* (1965). Ostachowicz's work is a pastiche, written as a conventional pulp-fiction thriller. The protagonist, a young paver with a university degree, witnesses how, due to their uncanny magical powers, a cadre of the Jewish »undead«, long buried underneath the houses of Muranów, begin to leave their underworld and to haunt the quarter's contemporary inhabitants. If the Hieronymus Bosch-like vision of zombies overrunning Warsaw is decidedly unrealistic, the reasons for this Jewish return reflect pressing contemporary concerns. The Polish capital is a space poisoned by trauma, suggests Ostachowicz, and an epicenter of »evil radiation«, which contaminates the whole of Poland. His protagonist, who decides to help the Jewish undead find peace again, speaks of the stigma of living in the country where the Holocaust took place:

I'm just furious with myself and fate that I wasn't born somewhere else, or at a different time, in some peaceful place that from the deep groundwater through sand, clay, concrete and bricks, roots, trees, cats, windows, roofs, the air, birds, clouds and the people with their belongings would not be permeated with a sense of guilt and pain. All of this damned latitude is totally soaked through with pain and fear, which I merely touched. All of those moans and screams, the tears and blood… each atom is befouled with evil. If the ore of evil abounds in the whole world, it is here that pure evil was refined in ovens. In the greatest production of purest evil in ovens, where people incinerate people. Evil is a radioactive element, and everything is contaminated with this radiation here, everything is active evil. (2012: 205)[6]

Ostachowicz's Jewish ghosts are therefore what Michael Mayerfeld Bell calls »ghosts of place«, an embodiment of the connection between the past

---

6   All translations, unless indicated otherwise, are by the author.

and present that humans perceive and construct in historic sites (1997). In a classic ghost story, the spirit returns to the site of its death, particularly if it was a violent one, or if its body was not properly buried. Ostachowicz uses this motif, choosing as his setting one of the most symbolic sites of Jewish martyrdom, the Warsaw ghetto.

Sylwia Chutnik, another young Warsaw-based author and feminist activist, is likewise fascinated with Muranów and ghosts of place. Her literary debut, *Pocket Atlas of Women*, is a collection of four minimally intertwined short stories, in which Chutnik concentrates on four women (one of them transgender) who are all, in one way or another, marginalized. Skillfully playing with language, she creates poignant portraits of everyday life in contemporary Warsaw, still scarred by the war. One of her characters is Maria Wachelberg-Wachelberska, a Jewish woman who escapes the Warsaw ghetto and joins the Polish underground army during the Warsaw Uprising in 1944. Maria survives the bombing of the city, miraculously escaping death, while all the inhabitants of her tenement house, having taken shelter in the cellar, die from a German grenade. After the defeat of the uprising, Maria witnesses the atrocities committed on civilians by the Vlasov Army. The most traumatic of her memories is that of her mother, who, wanting to protect her from rape, was killed by a Russian soldier. Maria, who blames herself for this death, decides to conceal her Jewish identity after the war and remains in the very building where she survived the war. Maria's neighborhood is a space marked with suffering, where the old woman is constantly confronted with her trauma. The heart of darkness is the cellar of her house:

The cellar in the tenement house in Opaczewska Street. It couldn't serve people in a normal way anymore, despite the fact that they gave it an overhaul and carefully scraped the corpses off the walls. The cellar walls saw things after which they couldn't store bikes, deckchairs and preserves. Such places are monuments. But what if a monument is part of the present-day reality, a block of flats inhabited by the living. Fill the cellar, pretend nothing ever happened there. Open a little shop, or a community club there. A tanning studio. Cover up the crime scene with new, useful contents. Make people domesticate it again. Don't be scared, come get your tan here. The war was long ago, it practically never happened. (2008: 124)

Inhabiting the places of death breaches a taboo. The (non-Jewish) living trespass in a space that belongs to the (Jewish) dead. The anxiety resulting from this sense of interloping makes normal daily life impossible. Such spaces of death seem apposite for only one purpose – dying. Therefore, when, in old age, Maria feels the end is near, she descends the stairs to await death where she once escaped it – in the cellar. She encounters the ghost of her mother there, who takes her to the spot where she was murdered. Walking through present-day Warsaw, they see the war-time city; memory and reality collapse into a vision of the space as seen through the prism of trauma.

The living and the dead cohabit Chutnik's Warsaw; and if the former are tempted to make spaces of death livable again by pushing aside the memory of what happened there, the ghosts of the dead reclaim those spaces, make history visible again. This territorial struggle, however, has an important ethnic dimension too. Today's Varsovians (predominantly non-Jews) live in a space marked by both Jewish and non-Jewish suffering, exemplified most powerfully by the Ghetto Uprising of 1943 and the Warsaw Uprising of 1944, respectively.[7] While the memory of the 1944 rising enjoys a high visibility in the urban space of Warsaw, the district of Muranów, roughly corresponding to the area of the former ghetto, remains a contested space, where the spaces of Jewish suffering and resistance are overlaid with a plethora of commemorative sites dedicated to Polish war losses.[8] The figure of *Jewish* ghosts is, therefore, an admonishment for Polish non-Jews to remember the dead »Others«.

---

7   The distinction between the Ghetto Uprising of 1943 as an instance of Jewish suffering and the Warsaw Uprising of 1944 as an event that concerned only non-Jews is an oversimplification as Jews (some of them survivors of the Ghetto Uprising) also fought in the Warsaw Uprising in 1944, but I juxtapose the two events in this way because of the incommensurateness of the memorial effort invested in Warsaw to commemorate both uprisings, with the 1944 uprising decidedly dominating the collective memory as the Polish act of heroic resistance against the Nazis.

8   Elżbieta Janicka's *Festung Warschau* (2011) depicts how Polish (non-Jewish) memory invades the most symbolic of Jewish spaces – the area of the Warsaw Ghetto – filling the urban space with plaques, monuments, memorial stones and shrines devoted to the non-Jewish heroes of the Warsaw Uprising of 1944, but also, spatially-unrelated events, such as the Battle of Monte Cassino (1944), or the assassination of Catholic priest, Jerzy Popiełuszko, by the Communist secret police in 1984.

Chutnik continues her reflection on Warsaw's scarred topography in her 2012 play *Muranooo*, where she returns to the topos of the haunted cellar, located this time in the former ghetto. As spaces of death, cellars full of rubble and incinerated bones are both loci of taboo and irresistible attraction. Chutnik's protagonists, present-day non-Jewish inhabitants of a block of flats in Muranów, descend into this underworld to seek Jewish treasures, but what they find instead is a ghost of a little Jewish boy, who asks them to help him look for his missing toy. The relationship of the living and the dead, argues Chutnik, is not only that of haunting, but also a symbiosis of sorts. In the epilogue of her play, she suggests that the living can soothe the suffering of the dead. »Live my life for me a little bit, will you? Live for me up there, with the air and sky above« (2012: 22) implores the ghost of the Jewish boy.[9] In Chutnik's play the living receive the mission not just to remember the dead, but also to live for their sake. »Muranów lives the unfinished life of the others« (ibid: 23), writes Chutnik. The present and the past are superimposed and simultaneous. Assimilating Warsaw's dark underworld and adopting its Jewish ghosts is in Chutnik's prose a gesture of respect and also redemption.

Negotiating the boundary between the living and the dead is a way of redrawing the boundary between the self and the other. Michael Mayerfeld Bell argues that ghosts »help constitute the specificity of historical sites, of the places where *we feel we belong and do not belong*, of the boundaries of possession by which we assign ownership and nativeness« (1997: 813; italics mine). In other words, spaces inhabited by the ghosts of our own dead are the spaces that shape our identity and give us a sense of belonging. By the same token, however, ghosts of the other might undermine our possession of space, question the legitimacy of our existence, trigger a sense of guilt and displacement.

Quoting the recent surveys of social psychologists who interviewed today's inhabitants of Muranów, Beata Chomątowska writes that many of them are anxious and unsure about how to factor themselves into the space of the sacrum in the former ghetto (2012: 340-341). While this problem of domesticating spaces formerly belonging to someone else is, in the Polish case, not limited to Muranów only, the dimensions of destruction and death that took place in this area make the reconstruction and repopulation of the district a particularly alienating undertaking.

---

9   I am indebted to Michael Meng for providing me with the manuscript.

The Second World War and its aftermath was the time of mass migrations and mass dispossession in Poland. As the real estate of deported Jews was being taken over by the new occupants and millions of Polish citizens were migrating into the so-called Recovered Lands in the West, the success of the project of a socialist Poland inside the new borders required severing the ties between spaces and their »ghosts«. Clearing the rubble and starting anew was a pressing objective, and the detritus of the Holocaust only stood in the way of returning normalcy to urban life. Muranów, where the trauma of the past was to be erased by the new plan for a perfect socialist residential district, was perhaps the most poignant example of the fervor to reclaim the spaces of death (cf. Meng 2011; Chomątowska 2012). The price to pay was the repression of narratives about the country's former residents. The ghosts banished in the post-war period, however, have begun to come back as Poles have taken steps to confront the dark chapters of their history since the fall of Communism.

In contemporary Polish literature, the unease about living in places contaminated by history is also accompanied by the discomfort about living in a country marked by persistent antisemitism. *The Flytrap Factory* by Andrzej Bart is a very particular fantasy of Jewish return. Set in contemporary Łódź, Bart's novel is a report from the imaginary trial of Chaim Rumkowski, staged by the Jewish ghosts of the Litzmannstadt ghetto. At one point, the protagonist and alter ego of the novelist, who is invited to participate in the hearings, takes Dora, one of the ghost-spectators of the proceedings, for a walk around present-day Łódź. The ›guided tour‹ with the ghost, who wishes to visit the house she lived in before her deportation, mirrors the experience of many actual Jewish tourists to Poland. When the couple is refused entry into the woman's former apartment and Dora spots countless stars of David and the word *Jude* graffitied on the walls, she asks her guide for clarification. Her Polish companion comes up with an alternative genesis of today's antisemitic slurs on the walls, which Łódź has become particularly notorious for.[10]

---

10 Much of today's antisemitic graffiti in Łódź is related to football hooliganism and the competition of two local football clubs: ŁKS and Widzew, the latter of which is seen by the fans of ŁKS as a ›Jewish‹ club. Anti-Widzew graffiti, therefore, heavily relies on antisemitic content and imagery (cf. Desperak 2008).

The Nazis used such signs to mark formerly Jewish houses that were designated for demolition. Did you ever read *Ali Baba and the Forty Thieves*? Remember how Ali Baba marked with chalk all the houses around the one tagged by thieves? People of Łódź did the very same thing. They painted the signs by night and the Nazis, if they were to follow their plan, would have to demolish half of the town. Later, the signs were covered with transparent varnish, so that they can remain an eternal monument to the heroic stratagem of the local people. (Bart 2008: 194)

Revisiting Poland's Jewish spaces – whether accompanied by a Jewish ghost or not – poses a challenge to contemporary Poles, who may be confronted with uncomfortable truths. Bart's attempt at translating a sobering reality of daily antisemitism into a tale of resistance is inspired by shame and a sense of guilt. His prose, like that of Chutnik's and Ostachowicz's, addresses some of the central anxieties triggered by recent debates on the Polish-Jewish past. Taking up themes of antisemitism, anti-Jewish violence, and also the dispossession of Jews, the authors put a finger on key sources of Polish moral unease. Engagement with these subjects in popular literature, on the one hand, can be seen as a reverberation of the recent scholarly debates addressing Polish complicity in extorting, robbing, and reporting Jews to the Nazi occupiers, as well as desecrating Jewish mass graves during and in the aftermath of the Holocaust.[11] The body of new historiographical, anthropological and sociological work, with path-breaking publications like Jan T. Gross's *Neighbors* (2001 [2000]) and *Fear* (2008 [2006]), has not only challenged the Polish myth of innocence, bringing the question of Polish violence against Jews to a wide readership, but has also changed the way Poles perceive the everyday spaces around them. Realizing the dimensions of pre-Holocaust Jewish life in Poland as well as the manner in which Jewish spaces came to be repopulated, adapted, or obliterated in post-war Poland, Poles discover what Svetlana Boym termed the »porosity« of space.

In *The Future of Nostalgia*, Boym defines porosity as a »variety of temporal dimensions embedded in physical space« (2001: 66-67). A porous space is one where the past becomes evident, and where layers of different

---

11 Much of the most recent Polish research on the implication of Poles in anti-Jewish violence during and after the Holocaust centres on dispossession (cf. Gross/Grudzińska-Gross 2012 [2011]; Grabowski 2013 [2011]; Tokarska-Barkir 2012).

epochs are superimposed on each other and readable as with a palimpsest. As a result of Poland's regaining its memory of its lost Jews, urban spaces once marked with Jewish life – or those that became sites of Jewish death – have *become* porous.[12] The history of persecution and dispossession is coming slowly into view. The sense of anxiety and alienation this discovery may trigger in those who came to inhabit these formerly Jewish spaces finds its metaphor in the genre of the ghost story. But the topos of the Jewish ghost is more than just a reflection of current historiographical revelations. Narratives of living Polish inhabitants who share their space with Jewish ghosts also suggest the possibility that contemporary Poles develop an emotional attachment to such spaces »contaminated« with the suffering of the Others, and a form of empathy towards those who inhabited them before. The return of ghosts, as in classic stories of haunting, offers an opportunity to amend past injustice and restore harmony. In this sense, fiction writing featuring Jewish ghosts offers a mode of coming to terms with the traumatic past and, *in the form of a symbolic exorcism*, closure.

HAUNTING AS A FORM OF RETRIBUTIVE AND RESTORATIVE JUSTICE

An important prerequisite of restoring an imagined harmony between the living – in this case, Christian Poles – and the dead – the murdered Jews – is the enactment of justice. In the narratives presented here, haunting becomes, therefore, a form of retributive or restorative justice, which allows a kind of closure – providing a medium for an imagined rapprochement of the Jewish dead and the Polish living who directly caused their suffering or feel a moral unease about the implication of their in-group in the historical harm-doing. By enabling the impossible, ghost fiction in which gestures towards easing the pain of victims are combined with declarations of forgiveness on the part of the harmed offers a form of closure for Polish readers that, even if based

---

12 »Porosity« of space in which the past and the present coexist in post-Holocaust Warsaw is also the subject of Piotr Paziński's recent novel *Ptasie ulice* (2013), where the protagonist, wandering around the former ghetto, descends into a cellar and ventures into a parallel world populated with mysterious spectral creatures.

on an *imagined* encounter, opens a space to speak about past injustice and ponder on the possibilities of retribution and reconciliation.

In *Between Vengeance and Justice*, Martha Minow provides us with the definition of restorative justice as an alternative to the more institutionalized retributive approach, typically represented by the adversarial lawsuit (1998: 91-92). If retributive justice stands for vengeance, restorative justice prioritizes the task of repairing the harm and rebuilding the relationship between victims and offenders. Contemporary Polish fiction frames the return of Jewish ghosts into both paradigms. Haunting becomes here, on the one hand, a form of punishment, retaliation, and vengeance; on the other hand, it is a chance for victims to speak about the suffering, and for the perpetrators to offer an apology. While Ostachowicz and Bart see haunting as a form of retributive justice and Słobodzianek and Chutnik picture Jewish ghosts rather as forgivingly »accompanying« the living, each of the narratives eventually suggests that the connection between the victims and perpetrators/witnesses and their descendants can and should be reestablished.

Igor Ostachowicz's *Night of the Living Jews* touches on one of the most widespread forms of Polish complicity in anti-Jewish persecution – that of the appropriation of Jewish possessions. In this respect, his novel reflects the concerns of Jan T. Gross and Irena Grudzińska-Gross, whose recent and highly controversial book *Golden Harvest* (2012 [2011]) discusses the involvement of Poles in dispossessing Jews during the Holocaust and desecrating mass graves in search for gold in its immediate aftermath. Raising the question of Poles appropriating Jewish belongings, Ostachowicz also addresses the Polish fear of Jewish restitution claims. In a passage that summarizes his moral dictum, the main protagonist states:

At a certain point, you can't avoid it anymore and you need to face the truth. And tell your aunts and uncles, your neighbors and your entire Polish family, who have just made themselves comfortable in front of the TV set: Yes, it's true, corpses ramble around the town and I wonder myself what the sanitary-epidemiological station says to that, and it's not inconceivable that they'll start looking for their cutlery and other junk, not to mention the real estate – and I don't even know if they like you. They seem to tolerate me to an extent, because I'm so utterly confused that, in the face of the truth that you already know, I'm bent on fighting to the bitter end for their right to wander around and otherwise do whatever they please. You don't like it? So I'll whomp you with my club. (2012: 235)

This militant declaration not only positions the main protagonist – representing the Polish everyman from Muranów – as the hero protecting the Jewish undead from the attacks of local neo-Nazis, but it also articulates the core of the Polish anxiety vis-à-vis Jews: the fear of property claims. Jewish zombies coming to search for their cutlery stand for the dispossessed victims who return to haunt those who profited from their death.

In Freudian psychoanalysis, the ghost was an embodiment of a sense of guilt and its apparition was linked to the breach of a taboo (cf. Smale 2009: 784). *Night of the Living Jews* can be therefore read as an allegory of the Polish guilty conscience. The return of the Jewish ghosts is here a form of coming to terms with Polish participation in the dispossession of Jews. The novel therefore hits a nerve.

But the text also provides a sense of closure, and it is here that we should focus our moral attention. Ostachowicz visualizes the ultimate Polish nightmare – Warsaw invaded by Jewish zombies. Yet he offers, simultaneously, a catharsis. His fantasy suggests, namely, that retaliation (here, a joint Jewish-Polish armed uprising against neo-Nazis who want to take control of Warsaw) and reparation (here, enabling the Jewish undead to experience joy, by taking them on a shopping spree to the local mall) can redeem the ghosts and reinstate peace between those who died in the ghetto and today's Varsovians who inhabit this site of death. The Polish everyman from Muranów takes the side of the wronged victims, empathizes with them (by travelling in time to a place similar to Auschwitz), avenges them (by means of bulldozing antisemitic crowds attacking the Jewish undead), and ultimately dies a heroic death for their cause. The story of the brave paver who organizes armed resistance against the neo-Nazis consoles us with a vision of the world where justice triumphs and suggests the possibility that some form of reparation on the part of Poles who inhabit places marked by Jewish death can reinstate harmony between the Jewish ghosts and the non-Jewish living.

In the final scene of the novel, the Jewish undead, all dressed in new clothes from the local shopping mall *Arcadia*, come to life again and mingle with the crowds in the streets of Warsaw. The visit to the shopping mall is here a metaphor of reparation. The joys of consumption provided by *Arcadia* help the Jewish undead forget their past suffering, but the act of clothing the zombies has also an aspect of symbolic and material recompense. Shedding their rags, the undead regain their human appearance and dignity. Indeed, they even seem to regain life: »As soon as all these Jews, clad in brand-new clothes, left Arcadia [...] they departed home, like normal people.« (Ostachowicz 2012: 249) The act of providing Jewish ghosts with personal possessions can also be read as a form of restitution – a necessary element of reconciliation. Although Ostachowicz's fantasy ends with a dreamlike vision of an impossible catharsis in which the intervention of a Polish hero lifts the curse from the city of ruins and brings the unmourned dead back to life, *Night of the Living Jews* expresses not only a naive longing for the *status quo ante*, but addresses the necessity of a (material) reparation as a prerequisite of any Polish involvement with the Polish-Jewish past.

If Ostachowicz paints a vision of retributive justice of a rather picaresque variety, Bart gives it a more conventional setting. *The Flytrap Factory* can be read as a pastiche of Hannah Arendt's report from Eichmann's trial: the narrator, an observer of proceedings staged by ghosts, listens to the testimonies of the witnesses (Arendt is one of them) pondering the problem of ethics at the time of the ultimate moral demise. In giving voice to the ghosts, Bart seems to follow Primo Levi's dictum that only the dead are the »true witnesses« (1989: 83). Rumkowski's trial gathers historic figures who personally knew the head of the Łódź Judenrat, such as Janusz Korczak[13] or Hans Biebow,[14] as well as others who, like Hannah Arendt, took part in the public debate about Rumkowski (2006 [1963]: 119). Even though the stories reported during the imaginary trial are based on documentary sources such as the published diaries of ghetto inmates, Bart constantly maneuvers between fiction and reality.

The Flytrap Factory suggests that literature gives us a particular vantage point on the Holocaust, because, with its capacity to reflect on human nature, it can contribute to our understanding of history. At the end of Rumkowski's trial, no sentence is passed. The proceedings finish, instead, with a theatre performance: a medley of Shakespeare's plays, which comment on the abuse of power (2008: 212-235). Literature is here a lens with which to look at history, and theatre a medium to unveil the human nature of perpetrators. Ghosts in Bart's novel seek retributive justice in that they compel the living to engage with the past and contemplate the impossible choices Jews in Poland were forced to face. Yet, by giving the victims a space to speak about

---

13 Polish-Jewish educator and pediatrician, director of an orphanage, who in 1942 was killed, together with his Jewish wards, in Treblinka.
14 Head of the Nazi administration of the Łódź Ghetto.

the injustice they experienced and emphasizing the humanity of those who, like Rumkowski, made themselves complicit in the Nazi persecution of Jews, Bart's ghosts' trial also has a dimension of restorative justice.

Notably, however, Bart's ghosts do not haunt Poles nor address Polish complicity in anti-Jewish violence. Bart's alter ego is merely a casual bystander; Rumkowski is a Jewish ›villain‹, and the testimonies all concern the culpability of Jews who decided to collaborate with the Nazis. What is more, while the question of Rumkowski's guilt remains unresolved, Poles seem to receive compassion from the Jewish ghosts. When Dora, the Jewish ghost in Bart's novel, comes across a volume of Rimbaud that she received as a gift from her father, stashed on the bookshelf of the elderly woman who lives in her apartment, she decides to leave this precious keepsake with the present owner. »If this lady keeps it here, it must be important for her«, she says, »it should stay here« (ibid: 152). Presenting the book to those who appropriated Jewish belongings after their owners were deported from Łódź, Dora performs a symbolic gesture of reconciliation and forgiveness. The Jewish ghosts, it seems, are not there to accuse the living.

The motif of Jewish absolution appears, too, in Tadeusz Słobodzianek's drama *Our Class*. The play, which takes as its theme historical events surrounding the Jedwabne pogrom of 1941, features characters modelled on real inhabitants of the town. Inspired by Tadeusz Kantor's famous *Dead Class* (1975), Słobodzianek also chooses a schoolroom as the setting of his drama. In bringing former classmates together, Jews and non-Jews, the dead and the living, Słobodzianek creates a space that is both very specific (by its clear reference to Jedwabne) and aspiring to a broader national relevance (as a metonym for Poland as a whole). The students entrapped in the timeless classroom narrate their lives and deaths, seeking to come to terms with their traumas.

The plot of the drama presents, in fact, an unending cycle of suffering. Rysiek, a Catholic, is in love with his Jewish classmate Dora, but Dora marries Menachem. When the Soviets retreat from the village in 1941, Rysiek, with a group of colleagues, rapes Dora and, soon afterwards, while taking part in the pogrom, ignores her cries for help. While Rysiek indifferently witnesses Dora's death in the barn, his classmate Władek manages to hide Rachela, another Jewish woman, and save her from the massacre. Władek later marries Rachela, who gets baptized and takes the Christian name of Marianna. The girl thus remains in town, but her life is at risk once again when Rysiek decides to deliver her to the Germans, to get rid of the last Jewish witness of the pogrom. Władek finds out about the scheme as Rysiek is leading Rachela to the police station, and he kills Rysiek to free his wife. As Rysiek dies, the ghost of Dora comes to greet him »on the other side«.

Rysiek: Where are we going Dora?
Dora: Nowhere Rysiek. We're already here. (2009 [2008]: 69)

And thus ghosts appear to accompany the dying throughout the play. They witness their moral downfalls and assist them in the hour of death; their passive, seemingly forgiving, presence suggests that both victims and perpetrators are mortal and in need of compassion. When Władek is dying of old age, it is the ghost of Rysiek that appears by his deathbed.

Once... I'm not sure if I was dreaming or if it really happened... Rysiek was there. I tried to say I was sorry but the words stuck in my throat. I said Rysiek. He didn't speak. Just walked up to me and threw his arms around me. I started sobbing. (Ibid: 103)

In one of the interviews, Słobodzianek said that in order to achieve reconciliation, »Germans should make films about Auschwitz, Russians about Katyń and Poles about Jedwabne« (Zielińska/Słobodzianek 2008). But despite the importance that he seemingly attaches to confessing national sins, Słobodzianek creates a *relativizing* narrative, where all are guilty, all have suffered, and all are victims of the ruthless wheel of history. Although the pogrom staged by Poles is at the centre of the narrative, Słobodzianek's drama features a Jewish perpetrator, too. Menachem, who loses his wife and child in the pogrom, joins the Communist political police after the war and shows particular cruelty during interrogations, torturing, among others, former Polish resistance fighters. In this way, both Poles and Jews are pictured as complicit in violence and needing forgiveness. The presence of ghosts haunting the living also suggests a transcendent idea of retributive justice or a punishing God. All evildoers receive their due punishment: thirty years after Zygmunt murdered the Jewish Communist Jakub Kac, his son drowns. But that very same year Menachem's son also dies in a terrorist attack in Israel. In Słobodzianek's drama, guilt and suffering are distributed equally and ghosts do not accuse but herald absolution.

Jewish ghosts therefore return in Polish literature both to haunt spaces where anti-Jewish violence took place (and where it was forgotten) and to open a possibility of »healing« past injustices. By means of punishing or pardoning the guilty, the Jewish ghosts take the position of agents of authority. Belonging both to the category of Holocaust victims and to the realm of fantasy, they play the role of spokespersons for the (murdered) Polish Jews, on the one hand, and divine characters devoid of human emotions, on the other. Consequently, their acts of forgiveness, like those performed by Słobodzianek's or Bart's protagonists, both possess a god-like dimension, and are not really comprehensible from a human point of view.

TRAUMATIC SURREALISM: THE *UNHEIMLICH* AND THE ABSURD

Despite the fact that the topos of returning ghosts has its tradition in Polish literature, with Adam Mickiewicz's poetic drama *Dziady* [Forefathers' Eve, 1982] as the most emblematic vision of conjuring the dead, the language that Chutnik, Ostachowicz, Bart and Słobodzianek employ has little to do with the pathos of the Romantic poets. Instead, all four authors rely on dissonance, combining a somber theme with black humor, pop-cultural references, and the absurd. By doing so, they employ the element of the *Unheimlich*, which belongs to the usual tropes of a ghost story, in a subversive way, to articulate both trauma and the ways of suppressing it; both national anxiety and its abreaction via the absurd. With its experimental approach to genre and language as well as the tendency to create dissonance between a somber theme and ostensibly unbecoming means of expression, this particular kind of prose might indicate that contemporary Polish literature has found a new language of loss, which has not only aesthetic, but also moral implications.

Sigmund Freud, who analyzed the effect of the *Unheimlich*, the uncanny, both in literary fiction and in daily experience, pointed to its paradoxical nature of combining the frightening and the familiar (2003 [1919]). The uncanny occurs, according to Freud, when the well-known but repressed returns and challenges our understanding of reality.[15] The return of the well-known

---

15 Freud distinguished between the effect of the Unheimlich that can be traced back to »primitive« beliefs, for example, about the return of the dead, and to childhood

is also the recurrent motif of the new Polish narratives about Jewish ghosts. In Słobodzianek's *Our Class*, it is the ghosts of former colleagues that secure the passage of the protagonists into afterlife; in Chutnik's *Pocket Atlas of Women* it is a family member that comes to haunt the protagonist; and in *Muranooo* and Ostachowicz's *Night of the Living Jews* it is not just any Jews, but the former inhabitants who return to their houses. Thus emotional proximity – love, compassion, but also hatred – a shared past, or a shared space, inscribes the Jewish ghosts into the realm of the familiar – as *our* Jews. Their homecoming, however, is not tranquil; it also stands for the return of the repressed.

Although the source of anxiety that lies at the basis of these ghost stories is real – the returning question about the degree of Polish complicity in anti-Jewish violence during the Second World War – fiction can also render what is objectively *Unheimlich* less fearful. The Polish ghost narratives achieve this by creating a sense of dissonance. Sylwia Chutnik, for example, has her characters speak of trauma in a casual language, discordant with the substance of their narratives. In a scene that forms the dramatic climax of the story, Maria Wachelberg-Wachelberska and the ghost of her mother converse in a manner that seems both stoical and nonchalant.

›Mom, what would you like to snack on?‹ ›Some potato peels, perhaps. Remember, in the ghetto, how we would cook rotten potatoes from the bin? How they would foam and rattle in the pot. They were disgusting, but we thought they tasted like an exquisite hors d'oeuvre.‹ (Chutnik 2008: 135)

Having her protagonists speak about their ordeals in the ghetto in seemingly inapposite language, Chutnik discards the prescription that narratives of suffering require an elevated register. In Chutnik's prose Jewish suffering is written into Polish space, and trauma anchored in everyday language itself.

Słobodzianek also relies on dissonance, if achieved by different means. In *Our Class*, he contrasts the infantile and the gruesome by punctuating scenes that portray ultimate human cruelty with children's songs and rhymes.

---

complexes, such as the fear of castration. In both cases, our fear is generated by something familiar which we ousted from our memory and banned into oblivion: »The uncanny [the ›unhomely‹] is what was once familiar [›homely‹, ›homey‹]. The negative prefix un- is the indicator of repression.« (2003 [1919]: 151).

The disharmony between the naivety and innocence of these playful interludes and the brutality of the recounted events contributes to the disconcerting effect that Słobodzianek's play produces.

If Chutnik and Słobodzianek create dissonance by applying registers seemingly incompatible with the message of their texts, Ostachowicz's *Night of the Living Jews* maximizes this effect by adopting the genre of horror, heavily referencing pop-culture and saturating his prose with black humor, parody, and absurdist touches. The climax scene of the novel exemplifies his style. It pictures the spectacular final siege, with the Jewish undead, who took shelter inside a shopping mall, facing a massive attack of neo-Nazis and other emissaries of evil. In the heat of the battle, the main protagonist encounters a Jewish zombie who manages to escape the street fighting and reports on what he has seen:

›It's a miracle I managed to get out of there‹ – he moaned. ›They're catching us in the streets, searching the cellars‹ [...] agitated he kept on repeating some nonsensical hearsay about select mechanized units of female German pensioners with permed grey hair. Thanks to the high-tech coaches at their disposal, they are apparently very mobile and can be quickly transported to the toughest sectors. Equipped with expensive, ergonomic digging shovels, they grind their snow-white dental implants and mutter their favorite passage from the Grimm brothers: ›Why do you have such big eyes? Why do you have such big ears? Why do you have such a big nose? And why do I have such big teeth? The better to eat you, to eat you, to eat you!‹ (Ostachowicz 2012: 232-233)

Ostachowicz's apocalyptic scenes of violence are particularly dissonant in this context, as his absurdist accounts of the Warsaw street skirmishes echo the imagery of the liquidation of the ghetto. While the Jewish undead are being chased out of the cellars and loaded on trucks to be deported, Ostachowicz frames this final battle of good and evil drawing on both the aesthetics of computer games and the Polish popular imagination of the war. The portrayal of Germans as at once beastly and ridiculous fits this macabre tableau of excess, and allows Ostachowicz to derisively caricature Polish phobias.

Using colloquial language, hyperbole, and action-film aesthetics, Ostachowicz nevertheless poses serious questions. His mocking humor is aimed not only at neo-Nazis, antisemites, and Polish »patriooots‹ (the long »ooo« suggesting their political querulousness), but also at philosemites.

Mocking his esoteric girlfriend, Chuda (Skinny), the protagonist comments with biting sarcasm that the return of Jewish ghosts is in fact a fulfilment of the philosemitic fantasy: »She would finally get her Poland with Jews and maybe she would stop talking about them non-stop and looking for her non-existent Jewish roots« (ibid: 243). Invoking the stereotypes of the Other (the Jew, the German), on the one hand, and addressing the contemporary nostalgia for Poland's past multi-ethnicity, on the other, Ostachowicz captures the ambiguous position of the Other in contemporary Poland.

The new language of haunting evident in the latest Polish prose might point to a particularly *Polish* need for narratives beyond either the realist tradition of representing the Holocaust or the anti-realist approach, which treats the Holocaust as a sublime object, defying representation itself. Stories of Jewish ghosts invading contemporary public spaces and involving the living in their acts of retributive justice implicate readers in the dispossession of and the historic wrongdoing towards Jews, unsettle them via the dissonant and inapposite form of narrating Jewish suffering, but also suggest that the relationship between the victims and perpetrators/witnesses can be repaired. Using colloquial language and references to contemporary pop culture, this new Polish prose addresses the Holocaust as an event that has had a transgenerational effect on Poles, who inhabit the spaces of Jewish life and death. Raising the question of postmemory in the country where, as Barbara Engelking put it, people to this day are witnesses of Jewish death, just because of the »place of their birth« (2011: 8), this kind of literature indicates the need not only for sustained confrontation with the legacy of bystanding and perpetratorship, but also sustained healing.

Adopting literary motifs usually considered escapist (ghost stories, horror) and offering a surrealist vision of history which blends the conditions of reality and dream, these narratives thus offer a medium to help the young generation of Poles come to terms with the painful knowledge about Polish involvement in anti-Jewish violence and factor it into the image of the collective self and the national topography. This particular capacity makes this fiction akin to Michael Rothberg's »traumatic realism«, in that it urges the readers to »acknowledge their relationship to posttraumatic culture«, but its ultimate goals are different (2000: 103). In his book of the same title, Rothberg defines »traumatic realism« as a way of representing the Holocaust that is both epistemological, in that it seeks »to construct access to a previously unknowable object« and pedagogical, in that it »instruct[s] an audience in how to approach that object« (ibid.). The new Polish prose tackling the subject of the Holocaust, which might perhaps be better subsumed under the category of »traumatic *surrealism*«, follows neither of these objectives. It does not contribute to producing knowledge, but rather aims at processing it. It is therapeutic rather than epistemological. Referencing real historical events that have been subject to nationwide debates, such as the pogrom in Jedwabne, this Polish traumatic surrealism is a mode of *response* to the revelation of facts and, offering fantasies of restorative justice and redemption, it opens a space of *abreaction* to difficult knowledge. Employing unconventional and dissonant means of expression, this Polish prose speaks of the impossibility to escape the shadow of the past, but it is by no means prescriptive. Rather than providing instruction on how to deal with the past, it offers a space of experimentation where the pop-cultural, the shocking and the iconoclastic all provide a new vocabulary to speak about loss, guilt and pain.

But, while traumatic surrealism might supply a new language to speak about the difficult Polish-Jewish past, it should also be dosed with caution. Redemptive narratives like that of Ostachowicz, in which the Polish everyman joins the »Jewish cause« and Jews and non-Jews triumph together over an external evil, or the motif of Jewish ghosts providing absolution, risk providing relief before the process of mourning has been completed.

In his writing on the representation of trauma Eric Santner distinguishes between two responses to loss: the Freudian *Trauerarbeit* or »work of mourning«, and »narrative fetishism«. *Trauerarbeit*, he believes, consists in remembering and repeating the »traumatic shock« in symbolically mediated doses, to come to terms with loss. »Narrative fetishism«, by contrast, marks an inability or refusal to mourn, which manifests itself in a »strategy of undoing, in fantasy«, and in »simulating a condition of intactness« (2003: 214). While the new Polish traumatic surrealism might shock and unsettle readers, thus pointing to the ways historical trauma contaminates Polish spaces and minds, its propensity towards *exorcism* risks devolving into »narrative fetishism«.

The very presence of themes like the Warsaw ghetto uprising or the Jedwabne pogrom in cutting-edge contemporary Polish prose may suggest a demand for new, uncompromising ways of addressing the painful Polish-Jewish past, and indicate a frustration with conventional memory-work. Yet the longing for Santner's »intactness«, suggested by the redemptive nature of these narratives of Jewish return, points to the dangers inherent in the trope.

In summoning Jewish ghosts, we must ask ourselves what lessons might be found in the haunting itself, before rushing to silence those things that go bump in the night.

LITERATURE

Arendt, Hannah (2006 [1963]): Eichmann in Jerusalem: A Report on the Banality of Evil, London: Penguin Books.
Bart, Andrzej (2008): Fabryka muchołapek, Warszawa: WAB.
Bartana, Yael (2007): Nightmares (http://www.artmuseum.pl/filmoteka /?l=0&id=200).
Bell, Michael Mayerfeld (1997): »The ghosts of place.« In: Theory and Society 26/6, pp. 813-836.
Boym, Svetlana (2001), The Future of Nostalgia, New York: Basic Books.
Carroll, Noël (2007): »Narrative Closure.« In: Philosophical Studies 135/1, pp. 1-15.
Chomątowska, Beata (2012): Stacja Muranów, Wołowiec: Czarne.
Chutnik, Sylwia (2008): Kieszonkowy atlas kobiet, Kraków: Ha!art.
Chutnik, Sylwia (2012): »Muranooo.« Unpublished manuscript.
Desperak, Iza (2008): »Nienawiść na łódzkich murach: antysemityzm i homophobia.« In: Folia Sociologica 33, pp. 204-222.
Dziuban, Zuzanna (2014): »Memory as Haunting.« In: Hagar: Studies in Culture, Polity, and Identities 12/Winter, pp. 111-135.
Elżbieta, Janicka (2011): Festung Warschau, Warszawa: Wydawnictwo Krytyki Politycznej.
Engelking, Barbara (2003): Szanowny Panie Gistapo: Donosy do władz niemieckich w Warszawie i okolicach w latach 1940-1941, Warszawa: Stowarzyszenie Centrum Badań nad Zagładą Żydów.
Engelking, Barbara (2011): Jest taki piękny słoneczny dzień: Losy Żydów szukających ratunku na wsi polskiej 1942-1945, Warszawa: Stowarzyszenie Centrum Badań nad Zagładą Żydów.
Freud, Sigmund (2003 [1919]): »The Uncanny.« In: Sigmund Freud, The Uncanny, London and New York: Penguin Books, pp. 121-161.
Grabowski, Jan (2013 [2011]): Hunt for the Jews: Betrayal and Murder in German-Occupied Poland, Bloomington: Indiana University Press.

Gross, Jan Tomasz (2001 [2000]): Neighbours: The Destruction of the Jewish Community in Jedwabne, Poland, 1941, Princeton: Princeton University Press.
Gross, Jan Tomasz (2006): Fear: Antisemitism in Poland after Auschwitz, Princeton: Princeton University Press.
Gross, Jan Tomasz/Gross-Grudzińska, Irena (2012 [2011]): Golden Harvest: Events at the Periphery of the Holocaust, New York: Oxford University Press.
Grözinger, Elvira (2003): Die schöne Jüdin: Klischees, Mythen und Vorurteile über Juden in der Literatur, Berlin: Philo.
Hirsch, Marianne (2008): »The Generation of Postmemory.« In: Poetics Today 29/1, pp. 103-128.
Huelle, Paweł (1991 [1987]): Who Was David Weiser? London: Bloomsbury.
Janion, Maria (2000): Do Europy tak, ale razem z naszymi umarymi, Warszawa: Sic!
Janion, Maria (2009): Bohater, spisek, śmierć, Warszawa: WAB.
Keff, Bożena (2001): Postać z cieniem. Portrety Żydówek w polskiej literaturze, Warszawa: Sic!
Krall, Hanna (2005 [1995]): »The Dybbuk.« In: Hanna Krall, The Woman from Hamburg and Other Stories, New York: Other Press, pp. 137-154.
Lehrer, Erica/Waligórska, Magdalena (2013): »Cur(at)ing History: New Genre Art Interventions and the Polish-Jewish Past.« In: East European Politics and Societies 27/3, pp. 507-540.
Levi, Primo (1989 [1986]): The Drowned and the Saved, New York: Vintage.
Meng, Michael (2011): Shattered Spaces: Encountering Jewish Ruins in Postwar Germany and Poland, Cambridge: Harvard University Press.
Minow, Martha (1998): Between Vengeance and Forgiveness: Facing History after Genocide and Mass Violence, Boston: Beacon Press.
Ostachowicz, Igor (2012): Noc żywych Żydów, Warszawa: WAB.
Paziński, Piotr (2013): Ptasie ulice, Warszawa: Wydawnictwo Nisza.
Rothberg, Michael (2000): Traumatic Realism: The Demands of Holocaust Representation, Minneapolis: University of Minnesota Press.
Santner, Erik L. (2003): »History Beyond the Pleasure Principle: Some Thoughts on the Representation of Trauma.« In: Neil Levi and Michael

Rothberg (eds.), The Holocaust: Theoretical Readings, Edinburgh: Edinburgh University Press, pp. 214-220.

Shallcross, Bożena (2011), The Holocaust Object in Polish and Polish–Jewish Culture, Bloomington: Indiana University Press.

Słobodzianek, Tadeusz (2009 [2008]): Our Class, London: Oberon Books.

Smale, Catherine (2009): »Ungelöste Gespenster? Ghosts in Ruth Klüger's Autobiographical Project.« In: The Modern Language Review 104/3, pp. 777-789.

The Jewish Renaissance Movement in Poland (2011): »A Manifesto.« In: Sebastian Cichocki and Galit Eilat (eds.), A Cookbook for Political Imagination, Berlin: Sternberg Press, p. 121.

Tokarska-Bakir, Joanna (2012): Okrzyki pogromowe, Wołowiec: Wydawnictwo Czarne.

Tokarska-Bakir, Joanna (2018): Pod klątwą: Społeczny portret pogromu kieleckiego, Warszawa: Czarna Owca.

Tryczyk, Mirosław (2015): Miasta Śmierci: Sąsiedzkie pogromy Żydów, Warszawa: Wydawnictwo RM.

Zielińska, Alicja/Słobodzianek, Tadeusz (2013): »Tadeusz Słobodzianek o ›Naszej klasie‹.« In: Kurier Poranny May 30 (http://www.poranny.pl/apps/pbcs.dll/article?AID=/20080530/ROZMOWY/592698555).

Of Ghosts' (In)ability to Haunt: ›Polish Dybbuks‹

ZUZANNA DZIUBAN

Of the many figures who might have served as a metaphorical frame for the (re)surgence of Polish memory about Jews, it is the dybbuk, the possessing spirit of Jewish mythology that has been most favored. No doubt, the dybbuk's Jewish provenance alone must have resonated powerfully with the Polish ›rediscovery‹ of Jewish prewar presence, which unfolded in the almost complete absence of a Jewish community in the country. Well underway since the early 1980s and gaining momentum after 1989, this process of ›rediscovery‹ translated into a wide range of initiatives that in turn reflected a growing public interest in all things Jewish. This included the publication of books on Jewish history and (religious) tradition, the organization of Jewish-themed festivals, and the restoration of synagogues and cemeteries. The mere attribute of ›Jewishness‹ transformed non-existent culture, customs, and people into objects of nostalgic longing. Dressed in the language of ghosts, this phenomenon has nevertheless required the figure of the dybbuk to be appropriately (re)framed, revised and edited in order to capture its specificity – a fate that has befallen many ›Jewish things‹ in post-Holocaust Poland.

In *Virtually Jewish*, Ruth Ellen Gruber allows the figure of the dybbuk to haunt accounts of Poles narrating their preoccupation with Jewish culture, literature and religion. Locating the roots of the phenomenon in the feeling of »cultural loss«, she reports on experiences of individuals for whom an often accidental encounter with the Jewish past, mediated through film or literature (in many cases that of Isaac Bashevis Singer), translated into a fascination, if not an outright obsession with Jewishness – hence, the possession by the dybbuk (2002: 41-42).[1] Piotr Cywiński is even more explicit, positing the figure of the dybbuk as a metaphorical framing for a new cultural sensitivity:

> Among many explanations of the new interest in Jews and Judaism in Poland, the most beautiful, and in many ways very convincing, is the poetic thesis that what has been left from the annihilated world of Polish Jews is a dybbuk – a mythological spiritual presence, which permeates present-day Polish reality. And it is there. And it propels people to see and to fill in the absence […]. (2005: 24)

The absence described by Cywiński permeates Poland in her entirety: it is inscribed in urban and rural landscapes, architecture, literature, culture. In his view, the dybbuk, through its ghostly presence, destabilizes this absence and renders it ›visible‹, ›present‹, felt. Cywiński, Gruber and others (cf. for instance Kącki 2015) employ the metaphor to capture the driving force behind the so-called ›Jewish turn‹ in Poland and the practices undertaken by individuals seeking to ›rediscover‹ Poland's Jewish past. But the ostensible »beauty« and cogency of the dybbuk as metaphor is primarily derived from the realm of cultural production and art. Since the late 1980s, dybbuk(s) have proliferated, both literally and figuratively, in dramas, performance art and film. Constructed and reconstructed by Polish authors engaging with ›Jewish themes‹ and asking (or making assertions) about the positionality of Poles towards the absent Jews, the dybbuk, in its Polish artistic renditions, is highly sensitive to transformations in cultural, political and affective constellations. But one thing is consistent across the various framings and reframings of the figure (as much by the authors themselves as by the critics of their work): the dybbuk is firmly established as a figure of memory, in particular of Polish memory about Jews – its ghostliness bridging the impassable hiatus between

---

1 In 1978, Isaac Bashevis Singer, the leading figure of the Yiddish literary movement, received the Nobel Prize for Literature. For many in Poland, it was the moment when they had their very first encounter with his writings and realized that, in fact, Jewish communities existed in the country (cf. for instance Tuszyńska 1998: 3). It is perhaps also for this reason that their image of Jews remains so persistently tinted by the folkloristic, exotic, imaginary (and phantasmatic).

absent/present, present/past, living/dead. In this chapter, I work against this dominant interpretation.

What I propose, instead, is a reading of the figure of the dybbuk through the prism of a series of ›unacknowledged continuities‹. These continuities are inscribed in the Polish framings of the dybbuk and also in the obdurate symbolic/political/material realities through which it travels. In *Ghostly Matters: Haunting and the Sociological Imagination*, Avery Gordon writes that following ghosts, both figurative and non-figurative, »produces its own insights and blindnesses« (2008 [1997]: 22). In her book, where she reclaims ghosts and haunting as consequential objects of sociological interest and investigation, Gordon focuses on the intimate relationship and the complex traffic between (and among) the visible and invisible, the present and absent. These interactions are, she suggests, constitutive of repressive configurations of power, if not to every social order. And yet, most scholars drawing from Gordon in their intellectual and political engagements with ghosts have focused exclusively on the affective insights, shadowy knowledge and visibilities opened by ghost stories and ghostly figures, which are understood within the struggle against silencing, absenting, invisibilization and exclusion. This orientation towards past injustices and their subsequent hegemonic erasures casts haunting as a point of access to the lingering traces of historically situated violence; it suggests a transformative knowledge of »blind spots«, of what is lost or obliterated and nonetheless exerts an unobtrusive affective impact.[2]

In this chapter, I am interested in those regained visibilities and uneasy absences/presences, but even more so in the »blindnesses« that ghost stories can create: that which is rendered unacknowledged, silenced, erased, or invisible but which *lives on*. In what follows, I will attempt to illuminate what the Polish dybbuks unveil and simultaneously occlude in their engagements with ›things Jewish‹. I argue that the responsibility for the »blindness« of Polish ghost stories rests, first and foremost, with those who invoke such stories and conjure ghosts for various purposes. But even in cases such as these, I suggest, ghosts have the ability to resist dominant interpretations and to *act back*: the meanings of the dybbuk, which not only predate, but also challenge and disrupt its Polish framing, subversively ›haunt‹ the figure – based, as it is, on the appropriation and alienation of the concept from its

---

2   For a more detailed discussion, see the introduction to this volume.

›owners‹.[3] The question is, if the dybbuk is not a figure of memory, then what is it?

In Polish renditions of the dybbuk, the trajectories, transformations and directionalities of which I follow in this chapter, the figure conveys a relationality: an encounter with and positioning of contemporary Poles toward Jews, constructed in their absence. It is an absence resulting from the extermination during the Holocaust, in which Poles, as we know today, were complicit; but also from the various incarnations of postwar anti-Jewish violence, which cost Jews their lives or drove the last remaining Jews from the country.[4] Yet, it would be inaccurate to claim that the absence of people has a

---

3   I consider this appropriation an operation similar to that of colonial translation, as conceptualized by Eric Cheyfitz in *Poetics of Imperialism* (1997 [1991]). Focusing on material and rhetorical practices through which Europeans constructed the Native American Others in the course of colonization, Cheyfitz shows how Native American terms, narratives, objects were ›translated‹ by Europeans, that is, at once acknowledged, »cut off from a proper (cultural) meaning« (1997 [1991]: 42), and invoked politically to objectify a particular image and positionality of the indigenous populations, legitimizing imperial practices of othering and exclusion, and dispossession of the land. Cheyfitz writes that »translation means precisely not to understand others who are the original (inhabitants) or to understand those others all too easily – as if there were no questions of translation – solely in terms of one's own language, where those others become a usable fiction; the fiction of the Other« (Cheyfitz 1997 [1991]: 105).

4   The scale of anti-Jewish violence perpetrated by Poles during the Holocaust is meticulously documented in Engelking (2011); Grabowski (2013 [2011]), Engelking/Grabowski (2018), to list just a few publications. The violence did not stop with the end of the war. According to estimations by Andrzej Żbikowski, in the immediate postwar years at least 650 to 750 Jews were killed by their Polish fellow citizens (2012: 93); Gross (2006) gauges the number at several thousand. Although there were many reasons driving Jews out of the country in the aftermath of the Holocaust – emotional, economic, political (cf. for instance Aleksiun 2002; Hurwic-Nowakowska 1996) – the »fear of being a Jew« (Grynberg 2001: vii) and the consequences that could follow from being recognized as/constructed as/made into one, acted as a major incentive for emigration. After the notorious Kielce pogrom of July 1946 alone, which cost the lives of over 40 individuals, the number of people officially registered in various Jewish organizations shrank

material counterpart that could materialize and be rendered visible via the dybbuk (as memory). Recent research has shown that the Holocaust was, from the outset, a source of considerable material benefit for the local non-Jewish communities in Poland. Civilians confiscated, dispossessed, looted, and redistributed wealth – taking possession of the property and personal valuables left behind by deported Jews, moving into forcefully vacated houses, taking part in the widespread plunder of assets of those still alive, blackmailing, and committing economically motivated murder. These ›property transfers‹ reenacted and sustained the prewar boundaries of othering and belonging, investing the economic violence with an essentially political dimension: even during the war the loot was constructed as »post-Jewish«, and legitimized (and justified) in these terms.[5] This process continued long into the postwar period, with substantial state involvement. ›Abandoned‹ houses, buildings and land were seized and nationalized, and objects were confiscated on behalf of the State Treasury. Indeed, as Andrzej Leder (2014) recently argued, the events of the war and its immediate aftermath brought about a radical social revolution in Poland, facilitating a final departure from the prewar social order shaped by the legacy of a serf labor economy. The appropriation by Poles not only of properties but also of occupational and social positions traditionally held by Jews opened up a space for the development of the Polish middle class, until then relatively weak and represented mostly by the Jewish minority. The violence perpetrated on a community which for centuries had been treated as culturally distinct and economically threatening (cf. Michlic 2006; Cała 2012) was constitutive of this new

---

from 240,489 to 89,060 (Cichopek-Gajraj 2014: 118). The antisemitic campaigns of the 1950s and the 1960s forced remaining Jews from the country. Those who stayed often decided to submerge their Jewish identities once and for all. Consequently, as justly observed by Elżbieta Janicka and Tomasz Żukowski in their contribution to this volume, »it was not the Holocaust but its extension – carried out by Poles – that ended the Jewish presence in Poland«.

5   For assessments of the scale and dynamics of economic violence accompanying the Holocaust in Poland, see for instance Wyka (1957); Grabowski/Libionka (2014a), (2014b); Engelking/Grabowski (2018); for a detailed and excellent discussion on the »post-Jewish« property (and space) in Poland, see Matyjaszek (2013; 2018).

social/political/economic order – an order founded on the genocidal destruction and dispossession of the Jewish other.

The material manifestations of this fact were either obliterated or naturalized after the war – by means of legal regulations, legitimizing the ›property transfers‹, or through the obliteration of markers of their provenance and former ownership. Jewish cemeteries were dismantled, synagogues reused, doorframes stripped of mezuzahs, movable and immovable assets swiftly integrated into national and local economies (cf. Meng 2011: 111-154; Matyjaszek 2018; Charnysh/Finkel 2017). The production of Jewish ›absence‹, as discussed by Cywiński, was integral to the process of (re)constructing the state, local communities and individual welfare. The process was as much material as it was political and symbolic. The absenting/invisibilising of Jewish presence occurred on all three levels and worked together to create the social order as we know it. This fact remains largely unacknowledged, even today. However, it constitutes a critical backdrop for my readings of the Polish dybbuks and the »insights and blindnesses« they produce, as well as providing an empirical grounding for the concept of ›unacknowledged continuities‹. My argument is that rather than being a figure of memory, the dybbuk speaks of the ability to unveil and/or disavow, to perpetuate and/or transform the continuities in the material, economic, social, and symbolic order in Poland. Thinking through its various renditions, both those from the 1980s and more contemporary versions, such as the 2015 movie *Demon* – renditions which in turn reflect shifts in affective, symbolic and political economies in Poland – I ask about the (potential) transformative power of the dybbuk; in other words, about its ability or inability to haunt.

SETTING THE SCENE

The emergence of the figure of the dybbuk in the Polish post-Holocaust imagination could be traced back to Andrzej Wajda's staging of *Dybuk: Na pograniczu dwóch światów* [Dybbuk, or Between Two Worlds] at Cracow's National ›Old Theater‹ in March 1988. In its revival of a classic Yiddish drama written by Szymon An-sky more than eight decades previously, Wajda's *Dybbuk* sketched the contours of the figure (and of the metaphor), and opened the door to its continuous resonance in Poland. Wajda's adaptation of the play was not the first to be performed in the country after the

Second World War. In 1957, in 1970, and again in 1973, An-sky's piece was staged at the Ester Rachel Kaminska State Jewish Theater in Warsaw under the direction of Abram Morewski, Chewel Buzgan, and Szymon Szurmiej, respectively. Performed in Yiddish and tailored for Yiddish-speaking Jewish publics, these productions were never likely to reach wider, non-Jewish Polish audiences.[6] But the 1988 version, headed by acclaimed Polish director Wajda and translated into Polish by poet and playwright Ernest Bryll, did exactly that: without introducing any major changes in the original plot, it brought *The Dybbuk* directly into the Polish context.[7]

Set in the Eastern European shtetls of Brinnitz and Miropolye in the early nineteenth century, An-sky's *Dybbuk* (2000 [1914/1919]) artistically actualized, and revised, a trope well established in Jewish cultural tradition, especially in Hasidic folklore (cf. Neugroschel 2000; Goldisch 2003; Chajes 2003). The word dybbuk, which stems from the Hebrew for ›adhere‹ or ›the one that claves‹, indicates a restless, wandering soul of a deceased person. Sinner in life, denied access to the world of the dead and, therefore, suspended »between two worlds«, the dybbuk seeks shelter in a living person.[8]

---

6   In his staging of *The Dybbuk*, which premiered on February 17, 1957, Morewski emphasized the folkloristic dimension of the play, its partially realistic, partially magical portrayal of Jewish traditions and customs (Morewski 1957). For Buzgan and for Szurmiej, who drew inspiration from Buzgan's interpretation of An-sky's play, of importance was also the theme of class struggle, but more than this, the intention to aestheticize the play in order to »erect an angry monument to vanished traditions, myths, and miracles; a monument to all that that no longer exists« (Buzgan 1970). In 1979, Szurmiej's *Dybbuk* was shown on the Polish Television Theatre (again in Yiddish).

7   The same year, Wajda's *Dybbuk* was staged in Tel Aviv at the National Habima Theatre. It is not without importance that, as Maciej Karpiński stressed in his interpretation of both stagings, the Polish and the Israeli, they differed considerably, positing »one could even speak of two disparate interpretations« (1991: 179). This alone suggests that when working on the Teatr Stary version of *The Dybbuk*, Wajda tailored it specifically for the Polish audience.

8   Already in its first textual descriptions, dating back to the sixteenth century, the dybbuk was cast as malevolent or penitential (Unterman 1991: 62). This malevolence rendered the dybbuk needful of an exorcism, but not for its malevolence alone. Initially closely linked with particular metaphysical beliefs (mysticism and

In the plot of An-sky's drama, this fate befalls a poverty-stricken yeshiva student, Khonen. Khonen, the son of Nissan, is in love with Leah, daughter of a rich merchant, Sender. Against her will, Leah's father arranges her betrothal with another, much wealthier man. In order to gain wealth and be able to compete for Leah's hand, Khonen resorts to sorcery and forbidden Kabbalistic practices – a decision that costs him his life. On the day of the wedding Khonen returns in the form of dybbuk, summoned by Leah, and enters the body of his beloved. Upon discovering that Leah is possessed, her father asks a Miropoler Tsadik to exorcise Khonen's ghost. It is in the presence of

kabbalistic theology), the dybbuk soon began to travel, acquiring new cultural meanings and opening up new interpretive dimensions. In many folkloristic, literary and artistic incarnations, the figure hovers »between two worlds«, capturing the interplay between the living and the dead but also coding particularly burning social issues. The dybbuk epitomized and channeled historically specific conflicts around the use of and struggle against social control, tensions between the ›new‹ and the ›old‹ in times of dramatic social transition, and those pertaining to gender and sexuality (Elior 2008; Legutko 2012). The presence of a dybbuk and its unsettling clinging signaled the refusal (of an individual) to conform to prevailing (traditional) cultural norms, or resistance against violence inherent to imposed social/cultural/gender roles. Caught within close circuit dynamics of possession and exorcism, dybbuk tales told stories of (temporarily) threatened but almost invariably restored social order (a point I will return to later on). After the Holocaust, the dybbuk also attracted (retroactive) trauma theory interpretations. Agnieszka Legutko, for instance, suggests reading in these terms not only An-sky's *Dybbuk* (including its post-Holocaust incarnations, both Jewish and Polish), but also earlier instances of dybbuk possession. She writes: »The reasons behind the [first] possession endemic [in the fifteenth-century Safed], I propose, may be attributed to the trauma of expulsion from Spain in 1492 and the Spanish Inquisition persecutions«; in the Eastern European context they »might have been triggered by the profound trauma of the Chmielnicki massacres (…).« (2012: 39-40) For An-sky, as for many of his contemporaries, whose prose was, too, haunted by the dybbuk (Isaac Bashevis Singer, Sholem Aleichem, and Isaac Leib Peretz among others), this would be the trauma of prevailing antisemitic violence, of pogroms, and of the First World War (ibid: 14). As mentioned above, I intend to challenge this interpretive shift towards memory and/or trauma, which also characterizes Polish framings of the figure.

the Tsadik, rabbi Azriel, that the full reasons behind the possession are disclosed. It was begotten by Khonen's thwarted love for Leah but also by a vow between Sender and Khonen's father Nissan before Leah and Khonen were born that they would betroth their children should they be a girl and a boy. After Nissan's premature death, Sender forgets the oath and, driven by greed, eventually breaks it. Summoned to a rabbinical court held at the Miropolye synagogue, Nissan's spirit demands justice (in vain) for Sender's betrayal and for the death of his son; Khonen, in turn, obstinately declines to leave the body of his beloved. Finally, after pronouncing the vow between Sender and Nissan invalid (since the children were not yet born when it was made), rabbi Azriel chases away the dybbuk. In the final scenes, Leah dies in the synagogue before rejoining her unwanted fiancé and her spirit merges with that of her deceased lover.

Organized, in Seth Wolitz's words, around classic »themes of love, generational conflict, personal autonomy, and the emancipation of the individual from communal and religious pressures« (2006: 167), An-sky's drama was preoccupied with the spiritual beliefs that shaped traditional Jewish culture, in particular the insistence on the continuous interplay between the living and the dead, the earthly and the otherworldly. The eponymous phrase »between two worlds« carried multiple meanings: between life and death; between different religious movements and doctrines; between clashing generations; between social classes, the rich and the poor; between the ›old‹ and the ›new‹; between prevailing repressive cultural/gender norms – including the violence of arranged marriage – and the desires of an individual; but also between tradition and modernism constructed as a specific historical condition of the Eastern European Jews at the end of the nineteenth and the first decades of the twentieth century. This in-betweenness had, in fact, an indelible impact upon the inception and immediate reception of *The Dybbuk* (cf. for instance Steinlauf 2006: 240-241; Zipperstein 2006; Rosenberg 2011).

An-sky (Shylome Zanvl Rappaport) based his play on materials collated during ethnographic expeditions in the Russian Pale of Settlement between 1911 and 1914 in which he had been both participant and leader. Traveling through the Jewish shtetls of Volhynia and Podolia, the Jewish Russian writer, intellectual, and ethnographer sought and documented traditional Jewish cultural practices, beliefs, folktales, legends, and art. Deeply embedded in the East European Jewish tradition, especially that of Hasidic mysticism, An-Sky's play paid tribute to the culture of the shtetl and its spiritual underpinnings, but it did so from a secular perspective and through recourse to a modernist aesthetic (cf. Wolitz 2006). This mirrored central traits of An-sky's own intellectual biography: born in 1863 into a Hasidic family, Rappaport received a traditional upbringing, which he later abandoned for Haskalah (the Jewish Enlightenment) and political involvement with socialism. Nevertheless, at the beginning of the twentieth century, like many of his contemporaries, An-sky reclaimed his Jewish roots. Written during the First World War in Russian (and later translated into Hebrew and Yiddish), *The Dybbuk* was intended to contribute to the strengthening and renewal of *yidishkeit* (›a Jewish way of life‹), but it also gave voice to An-sky's self-perception »as a mediator between cultures« (Safran 2000: 767) – first and foremost, between the culture of Eastern European shtetls and that of assimilated Jews, then between the culture of Jewish and non-Jewish subjects of the Russian empire and its political successors.

The Dybbuk was also a response to a particular point in historical and cultural time. As rightly pointed out by Michael Steinlauf, economically-motivated emigration, widespread discrimination, ethnic/religious violence (pogroms), and, finally, the bloody war, resulted in »the centuries-old Jewish life rooted in the small towns of Eastern Europe [being] profoundly shaken« (2006: 241). It is for this reason that Gabriella Safran frames An-sky's work as an exercise in »salvage ethnography«, a concept she borrows from James Clifford. In documenting and artistically representing Hasidic mysticism and the folk heritage of the shtetls, *The Dybbuk* affirmed and ›salvaged‹ endangered forms of life and the traditions of an irrevocably decaying Jewish culture. At the same time, it artistically articulated the hopes and anxieties that this historical time brought upon Eastern European Jewish communities: the experience or constant fear of antisemitic persecution, of the violence shaping daily life even beyond the wartime period. This is perhaps best indicated by the fact that An-sky dedicated his drama to a friend and longtime collaborator, writer A. Vayter (Ayzik Meyer Devenishski). In 1919, Vayter, who was falsely accused of being a Bolshevik, was executed in Vilna by Polish Legionaries in a wave of anti-Jewish violence that reigned in the first months of Polish independence. In the eyes of his contemporaries, Vayter's death became a symbol of shattered hopes in the face of antisemitism and its violent outcomes, which accompanied the establishment of the Polish state.[9]

The drama was first performed in Yiddish in December 1920, one month after An-sky's death, by Jewish theatrical company the Vilna Troupe at Warsaw's Elizeum Theater. It immediately enjoyed enormous success. In 1922, the Moscow Hebrew-language Habima Theater adopted Hayim Nachman Bialik's 1918 Hebrew translation of *The Dybbuk* (staged in Poland in 1926). Throughout the 1920s and 1930s, both theater troupes traveled through Europe and beyond, reviving the play for Jewish and sometimes also non-Jewish audiences. Ballets and operas, too, were based upon it (cf. Peñalosa 2012; Legutko 2012). In 1937, An-sky's already classic drama became the subject of one of the most important films in the history of Yiddish cinema (Goldman 2011 [1983]: 84-87; cf. also Mazur 2007). Directed by Michał Waszyński and released in Yiddish (with Polish subtitles) by Polish film company Phoenix Films, *The Dybbuk* received great acclaim for its aesthetic qualities and sensibility to the cultural and spiritual reality of the shtetl. Perhaps more significantly, almost all adaptations and stagings of the play greatly appealed to contemporaneous Jewish audiences. Commenting on the reception of the 1920 performance in Poland – an important center of prewar diasporic Jewish life and a hub of Yiddish culture – Steinlauf observes that among Yiddish-speaking Jews (the representatives of working class, religious Jews, and intelligentsia alike), it became a source of genuine obsession (2006: 232-236). In its many incarnations, *The Dybbuk*'s melodrama and attentiveness to cultural tradition and identity strongly resonated with the existentially and politically precarious conditions of Jewish life in interwar Poland and Eastern Europe more generally.

The Polish reception of the play was not so unambiguously positive, however. While it is often claimed that Polish audiences reacted enthusiastically to the 1937 film adaptation, the reality is that some critics immediately (and reductively) accused *The Dybbuk* of imitating the greatest works of

---

9   Two other friends of An-sky, who shared an apartment with Vayter, were arrested that day, but spared. An-sky, who at that time lived in Vilna, personally participated in the burial of his colleague and, in the aftermath, conveyed his anguish in his 1919 article »Mute Despair« (Safran 2010: 284-285; cf. also Steinlauf 2006: 283).

Polish romanticism.[10] When in 1925 Mark Arenshteyn succeeded in bringing the drama to the Polish stage, his performances were frequented mostly by non-Yiddish speaking assimilated Jews and, to a much lesser extent, by Poles »attracted by the exoticism« of a culture they barely knew (Czapliński 2015). The process leading up to these performances was extremely difficult for Arenshteyn. As Steinlauf notes, »an attempt to stage the play on the Cracow Polish stage two years previously had closed after two performances because of bomb threats« (2006: 243). Similar threats surrounded the performances at Warsaw's small Scarlet Mask Theater, the only venue in the Polish capital willing to produce »so ›Jewish‹ a play« (ibid: 244). Other stagings of *The Dybbuk* also unfolded amid antisemitic reactions and pronouncements. This was the case, for instance, with the 1935 Warsaw premiere of Ludovico Rocca's opera, produced in 1934 for Milan's Theatro alla Scala. Among

---

10 This criticism was voiced by some leading Polish interwar cultural figures (for instance, Antoni Słonimski, Stefania Zahorska, Jan Lorentowicz or Henryk Łubieński), who suggested that An-sky's text borrows from Adam Mickiewicz's *Dziady* [Forefathers' Eve, 1860] – a classic Polish Romantic drama that artistically elaborates on the pre-Christian folk ritual of summoning the dead. In Mickiewicz's interpretation, this is entangled inextricably with Polish nationalism and the struggles for independence. Given that An-sky was immersed in Russian, and not in Polish culture, however, it is doubtful whether he even knew *Dziady* (cf. Czapliński 2015). Later on, thanks to Tadeusz Boy-Żeleński (1928) and Adolf Rudnicki (1987), this comparison became a means of articulating (or assuming) bonds/similarities between the cultures and the texts. Since 1988, it has accompanied every staging of *The Dybbuk* in Poland. Commenting on the reception of Krzysztof Warlikowski's 2003 adaptation of the play (which will be addressed later on), Bryce Lease critically observes: »I would suggest there is a symbolic price to pay for such a comparison that implicitly assimilates *Dybbuk* into the Polish Romantic canon, and thereby inadvertently endows it with a comparable set of values. [...] One would be surprised to encounter the inverse qualification of Polish literature in relation to Jewish culture«. (2016: 161) I would push this observation one step further: since such a practice belongs inherently to the repertoire of the dominant culture, constructing cultural practices of a minority as cheap copies or merely emanations of its own greatness, it is worth asking not only about the price but, first and foremost, about what is to be gained from such a comparison for those who so persistently insist on it.

some directly anti-Jewish comments, one remains particularly striking. A review titled »The Dybbuk Haunts in the Warsaw Opera«, which appeared in the right-wing daily newspaper *Dziennik Narodowy* on June 2, 1935, criticized the performance and its predominantly Jewish audience, concluding: »Oh how powerful, how dreadful an exorcism would be required to expel from us this four-million [sic!] ›Dybbuk‹!«

When Wajda started working on his version of *The Dybbuk* in the 1980s, this powerful, dreadful ›exorcism‹ was long completed. The ›spectrally human‹ Jews did not constitute a threatening, haunting and excessive presence in the country,[11] on the contrary – it was the absence of the people and of the culture ›wiped out by the Holocaust‹ that increasingly began to draw attention. Wajda's *Dybbuk* and its readings manifested and, to an extent, contributed to the construction of this new cultural sensitivity, reversing the vector of interpretation of the figure quoted in *Warszawski Dziennik Narodowy*. The performance, which premiered on March 12, 1988, came after a series of other artistic initiatives that sought to (re)create the contours of the ›traditional‹ prewar Jewish world for Polish audiences. In 1983, *The Fiddler on the Roof* began what was to be a glittering career in Poland; in 1986, an adaptation of Isaac Bashevis Singer's *Magician from Lublin* (1960) premiered at Wroclaw Contemporary Theatre (cf. Karpiński 1991). In the medium of film, »a nostalgic account of a lost Jewish world« (Haltof 2014 [2012]: 141) was perhaps most powerfully given in Jerzy Kawalerowicz's *Austeria* [The Inn, 1983]. Set in the 1910s, and based on the novel by Julian Stryjkowski (1966) – but also inspired by Waszyński's *Dybbuk* – the film depicted Jewish life in a small Galician shtetl on the verge of destruction brought about by the First World War (Haltof 2014 [2012]: 142; cf. also Safran 2000). The very fact that these productions passed through the filters of government censorship and, as was the case with *Austeria*, even became the subject of intense state marketing, indicated an important shift in both the cultural and political frame. More and more room was opened up for direct engagement with Jewish themes and, in Irena Irwin-Zarecka's words, for the »regime's celebration of Jewish culture« (Irwin-Zarecka 1988: 119). Although not paramount to

---

11 In the introduction to this volume I analyze the status of the Jewish Other before, during the war and in the immediate postwar period in terms of the spectrally human. Borrowing from Judith Butler, I construct the normative dynamics behind anti-Jewish violence in Poland as dehumanization through derealization.

this process, Wajda's *Dybbuk* provided useful insight into the conditions under which it had originally unfolded.

In Wajda's staging of the drama at Cracow's ›Old Theater‹, it was Bryll's poetic translation of An-sky's prose, intended to bring it closer to the Polish audience (Bryll 1988b), but even more so the scenography designed by Krystyna Zachwatowicz that played a pivotal role in framing the meaning of *The Dybbuk*. Throughout the performance, the action unfolded against the backdrop of an old, abandoned Jewish cemetery, fashioned on the necropolis of Cracow's Kazimierz.[12] Erected upstage and separated from the rest of the set by an almost entirely transparent scrim, the cemetery could be viewed only by looking through a large synagogue window, which constituted the actual spatial frame for the scenic action. In the opening scene, snow was falling and ravens hovered above the run-down, contorted tombstones – an image said to be so moving that it forced the audience to rise to its feet in a standing ovation. The presence of the cemetery, but also of the figures erring between the Matzevot (in the prologue and epilogue of the performance), suggestively evinced the closeness of death and the dead, and the interplay between the dead and the living. This sensation was further strengthened, but also slightly interpretatively redirected, by yet another stenographic decision: a thin veil of black tulle separated the stage from the audience, blurring the view of the actors and the scenic actions.

While the first scrim spoke to the porosity of boundaries between the worlds of the dead and living, the second imposed a spatial and temporal

---

12 The pictures of the cemetery, taken by Wajda and Zachwatowicz, were included in the performance programme. In a review for *Teatr*, Krzysztof Kopka further foregrounded the intended similarity between the Cracow's necropolis, and many others in the country, and the one constructed on the stage: »It is a forsaken cemetery, just like so many other Jewish cemeteries in Poland, today only monuments to a nation that used to live here, and whom they outlived.« (1988) It is worth noting that the abandoned cemeteries, with lone, deteriorating Matzevot, are considerably outnumbered by those robbed of all tombstones during and after the war. In his 2012 book, *Matzevot for Everyday Use*, Łukasz Baksik meticulously documents how Poles, through a variety of practical purposes, invested those ›monuments‹ with a second lease of life: they became cinder stones, pavements, building materials. Human remains still rest in the grounds transformed into parks, parking lots, or markets.

distance between the actors and the audience. Its importance for the modes of reception of the play was reflected in almost all reviews. Bronisław Mamoń wrote in *Tygodnik Powszechny* that this visual experiment transformed the stage into an image comparable to those of long forgotten and accidentally rediscovered old, »faded and ashen« photographs. »One looks at them«, he added »with interest, maybe even with sentimentality, surprised that the world has changed so much« (1988). In another critic's view, the veil created for audiences a reflection of »a world summoned from non-existence, creating an impassable temporal boundary between the viewers and the drama's protagonists« (Czapliński 2015; cf. also Karpiński 1991: 160). In other words, by putting on stage the reality and dramas of the shtetl, Wajda's *Dybbuk*, conjured up »an exotic lost Jewish world« (Steinlauf 2010: 110), a culture irrevocably decimated by the Holocaust.

While Wajda's reconstruction of the reality of the Eastern European shtetl differed significantly from the ›naively folkloristic‹ incarnations in stagings of *The Fiddler on the Roof* or *The Magician from Lublin,* he also went to great lengths to meticulously portray Hasidic clothing, customs and religious practices. The intention of the performance, as indicated in the program, was to educate: to »expand our [Poles'] knowledge of the Jewish nation« (Kopka 1988), both for those born after the war and those who remembered but never really knew (or wanted to know) the nuances of prewar Jewish culture. The community, its traditions and inner dynamics was, therefore, central to Wajda's staging, rather than the fate of individual characters (cf. Wach-Malicka 1989; Mamoń 1988). Placing particular emphasis on the metaphysical/philosophical/religious beliefs structuring the lives and practices of his protagonists, Wajda nevertheless failed to fulfill the expectations of those members of the audience who, according to two reviews published in *Trybuna Opolska,* were expecting to hear »żydzłaczenie« (the mocking belittling of ›Jewish‹ pronunciation) and see »Jews exaggerated, as we see them in our imagination [sic!]: with *payot* [sidelocks], speaking distinctive Polish« (Szczurek 1988; Anonymous 1989).[13] Instead, Wajda dressed his characters

---

13 In his contribution to the program, Bryll asserts that in preparing his poetic transcription of An-sky's text he aimed at avoiding exactly this: the Jewish protagonist speaking a language all too familiar from other Polish dramas, crippled and ridiculed. His choice was to bring the lines closer to the style of Old-Polish and Romantic tradition, the language of Polish stage characters (1988b). Apparently,

in a halo of mystery and gravity, emphasizing the depth and beauty of the world they shared. It is for this reason that Maciej Karpiński approvingly framed *The Dybbuk* as being driven by a »noble intention«. »Devoid of all colloquial and folklore elements, as a kind of challenge to the clichéd way Jewish themes have been presented in Polish theatre and drama« (often not free from explicit antisemitic subtexts), Wajda's staging was »constructed like a monument to a dead tradition« (1991: 159). The solemnity evoked by stenographic details, the presence of the eerie cemetery and of the veil, artistically manifested the in-betweenness inherent in the cultural and spiritual reality captured in An-sky's *Dybbuk*. Even more significantly, they brought to the fore further meanings of »between two worlds« that were pivotal to Wajda's interpretation of the play and its reception – those between the past and present; between absence and presence; and between the contemporaneous audience and the vanished culture of the shtetl; that is, first and foremost, between the ›Jews‹ and the ›Poles‹.

This ›Polish-Jewish‹ dimension of Wajda's performance was echoed most powerfully in immediate reviews. Although some critics accused the director of making a politically opportunistic decision in taking on such an unequivocally Jewish play (cf. Niziołek 2013: 138), many others recognized the staging as a historically and culturally specific gesture of deference and nostalgia (Pysiak 1988). Its roots lay firmly in the tradition of Polish Romanticism and its attentiveness to the dead, now cutting across not only ontological but also national lines.[14] On the stage of the Old Theatre, the play – a

---

this was not enough to satisfy the audience. Interestingly, Mark Arenshteyn met with a similar challenge when he attempted to stage the play in Polish in 1925. According to Steinlauf, he »had to labor against the ingrained tendency of his actors to »żydzłaczenie« – that is, to perform using the traditional intonations and gestures associated with the stage Jew of Polish farce. The performance succeeded artistically chiefly because Arenshteyn seems to have enabled the actors to find their own path, that of Polish Romanticism, into a world so alien to them«. (2006: 244)

14 This interpretive trajectory was, to an extent, set by Wajda himself when he decided to include in the performance programme an excerpt from Rudnicki's book *Teatr zawsze grany* [Theater Always Played, 1987], which draws similarities between *Dybbuk* and *Dziady* and ends with the assertion: »*Dybbuk* and *Dziady*, two national portraits« (1988a [1987]). Grzegorz Niziołek argues that even the

»monument to a dead tradition«, which cast the ›Jews‹ in the roles of the dead and the ›Poles‹ in those of the living – was to be explicitly and thoroughly ›Polish‹. It is perhaps unsurprising that Wajda's performance soon came to be perceived as »a gift of memory and reverence, brought by Polish artists – the writer, director, stenographer, composer, choreographer, and the actors – for the Polish Jews« (Mamoń 1988). Reframed in these terms (regardless of the director's original intention), Wajda's *Dybbuk* said more about those receiving the play than about the tradition it sought to capture. But it also decisively (re)defined the meaning of the eponymous figure, a shift so aptly expressed in the glowing review by Karpiński: the *dybbuk* entered the scene as »a symbol of Jewish tradition, philosophy and religion, which returns to us as if from beyond the grave, as an inheritance [sic!] from the murdered nation.« (1991: 160)[15] A consequential revision indeed.

OVERSHADOWING

Ira Konigsberg claims that the Holocaust has irrevocably transformed the way *The Dybbuk* can be, and is, read. Writing about Waszyński's cinematic adaptation of the drama, she posits that »it is impossible to regain the historical purity of a work and see it through eyes innocent of events that have happened since its creation« (1997: 25). Before the outbreak of the Second

---

scenography in Wajda's performance referred back to Stanisław Wyspiański's 1901 staging of Mickiewicz's drama. In his view, this testified to Wajda's intent in transforming the performance into a ritual of »belated mourning« informed by the tradition of *Dziady*, which was, nevertheless, not grasped or (intentionally) rejected by the audience, unwilling to submit to its transformative, affective economy (2013: 138-139). Though I agree that it was Wajda's and Bryll's intention to reframe one work in terms of the other, perhaps also for reasons other than ›strategic‹. I will not delve deeper into this topic here. To put it briefly: in line with my introductory remarks, I view this reframing, first and foremost, as a means of appropriation.

15 For a critical discussion of the concept of »inheritance« [dziedzictwo] which, in Polish discourse, pertains equally to intangible heritage and to tangible properties misappropriated by Poles during and after the war, and serves to disavow their provenance in economic violence, see Konrad Matyjaszek (2013; 2018).

World War, the play's portrayal of the cultural and spiritual reality of the shtetl was, no doubt, a response to the complex and threatening political situation faced by East European Jewish communities. After the Holocaust, the text emerges as ›contaminated‹ by the retrospective knowledge of the event: it turns into a harbinger of the things to come, a dramatic symbol of destruction and death. *The Dybbuk*, notes Konigsberg, »is a Kaddish, a prayer for the dead, that asks us to remember its dead« (ibid) – a precious relic of a decimated culture. A similar perspective informs many theoretical engagements with this text, but also with other artworks, artifacts, and visual representations depicting Jewish realities from before the Holocaust. Building upon the work of Susan Sontag, Ewa Stańczyk argues that photographs capturing the ordinary life of the shtetl also carry a haunting quality and, when looked at by contemporary viewers, remain tinted with »the image of impending annihilation« (2014: 365). This is exactly what Konigsberg means by lost innocence in relation to the reception of *The Dybbuk*. Watching it through the prism of the Holocaust, or, better yet, in its shadow, produces a different mode of viewing: »along with our nostalgia, we bring into the film a sense of the tragic that may not have been there to begin with but that makes the film more beautiful and more painful to watch« (1997: 25). While this mode of reading/viewing of *The Dybbuk* has often been conceptualized in terms of ›backshadowing‹, the version performed in 1988 in Poland could be better described by another term: to overshadow.

Backshadowing, as constructed by Michael André Bernstein in *Foregone Conclusions* (1994), imposes insights, judgments, affects, and images reserved for postwar positionalities and perspectives on pre-Holocaust cultural narratives. Moving backwards through temporal orders, this mode of reading retroactively assumes knowledge about accomplished futures and projects it onto the foretime. In this way, backshadowing renders prewar texts/actions/actors extremely vulnerable to critical appraisal, »as though they too should have known what was to come« (Bernstein 1994: 16). But viewed through a contemporary lens, pre-Holocaust narratives, deprived, in Konigsberg's words, of »historical purity«, also begin to act as disturbing prophecies and forewarnings. They point forward to and anticipate the Holocaust and the imminent destruction of the prewar Jewish world. In somewhat less naïve terms, Zehavit Stern writes about backshadowing as a practice of interpretive »flattening«, which eclipses the contingencies of cultural and historical time (and also the complexities of the cultural text in question) and folds them into an abridged image of a doomed pre-Holocaust world. Relating this directly to *The Dybbuk*, she writes: »Life in a Hasidic community of the nineteenth century, its literary stylization by An-sky in the early twentieth century, and its cinematic reworking by director Michał Waszyński – all these historical matters are likely to be reduced to a single conception, simplified and monolithic, of the pre-Holocaust world.« Moreover, she adds: »The concept of [*The Dybbuk*] as a remnant, even a holy remnant, creates a distance between the objects represented – the Jews of eastern Europe in the generation before the Holocaust – and the subjects beholding them today.« (Quoted in Rosenberg 2011: 3)

Summoned to the Polish stage by Wajda in 1988, the pre-Holocaust Jewish world was not constructed as doomed, it was instead cast as already effectively absent. This absence, pivotal for Wajda's framing and the immediate reception of *The Dybbuk*, certainly created an impassable distance between the reality portrayed on the stage and the Polish audience, but it also worked hard to revoke it. In this case, temporal othering (characteristic of backshadowing) went hand in hand with a specific (re)configuration of Jewish otherness: both extinct and culturally distinct, Jewishness was positioned in direct relation to contemporary Polish culture, and not so much to the destruction and death brought about by the Holocaust. Despite the claims put forward by many critics that Wajda's staging of *The Dybbuk* unfolded »in the shadow of the Holocaust« (Czapliński 2015; Steinlauf 2010: 110), the Holocaust and its contingencies in Poland were, in fact, carefully filtered out from the performance. For example, Wajda's initial idea to set the scenic action in a cattle car heading towards an extermination camp, explicitly pointing towards the imagery of the Holocaust, was rejected by the director himself as »too audacious« (Wajda 2011). Similarly, a poetic prologue addressing the events of the war that was added by Bryll to the original text was ultimately removed from the script. Its fragment, quoted in the programme, alluded to ›tensions‹ inherent in prewar Jewish life in Poland (»we quarreled, lived together, we were together…«), and ultimately framed the dybbuk as the soul of the prematurely dead, who return to haunt those closest to them before their death. The target of the haunting is not the murderers, the Nazis, who took their lives (»the Hasidim believe the murderer will be judged by the Righteous Judge«), but those with whom they ›shared‹ their existence, the ›fellow citizens‹, the Poles (Bryll 1998a).[16]

These resolutions seem particularly compelling in view of the fact that the performance was anticipated to be both an artistic and a social event (Pysiak 1988; cf. also Mamoń 1988). Wajda insisted that the play be staged on a day symbolically associated with the events of 1968; marking the twentieth anniversary of the political protests against the repressive state and even more so of the antisemitic campaign that forced the last remaining Jews from the country or into submerging their identities. In so doing, he cast *The Dybbuk* as a critical voice in the debates that were unfolding on the subject of ›Polish-Jewish‹ past. And indeed, the year 1987 marks an important breaking point in public engagement with the Holocaust in Poland. One year before the Cracow premiere of An-sky's text, the weekly *Tygodnik Powszechny* published Jan Błoński's article »The Poor Poles Look at the Ghetto« (1990 [1987]). This essay raised what were at that time profoundly troubling questions about the positionality of non-Jewish Poles vis-à-vis the extermination

---

16 Bryll writes: »When the murderers slaughtered this nation / It cannot be forgotten. On this soil / It had still so much life to live… And it has to return / To us as a dybbuk […] We had seen each other too easily throughout centuries / Lived together but didn't understand… / Maybe it is better to forget? / You will not forget / This would mean depriving the nation of its soul […].« (1988a) Only one of the two excerpts from Adolf Rudnicki's *Teatr zawsze grany*, quoted in the programme of *Dybbuk*, conveyed an explicit, though subtle, reference to the Holocaust as it unfolded on the Polish soil: »Jews are helpless. You can win their hearts by ensuring their safety. How could Poles guarantee safety to anyone during the Second World War? What kind of safety was even possible here? But it was Poland and the Poles were obliged to ensure their security. They could not? And this was their great sin.« (The question mark after »they could not«, I would posit, speaks volumes about Rudnicki's perceptions of the war and bearings of Poles vis-à-vis the Holocaust). In this excerpt, Rudnicki, a Polish Jew, hints, therefore, at an alternative interpretation of the dybbuk, which was, nevertheless, not picked up either by the creators of the play or by its audience: »The aftereffects of this sin will live long in movies and books. What this country is facing now, is the struggle with the specter of history.« (Rudnicki 1988b [1987]) When Rudnicki is referred to by the critics of *The Dybbuk*, it is only his piece on *Dybbuk* and *Dziady* that is mentioned.

of the Polish Jews. Błoński's argument, which centered around the moral implications of indifferent ›witnessing‹ of the Holocaust, explicitly constructing it in terms of guilt and tracing its roots to prewar hostile attitudes towards the Jews, sparked off a fierce public debate in Poland, perhaps the first of its kind, and one in which Wajda could be considered to be taking a stand.[17]

Instead, his *Dybbuk* safely glossed over the Holocaust and the complex realities of anti-Jewish violence, normative and otherwise, that shaped ›Polish-Jewish relations‹ before, during and after the war. In stark contrast to Konigsberg's reading of An-sky's text, which emphasized the impossibility of historical purity and innocence since the events of the Holocaust, the Cracow performance effectively *overshadowed* these events and strove towards ›innocence‹: the sentimental innocence of the pre-Holocaust world conjured up on stage; the innocence of Wajda's »noble intention«, wrapping this world in an air of mystery and solemnity, but passing over its threatening underpinnings; and, finally, the innocence of the Polish audience invited to embrace nostalgia for the absent Jews without having to »look at the ghetto«. Joanna Tokarska-Bakir argues that an »obsession with innocence« invariably shapes Polish responses to debates about the Holocaust, disallowing the acknowl-

---

[17] In 1985, after the release of Claude Lanzmann's *Shoah*, public opinion in Poland was brutally confronted with questions pertaining to Polish antisemitism and complicity in the Holocaust, formulated mostly by Western critics and reviewers of the film, but it mobilized unanimously in defense of the ›good name‹ of Poles and against their portrayal in the documentary. Lanzmann interviewed several inhabitants of former shtetls or towns neighboring extermination camps, mostly simple farmers now living in formerly Jewish houses, whose accounts shed light not only on the prevalence of antisemitism (prewar, wartime and postwar), but also on the involvement of Poles in the Holocaust. Almost all critics in Poland, many of whom had not even seen the film, unequivocally condemned Shoah, denouncing it as »anti-Polish« and mendacious. It was only the publication of Błoński's text in 1987 that brought the problem of Polish ›guilt‹ into the open. The fierce resistance against his arguments made manifest the extent to which the Poles were unprepared or, better said, unwilling to take the subject on, even though Błoński, with his insistence on indifference and passivity, barely scratched the surface of the problem. For a detailed discussion on responses to Lanzmann's *Shoah* and discussions following Błoński's text, see Forecki (2010: 132-165).

edgement of the wrongs and injustices inflicted upon the Jews by the Poles, even at the expense of ›facts‹ and historical accounts, all to uphold the national self-image (2004). Błoński's essay called for a substantial reconfiguration of the field of visibility pertaining to the Holocaust. Its author rightly expected that it would come into sharp conflict with the »readers' sensibility« (Błoński 1990 [1987]: 48) and with their ability to (re)imagine themselves as historical, ethical and political subjects. Perhaps Wajda anticipated that his production would inspire similarly adverse reactions if his invocation of the Jewish world were to intervene in symbolic economies structuring hegemonic representations of the Second World War, the Holocaust, and Polish collective subject positions. In order to bridge »between two worlds« – the ›Polish‹ and the ›Jewish‹ – his *Dybbuk* had to iterate, if not enact, the cultural and political frames (Błoński's »sensibilities«) that dictated the conditions under which their encounter was to be possible in the first place.[18]

To overshadow means to tower above and cast a shadow over, to eclipse, to render invisible. The word implies a certain level of control, privileging one modality of vision over another, but also an activity, a very specific one for that matter, that of obscuring, masking, making invisible. More than merely a historically/culturally positioned and affectively charged mode of reading, ›contaminating‹ through-the-prism-of or ›flattening‹ reading into, overshadowing constitutes a representational practice *par excellence* – one which operates through exclusionary effects, creating its own blank spots, blindnesses, and invisibilities. In this, unlike complete silencing or invisibilization, overshadowing simultaneously unveils and occludes or, better yet, unveils to occlude. While offering insight into Jewish culture and past in Poland, it does so in a way that prevents access to ›the thing itself‹. Relegating

---

18 Reflecting on the scenography of Wajda's *Dybbuk* and audiences' enthusiastic reactions to its allure, Niziołek writes: »The overwhelming beauty of the image perhaps masked the fear of the creators of the performance about the hostility or indifference of the audience towards the Jewish world summoned at the stage. The stirring up of enchantment allowed them to disarm such attitudes.« (2013: 139) I would suggest that it was not the ›Jewish world‹ as such, which was already at that time a subject of popular interest, if not fascination, but the questions that the staging could have posed – about Polish antisemitism or Polish involvement in destruction of this world – that were the potential source of hostility and/or indifference Wajda tried to disarm.

to the shadows the contingencies and complexities of *The Dybbuk* as a cultural text, the plethora of meanings saturating the figure in the Jewish tradition, and, most importantly, the violent history of ›Polish-Jewish relations‹, Wajda's staging has arrived at a simplified and monolithic image of the pre-Holocaust Jewish world, and at an equally idealized image of its Polish recipients. But, on a more fundamental level, the violent nature of the relationship between the two – inscribed in the very structure of their relationality – was rendered invisible by the control exerted through the conditions imposed on the encounter between them: a control based on the appropriation of the dybbuk (the ›Jewish world‹), and the act of using its absence/presence in order to uphold a particular norm and perpetuate a particular mode of vision – one historically based on, and actively invisibilizing, the exclusion and dispossession of the Jewish other. But it is exactly in this frame that the dybbuk has emerged as a potent figure in the Polish post-Holocaust imaginary, a figure of memory, of absence, nostalgia, and loss – a ghostly presence that is, effectively, unable to haunt.

POWERFUL/POWERLESS

Avery Gordon conceptualizes haunting as a »transformative recognition« (2008 [1997]: 8), which brings about a disruption and critical intervention into existing power structures, hierarchies and normative/symbolic/political orders. Affording a critical insight into »the ensemble of social relations that create inequalities, situated interpretive codes, particular kinds of subjects, and the possible and the impossible themselves« (ibid: 4), haunting produces or, at least, calls for a change, for the countering or revision of these social relations, for an alternative production of interpretive codes, affects and subject positions. This transformative power is a source of the fear traditionally associated with ghosts: to haunt means to instill terror, to disturb, unsettle, and disjoint. On a theoretical plane, it invests haunting with the ability to trouble and to work against the erasures, exclusions and invisibilities created by repressive regimes of power and dominant cultural (and analytical) discourses, »the possible and impossible themselves«. »Following ghosts«, writes Gordon, »is about making a contact that changes you and refashions the social relations in which you are located« (ibid: 22). The very presence of a ghost is, for her, »a sign, or the empirical evidence if you like, (…) that haunting is taking place« (2008 [1997]: 8). Drawing on my readings of the Polish dybbuk(s), however, I argue that the situation is somewhat more complex. Instead of simply serving as indications of haunting, ghosts need to be fathomed through an ever specific and contextual capability to affect, to change, disrupt, unsettle; in other words, through their ability or inability to haunt.

The idea that ghosts' ability to haunt may vary in scale and scope is suggested in Esther Peeren's conceptualization of the agency of ghosts in *The Spectral Metaphor: Living Ghosts and the Agency of Invisibility* (2014). In her book, Peeren explores the potential of spectrality as a metaphor for the condition of the »living ghosts« produced by late capitalism (servants, domestic workers, undocumented migrants). Although employed figuratively to convey modes of agency enacted by various dispossessed (living) subjects, her theorization of haunting also resonate in other analytical contexts: figurative or not, and across ontological lines, ghosts possess varying capacities to act and exert power, which require analytical attention. Peeren establishes haunting as a form of agency, understood in terms of being able to act and to be seen. Following poststructuralist conceptualizations of agency not as an autonomous capability driven by free will but as an *effect*, she constructs haunting as »at once made possible and restricted by social norms and power relations« (ibid: 14). The ability of ghosts to haunt, she claims, is always conditioned and constrained; their mere presence might not necessarily be a sign that haunting is taking place:

A ghost incapable of manifesting influence and presence or threatening to molest is [...] still a ghost, but not a haunting force capable of inducing the strong affects that grant it power over the living. Haunting, like agency, is not a property one simply has, but a conditional capability whose strength and (im)possibility are determined, to a large extent by contextual factors, both preceding and shaping the situation in question (power structures, established discourses and so on) and arising from it (the contingency of the event). (Peeren 2014: 182)

At the root of this framing of haunting, then, lies the assumption that haunting (as agency) is always formed within a specific social/cultural/political field, that it is a product of relational construction and a response to specific relations of power. While this reading corresponds with the one advanced by Gordon, which constructs ghosts as upshots of symbolic/political/material realities, it also invites a shift in analytical attention towards the conditions which impact ghosts' ability to enact agency, to the configurations of power that render haunting possible, or not.[19] For the purposes of my analytical context, this allows us to view ghosts as figures operating in conditions that are not only historical but also informed and shaped by a broader web of »relations of power« – between the living and the dead, between ghosts and the symbolic, political and affective economies that enable or confound their transformative potential. Put simply: in order to haunt, to instill terror, disturb, unsettle, and disjoint (or to refashion social relations and dominant cultural discourses), ghosts must be endowed with the power to do so. In this way, the figure of the ghost hovering between two worlds – life/death, present/absent, visible/invisible, present/past – encapsulates yet one more uneasy distinction: powerful/powerless.

Wajda's *Dybbuk* did not bring about a change – instead, it left intact and perpetuated the established discourses and power structures between the Poles and Jews, the living and the dead. His dybbuk was, then, effectively unable to haunt. It is the play's other theatrical incarnation, created in 2003 by Krzysztof Warlikowski, that was (and still is) considered to mark a major shift in the Polish framing of the dybbuk, and in the articulation of the positionality of Poles towards the absent Jews, thereby (ostensibly) investing the dybbuk with genuine transformative potential. According to Michael Steinlauf, Warlikowski's *Dybbuk* »represented something profoundly new« (2010: 111) – a statement with which many Polish critics would agree (cf. Cieślak 2003; Sobolewski 2003; Basara 2004).

---

19 For Peeren, who analyses »the ghostliness produced by the exclusions that occur within the realm of life, among the living« (2014: 24), the question of haunting pertains, first and foremost, to the very condition of the (social, political and cultural) invisibility of certain subjects and their ability to act against the systemic forces that relegate them to this position: the ability to challenge the mechanisms through which those subjects are rendered ghostly, invisible, irrelevant, unaccounted for. Therefore, unlike me, she is not so much interested in addressing the perspective of the haunted, as that of ghosts – her analysis pertains to the modes of »spectral agency« (and empowerment) enacted by living people from the position of invisibility. For me, it is the position of the haunted, and, thus, that of the symbolic/political/material order within which the ghosts appear, and which they have the (in)ability to challenge and/or struggle against, that is of interest.

The novelty lay, in part, in Warlikowski's unique interpretation and adaptation of *The Dybbuk*. His production, staged for the first time on October 6, 2003, at the Wrocław International Theater Festival Dialog, and later that year performed at the Warsaw Teatr Rozmaitości,[20] brought together Ansky's classic text and a contemporary short story, *The Dybbuk*, written by Polish (Jewish) author, Hanna Krall (2005 [1995]). In Krall's story, Adam S., an American Jew and child of Holocaust survivors, is possessed by the ghost of his step-brother, who at the age of six perished in the Warsaw ghetto. Warlikowski's staging performed both texts without an interval, constituting the structure of the play, which was framed by an additional prologue: seven actors sitting at the front of the stage narrating Hasidic tales and anecdotes for the audience. Taken from (adapted) Hasidic stories composed by Shlomo Carlebach (1996) or written by Hanna Krall, the tales are set in the 1930s and tell of famous rabbis, of the wisdom and miracles of prewar shtetls. The names of the recounted towns – those of Lublin, Kock, Radzyń, Turzysk, Góra Kalwaria, or Międzyrzecze – left no doubt to audiences that the events unfolded in Poland. Situating his *Dybbuk* within the (dis)continuity between prewar Jewish presence (in Poland), the Holocaust, and the contemporary world as constitutively affected by the event, Warlikowski made a play which directly engaged with the question of Jewish absence/presence and its relevance in Poland – a question all the more pertinent because posed in the aftermath (and as a theatrical response to) debates since 2000 surrounding the revelations about the Jedwabne massacre.

---

20 The Warsaw premiere took place on November 2, 2003. As with Wajda's Dybbuk, the dates of both premieres of Warlikowski's play were symbolically charged: in Wrocław it marked the day of Yom Kippur (in Judaism, the holiest day of the year, the Day of Atonement), in Warsaw, the Christian All Souls' Day, when the dead are prayed for and commemorated. The play was, in fact, to be staged first in the summer of 2003 at the Avignon Theater Festival, which was cancelled due to strikes. Although prepared for an international audience, it was, like Wajda's *Dybbuk*, intended to resonate primarily with Polish spectators. Commenting on the canceled French premiere of the play, one critic stated: »It is probably better this way, because the performance from the very beginning was aimed not at international but at the Polish audience, with which, in the last years, Warlikowski's theater ›holds a dialogue‹.« (Partyga 2004: 100) In 2004, the play was shown in New York; in 2008, in Israel.

Indeed, the publication in 2000 of Jan Tomasz Gross' *Neighbors: The Destruction of the Jewish Community in Jedwabne, Poland* (2001 [2000]), was to constitute yet another breaking point in Polish public debates pertaining to the Holocaust. In 1987, Błoński addressed the matter of guilt, which in his view lay in the indifference and passivity of Poles vis-à-vis the Holocaust. In 2000, Gross revealed Poles' role as perpetrators. He discussed the crime committed by Poles in Jedwabne in July 1941, when the vast majority of the hundreds of Jewish inhabitants of the town were burned alive in a barn – an act of mass murder that, until then, had been attributed to the German occupier. The sheer cruelty and scale of the massacre, meticulously reconstructed by Gross, could commove the reader. But in Poland, it was rather Gross' ascription of culpability to the Poles that violently shook and split public opinion. His intervention into the dominant representation of the Second World War, the Holocaust, and the Polish collective subject position – constructed thus far through notions of victimhood, oppression and heroism – caused outrage, indignation and resentment. Gross' theses, methods and integrity were fiercely discussed and questioned.[21] Yet, on a somewhat smaller scale, his investigation into Jedwabne acted, too, as an incentive for a critical reexamination of this and other crimes perpetrated by Poles during the war, of the received narratives of the Polish-Jewish past, of the national self-image, and of the »structural dynamics of antisemitism in Polish culture« (Lease 2016: 142). For Warlikowski, too, »the so-called ›Jewish question‹ arose in Poland with the emergence of Jedwabne«, prompting him to pursue new theatrical interests (Arvers/Warlikowski 2010: 88). Asked by Piotr Gruszczyński about his *Dybbuk*, and the play's explicit references to the Holocaust, Warlikowski said:

Jedwabne brutally confronted Poles with history, which for us, after the war, was pushed aside to some extent, passed over in silence […]. But if we do not rethink the situation of Jews in Poland in a different way, we will never be [at peace] with ourselves. Our words will not be sincere. (Gruszczyński/Warlikowski 2010 [2003/2005]: 94)

---

21 For an account of the debates that followed the publication of Gross' book, see Michlic and Polonsky (2004). Between 2000-2002, the crime was investigated by The Institute of National Remembrance (IPN), which reasserted Poles' culpability for the crime (cf. Machcewicz/Persak 2002).

In the context of Warlikowski's theatre, this statement could sound genuine. His work has been driven by an interrogative attitude to contemporary social reality, to the issues of exclusion, marginalization, and difference; it has addressed questions of otherness – of the ›other‹ within and in relation to Polish culture. Invariably stirring controversy, he has touched upon themes of homosexuality, of patriarchal violence and of identity, firmly establishing his theater as a space for self-questioning, for intellectual and emotional transformation, cathartic and therapeutic (Gruszczyński/Warlikowski 2010 [2003/2005]; cf. Niziołek 2010: 55; Drobnik-Rogers: 2009).[22] In fact, Warlikowski's decision to work on *The Dybbuk*, coincided with a moment when his interests shifted towards direct critical engagement with (his) Polish identity and the very notion of Polishness – its myths, hegemonic narratives, and silences. The Polish-Jewish past, so turbulently forefronted by the Jedwabne debate, became constitutive to this process. Warlikowski recognized the significance of Jewish history (and its postwar erasure) for present-day constructions of Polishness, and he came to realize that »the life and the annihilation of the Jews in Poland [is] the missing link within Polish identity today« (Gruszczyński/Warlikowski 2010 [2003/2005]: 94). The dybbuk was to ›haunt‹ the Poles.

Warlikowski's production did not draw from Jewish folklore. There was no klezmer, no traditional ›Jewish‹ clothes. The play achieved a more complex representation of Jewish otherness than the one proposed by Wajda. As early as in the prologue, the actors narrating Hasidic tales were dressed in modern clothes; only men's yarmulkes indicated their Jewishness. They sat on the proscenium, separated from the rest of the stage by two glass cages delineating the actual space of scenic action. This positioning of the actors on the stage, the fact that the cast faced and directly addressed the audience, along with the mention of Polish towns in tales about stories possessing the might of a prayer, about God who failed to meet the expectations of humans, about a Messiah for whom nobody waits, all served to establish relationality between the Poles and Jewish presence/absence. »The audience is confronted

---

22 In another interview with Gruszczyński, Warlikowski described his theater »as a real group therapy, a positive – or negative – discharge of fears and tensions, of all that we normally don't verbalize in our everyday work, in our scientific and political statements, through our racial, national, or religious identities.« (Gruszczyński/Warlikowski 2006: 165)

by these fantastic tales as *nasze* (ours), born in Polish towns, raised on Polish soil«, suggested Steinlauf (2010: 111). And indeed, this interpretation reverberates in many reviews: the Hasidic stories acted as reminders of historical Jewish presence in Poland, they evoked the emptiness their ›absence‹ left behind.[23] At the same time, they opened space for participation, for closeness between the actors and the audience, inviting the latter to engage with the narratives of a culture essentially foreign and unfamiliar to them, a culture which no longer existed in Poland.

The prologue ignited a certain affective economy, creating intimacy and transforming absence into loss – a »missing link within Polish identity today«. This convivial atmosphere is suddenly interrupted by the disturbing tone of the last story, told by the actor Andrzej Chyra (cast in the double role of An-sky's Khonen and Adam S. from Krall's short story), which marked the transition to the second part of the performance. Chyra's tale, which invoked the »memory of other worlds« and the need to transgress the everyday, was followed by an almost complete blackout of the stage. This produced an interpretive shift towards a deeper and more universal engagement with questions posed by An-sky's *Dybbuk* – those of spirituality, of mysticism, the transformative power of love, and death. Warlikowski reasserted its status as a classic.[24]

---

23 In a review titled »The Return of the Neighbors« for *Rzeczpospolita*, Jacek Cieślak writes (it seems, without irony): »Krzysztof Warlikowski brings our Jewish neighbors to life. Here they are, perhaps saved by the Poles [sic!]. They escaped Treblinka and Jedwabne, they sit in front of a restaurant, maybe their home, relating stories of good and sinful Jews, of love and tragedies, they remember the dead. An idyll, as if the Holocaust never happened!« (2003)

24 This universalizing approach to An-sky's text was acknowledged by many critics, who saw it also as an indication of Warlikowski's attempt to distance himself from Wajda's reading of *The Dybbuk* and its insistence on »historical distinctiveness and cultural alterity« (Lease 2016: 158). Warlikowski's *Dybbuk* was thoroughly modern and contemporary. This was conveyed through the actors' costumes and through the design of the spaces in which the staging unfolded: a mikveh which could just as well be a sauna or a traditional Polish wedding hall. Equally significant, the stenographic decision to locate most scenic action within a glass cage could be read as a response to Wajda's – while in Wajda's *Dybbuk* the tulle served to separate, to impose distance between the audience and the

In a similar vein, the transition between the second and the last part of the performance also imposed a strong interpretive shift: the scene of Leah's death and her union with Khonen is transformed into one featuring Adam S. and his wife (played by Magdalena Cielecka, also cast in the role of Leah). We are now in contemporary America, the Holocaust has already unfolded, Adam S. and his wife talk about his dybbuk, and about the possibility of freeing him from its troubling presence. The wife is impatient, she suggests therapy, insisting that something has to be done. This part of the performance, staged as a series of monologues, closely follows the story of Hanna Krall. Adam S. is an American academic who, in his scholarship, looks at the architecture of prewar wooden Jewish synagogues in Poland. His interest in »something that no longer exists« is driven by the possessive presence of his stepbrother's ghost, who has been with him his entire life. His stepbrother was the child of Adam's father – a Polish Jew – with his first wife. He perished in the Holocaust. The possession is a source of intense sadness and despair – the despair, Adam learns from his father, of a child thrown out of a hiding place in the ghetto and left on the street to die. It makes Adam feel »worse and worse«. And yet, when Samuel Kerner, an American Jew who became a Buddhist monk, finally manages to exorcise the dybbuk, Adam, filled with *rachmones* [compassion], calls him back: »Stay with me. You are my brother, don't go away!« The staging ends with a scene in which Adam runs on a treadmill to counteract a heart condition and prolong his life, and thus that of the dybbuk. It is only when the spirit wants to cling to his newborn child that Adam objects: »Oh no, don't you dare. No ghetto, no Holocaust. You are not going to inhabit my child.« He takes it upon himself to protect the child and host the dybbuk, its despair and troubling memories. The presence of his sleepless wife in the final tableau suggests, however, that this lack of closure remains and will remain unresolved until Adam's death.

The question of spirituality and of God (or his loss) after the Holocaust, runs through all parts of the performance. It reverberates in the Hasidic tales recounted in the prologue; in Warlikowski's interpretation of An-sky's text, read (again!) »in the shadow of the Holocaust« (Gruszczyński/Warlikowski 2010 [2003/2005]): 93); in the portrayal of an American Jew who seeks help not in a synagogue but in therapy; in the story of the Buddhist monk haunted

---

actors, in Warlikowski's staging, the transparency of the glass and its porosity, served to construct the otherness and alterity as complex and non-absolute.

by the question of »why God had allowed Treblinka«. Considered on this plane, Warlikowski's *Dybbuk* engages with questions that permeate the field of (cultural) Holocaust studies, organized around the (often contested) diagnoses of the irrevocability of the disturbance in the moral/symbolic/aesthetic order(s) brought about by the Holocaust, which casts the contemporary world as post-traumatic (cf. LaCapra 1998; 2001). The acceptance of the dybbuk, as entered into by Adam S., becomes synonymous with an ethical imperative to embrace the order as irrevocably shattered and to be willing to live on regardless.[25] It is in this sense that one can understand Krall's statement, recounted in many reviews of the play: »An-sky tells of innocent times. In our time we know that the dybbuk is not to be chased away [...]. Without our dybbuks we would be worse, and more foolish [human beings].« (Cieślak/Krall/Warlikowski 2003) In his interview with Gruszczyński, Warlikowski further strengthens this interpretive line: »we need the dybbuk to save our spirituality«, he says, »we cannot live without the dybbuk without sinking into the banality of existence«, instead, »we« are to embrace the »suffering« to which we are »effectively condemned«: the dybbuk, today, »is the personification of the memory that we don't want to let go of, that we want to cultivate within ourselves, the memory that might save us [sic!] today.« (2010 [2003/2005]: 94-95) The question is: whose memory, and of what?

There was no doubt, either for Warlikowski or for the reviewers of the play, that his staging spoke of »memory that creates identity« (Frei, as quoted in Matuszewska 2005) – the identity of contemporary Poles and their

---

25 In an article »Witnesses, the Unspeakable, and Tragedy«, reprinted in the programme of the performance, Maria Janion reminds the audience that art about the Holocaust cannot bring about catharsis. The art produced after the Holocaust, she writes, »Commands us to live in an excess of pain, with the sense of irreversible loss and mourning, which should have no end.« (2003 [2002]). This is the only text, apart from An-sky's *Dybbuk*, quoted in the programme. In his interpretation of Warlikowski's staging, Niziołek follows (only) this interpretive trajectory and reads the play as a morally ambivalent exercise in the ethics of mourning: establishing the trauma of the Holocaust as the deconstructive foundation of identity, it renders it a symbolic capital and a source of »social charisma« (2013: 511). In what follows I argue that such a trauma-orientated reading is much more problematic than this.

memory of the Jews. Moreover, this memory was constructed as inherently traumatic: »Each of us has our own dybbuk: our obsessions, anguish, traumas...«, asserted Warlikowski (Arves/Warlikowski 2010: 90). Warlikowski's play, as Agnieszka Legutko argues, »examines the essential role that the traumatic memory of the past plays in modern [...] Polish identity, using the dybbuk possession motif to explore the phenomenon of postmemory, and the haunting presence of the Holocaust in today's consciousness of [...] non-Jewish Poles.« (2012: 184) Indeed, the last part of the performance could be legitimately read through a trauma theory framework: Adam S., the son of Holocaust survivors, a representative of the second generation, carries within himself the traumas of his relatives. We are dealing here with an artistically elaborated instance of the generational transmission of trauma, as theorized by Marianne Hirsch (1997; 2012). In Warlikowski's staging, however, this becomes the experience of the Poles who are also constructed, explicitly and without further debate, as the carriers of the trauma of the Holocaust.[26] The difference between the Jewish and Polish experience and positioning vis-à-vis the Holocaust is effectively blurred, the former appropriated by the latter – Adam S. comes to represent the Polish memory of the Jewish past and of the Holocaust. Warlikowski writes:

His [Adam's] words: ›Stay with me. You are my brother, don't go away!‹, can be read as a message of the performance. In this way, the Poles and other European nations are included in this parable. Jews are our brothers, whom we carry within ourselves as a dybbuk and whom we don't want to forget. (Dasara/Warlikowski 2004)[27]

But Adam S. is not a Pole, he is an American Jew and, in fact, a real person. Krall based her story on the experiences of an existing individual, the scholar Michael Steinlauf. A descendant of Polish Jews (who left the country after the war), Steinlauf is haunted by his step-brother Mojsze/Michał, who,

---

26 For a more extensive discussion of the discourses of trauma in relation to the Holocaust and the problems with its application to Polish experience and memory of the Holocaust, see Janicka (2014-15), the introduction, and Konrad Matyjaszek's contribution to this volume.

27 In the context of history of ›Polish-Jewish relations‹ this invocation to ›brotherhood‹ seems, at the very least, problematic.

indeed, perished in the Holocaust.[28] The historical anchoring of the story is not without relevance to Krall. As she stressed in interviews, the narratives she wrote for the prologue of Warlikowski's staging also draw on real persons and events: Kock is for her the home town of a Polish woman (Apolonia Machczyńska), who, during the war, hid twenty-five Jews in her house. She was betrayed by another Pole and killed, as were the people she tried to help; Turzysk and Lublin, in turn, refer back to mass executions of the Jews, which took place in a nearby Krępiec forest (Cieślak/Krall/Warlikowski 2003; Sobolewski/Krall/Warlikowski 2003). The stories speak, then, to the specificity of the Jewish experience and memory of the war, and about the dangers posed to Jews in hiding (and those individuals who helped them) by their Polish fellow citizens. This focus on the Jewish perspective on the Holocaust, and its difference from or incompatibility with the Polish perspective (so sharply emphasized by the Jedwabne debate), runs through Krall's entire writing. It is perhaps most powerfully articulated when Krall, asked about what she feared in anticipation of the staging of *The Dybbuk*, responds: »The history of Adam S., who carries a dybbuk, is not invented. Someone entrusted their story to me and I entrust it now – through the director – to the audience. Will they be willing to embrace it?« (Sobolewski/Krall/Warlikowski 2003) Yes they would, without a doubt, but only on their own terms and conditions; in other words, through appropriation and erasure.

While this appropriation pertains to the trauma of the Holocaust and to the very figure of the dybbuk, which is constructed (again) as a metaphor of Polish memory about the Jews, the erasure unfolds at the level of the content: the staging establishes the subject of remembering (the Poles), but we learn nothing about ›what‹ is to be remembered. The historical and social specificity of the experience of the Holocaust, so important for Krall, is replaced by an empty signifier of ›trauma‹. It is in these terms that one can interpret Warlikowski's decision, praised by some reviewers, not to »theatricalize« the Holocaust. And indeed, the Holocaust, around which the staging is structured, is signaled and addressed solely through absence, it unfolds in the interval during which the second part of the performance, based on An-sky's text, suddenly devolves into the third, when Khonen turns into Adam S., and Leah into his wife – representing the world before and after the Holocaust.

---

28 See Cieślak/Krall/Warlikowski (2003). Steinlauf himself recounts the story in an extensive interview with Elżbieta Janicka (Janicka/Steinlauf 2014-15: 447-451).

Warlikowski creates an empty space, which, as one reviewer notes, »the viewer ha[s] to fill in with their own imageries of the Holocaust« (Bryś 2009: 18). Aesthetically this is incredibly powerful, when considered on an ethical and political plane, however, the opposite is true. The staging makes no comments about the Polish-Jewish past, it eludes direct engagement with the questions opened by the Jedwabne debate and offers no answers and insights that would allow the audience to »rethink the situation of Jews in Poland in a different way«. Instead, it creates an image of the Poles ›saved‹ by their willingness to embrace the dybbuk, to accept it and carry it as their own. But are they in the least bit transformed?

In his interpretation of Warlikowski's *Dybbuk*, Bryce Lease suggests that the figure stands for »the ethical imperative to remember and to confront one's own commitment to difference and plurality« (2016: 161). In an immediate review for *Gazeta Wyborcza*, Tadeusz Sobolewski asserts that the staging speaks of the necessity of »saving the dybbuk« (2003) – it is through saving the absent/present Jewish other that the Poles, apparently, save themselves.[29] Ironically, read through these framings, Warlikowski's staging emerges not as critical but as self-celebratory: in lieu of a decisive intervention into dominant cultural discourses and interpretive codes (the persistence of which was so powerfully illuminated in the course of the Jedwabne debate), it (re)establishes the ›Poles‹ as sincere, as open to otherness, as thoroughly ethical subjects, as ›better‹ and less ›foolish‹. In this, it bears more resemblance to Wajda's staging than anyone was ready to admit – Wajda *overshadowed* the Holocaust; Warlikowski ›emptied‹ it of any specific

---

29 There is a short dialogue in Krall's *Dybbuk*, partially repeated in Warlikowski's staging, that yields insight into the power the living exert over the ghosts and the conditions they impose on their ability to haunt, which was, nevertheless, not picked up in the reviews and interpretations of the play. The narrator speaks with Adam S. about his decision to undo the exorcism performed by the Buddhist monk: »›You shouldn't have called him back‹, I said. [...] ›Then what?‹ ›He would have gone to the light, wherever it is. He would have forgotten.‹ ›I know‹, Adam S. agreed. ›But when he began to go... When he was walking away like that, I felt... I don't know how to say this in Polish... I felt such *rachmones*...‹ ›Litość taką, such pity‹«. (Krall 2005 [1995]: 153) It is difficult not to ask, who has power over whom, who is ›saving‹ whom, who ›needs‹ whom in this case? Does Adam's *rachmones* pertain to the dybbuk or to himself?

historical content, leaving only the contours of the shadow. Here, then, the spectral figure also emerges and moves within a frame delineated by what Warlikowski decides to erase or simply leave unsaid – between »insights and blindnesses« constitutive to his interpretation of the *Dybbuk*. And while it might offer a way to escape the »banality of existence« and expand the spirituality of contemporary Poles, the role the dybbuk comes to play in this context can hardly be articulated in terms of haunting as a (politically charged) transformative force. Although constructed as such (as an agent of traumatic memory), the dybbuk does not disturb, unsettle, or disjoint the »inequalities, situated interpretive codes, particular kind of subjects, and the possible and the impossible themselves«. The power structures (between the Jews and Poles, the living and the dead, over whom they, again, retain full control) – invisibilized and unchanged – *live on*.

גייט אַרויס פֿון מײַן הויז

In Jewish cultural tradition, at least prior to the Holocaust,[30] the dybbuk does not speak of memory; rather, it acts as a figure of disturbance and dissolution directed against prevailing (traditional) cultural norms, against the established social order and the power structures it embodies. While its early, sixteenth-century incarnations are thought to signal specific shifts in the religious and theological landscape of Judaism (the birth of the kabbalistic doctrine of transmigration of souls), the idiom of possession was, from the outset, entangled with the question of power and control more generally (Trachtenberg 2013: 49-51). It was, therefore, always resonant with broader social and cultural realities. The power that dybbuk tales addressed was a power (unequally) distributed among the possessive (evil) spirit, the possessed – often themselves a ›sinner‹ –, and an exorcist. The presence of a dybbuk, a spirit of the dead taking control over a living person and forcing them to transgress established norms of conduct, invariably met with a powerful curative response, that of an exorcism. On the social and cultural plane,

---

30 In addition to Hanna Krall, other Jewish authors have also embraced the figure of the dybbuk as a means to articulate the experience and memory of the Holocaust: Paddy Chayefsky (2017 [1960]), Romain Gary (1968 [1967]), Julia Pascal (2009 [1992]).

this power dynamic was articulated through the distribution of roles between the subjects involved, which unfolded along the lines of gender, authority and/or positions in the communal hierarchy. As in An-sky's *Dybbuk*, the possessed was usually a woman who submitted to the power of a deceased male, and the exorcist was a respected and respectable rabbi, a carrier of morality, binding religious doctrines, and the law.

As Rachel Elior convincingly argues, this gendered configuration of possession constituted a response to the patriarchal order that governed Jewish communities in the Middle Ages, early modern era, and beyond (2008: 52-65). It was through the idiom of possession, delegating authority over one's conduct to the spirit of the dead, that women could act upon their wishes and sexual desires, and revolt against patterns of dominance, subordination, enforced sexual/social/religious norms, and disciplinary practices, including the violence of arranged marriage. Allowing for the suspension of those norms, the dramatic event and the condition of possession granted the ›haunted‹ some measure of agency over themselves. At least in the interim, by expressing their sexuality and opinions, women could act against the »powerlessness, speechlessness« and subordination (Elior 2008: 65) inherent in their gender roles, and challenge entrenched power relations. In this context, the dybbuk represented a disturbing and subversive force.

This culturally established meaning of the dybbuk is echoed in An-sky's text. The resistance against an oppressive social/cultural/religious/economic order is the driving force behind Leah's decision to (voluntarily) submit to the power of the dybbuk, a gesture of opposition to her father's will and the unwanted marriage Sender has arranged for her. Khonen too, resorting to forbidden kabbalistic practices, rebels against established religious and theological doctrines; against the class-based social stratification relegating him to a position of inferiority; against the power that disciplinary social conventions hold over his freedom of choice. Both Khonen and Leah lose their lives in a struggle against a dominant culture predicated upon patriarchy, inequality and Orthodoxy – conceding, perhaps, to the only possibility of escaping its underlying violence. And it is precisely this last thread (and not so much, as it is often claimed, the motif of voluntary possession, or engagement with the questions of memory) that renders An-sky's *Dybbuk* exceptional against the landscape of traditional dybbuk stories. According to the standard scenario, the tales of spirit possession culminate in a successful exorcism, in which the spirit is effectively chased away, the possessed freed from its transgressive influence (cf. Alexander 2003; Elior 2008). By regaining control over the dybbuk, which was forced to speak and confess its sins during the exorcism, both the possessor and the possessed are ›cured‹, allowing the former to finally rest in peace, and the latter to return to society and ›normalcy‹. On a more fundamental level, the exorcism serves to reestablish, if not to reinforce, the governing social norms: it lays bare and reasserts the existing boundaries between the permissible and the impermissible, the acceptable and unacceptable, »the possible and the impossible themselves«.[31] The traditional dybbuk tale revolves, therefore, around a (temporarily) threatened but almost invariably restored social order and, as such, imposes serious constraints on the agency of the dybbuk (and/or the possessed). And yet, within this frame, the figure remains invested with an ability to trouble – even if this entails merely the power to reveal the violence upon which the order inherently rests.

And it is within this interpretive frame, set by the traditional dybbuk story, that I will read one last Polish incarnation: the 2015 horror movie *Demon* created by the late director Marcin Wrona and directly inspired by the events and afterlife of the Jedwabne massacre. In Polish critical reception, the film, which is based on Piotr Rowicki's 2008 drama *Przylgnięcie* [Clinging, 2015 (2007)],[32] was immediately constructed as contributing to debates about the memory, if not the »trauma of the Holocaust« (Fortuna 2015; cf. Romanowska 2015). This time, the dybbuk was to embody the troubling presence of an unacknowledged and unmastered past, the turbulent engagement of Poles with the legacy of the Holocaust. This interpretive trajectory,

---

31 This, in fact, corresponds with the interpretive line which constructs the dybbuk as figure whose importance is reasserted in times of crisis and radical cultural/political/economic transformation. As maintained by Tamar Alexander, for the Jewish community »dybbuk tales [served] as a means to strengthen its religious norms for the preservation of the Jewish life« (2003: 314).

32 Rowicki's play, rewritten several times between 2007 and 2010, had a first staging at the Theater Confrontations Festival in Lublin in 2008 (directed by Aldona Wigura). It was inspired by a workshop on the history of Jews of Lublin organized in 2007 by the Drama Laboratory, which resulted, in fact, in several scripts, written by young Polish authors, on the wartime anti-Jewish violence, Polish antisemitism, and ghosts – for instance, Małgorzata Sikorska-Miszczuk's *Mayor* (2014 [2011]) on the haunted contemporary Jedwabne.

which uncritically reproduced the ingrained Polish reading of the dybbuk as a figure of memory (whether traumatic or not), was even presented by those involved in making the film and the play. In a conversation with Szymon Majewski, Rowicki framed his drama as engaging with the question of historical »truth«, of »forgetting«, and of the »guilt« carried by Poles vis-à-vis Jews. By taking up the theme of anti-Jewish violence perpetrated by Poles during the war, he aimed to contribute to the »Polish-Polish debate« that has stirred and divided public opinion in the country since the publication of Gross' book on Jedwabne (Majewski/Rowicki 2008). Paweł Maślona, the co-author of *Demon*'s script, also asserted that the movie was about »memory that returns to us«, memory of wartime violence against Jews (quoted in Romanowska 2015). This frame has governed the vast majority of (if not all) readings of both the drama and its cinematic adaptation, regardless of their significant dissimilarities.

Rowicki's drama does seem to fit the frame neatly. *Clinging* revolves around the story of a small-town gangster, Piotr Pytlakowski, alias Pyton [Python], who, upon deciding to marry and start a family, undertakes some steps to settle down and establish a legitimate business of his own. He does not want his children to be forced to explain themselves when asked about their father's profession and whereabouts. The way out of criminality is to be found through one final transgression. Resorting to violence and extorsion, Pyton acquires a piece of land in the center of the town from a local locksmith. It is a long-abandoned and overgrown parcel, on which he plans to set up a second-hand car shop. It is sentiment that underpins his decision to obtain this particular plot: he used to come here as a child, as did other children from the town, to eat wild-growing apples, smoke cigarettes, and undergo sexual initiations. Pyton never reflected upon the reasons behind the abandonment of the parcel. In the programme of the first staging of the play, Jagoda Hernik-Sapińska explains: »Almost in every Polish town in the times of PRL [Polish People's Republic] there was a parcel of this kind, called in parents' and grandparents' conversations ›this parcel‹, nobody knew why it was empty, overgrown, to whom it belonged« (2008). As the story unfolds, Pyton finds answers to questions he never intended to pose. During the war, the parcel belonged to the locksmith's father, Stasio, who moved to an ›abandoned‹ Jewish house after the war. But the whole truth is more troubling than that: it is also on this piece of land that local residents murdered (buried alive) the Jews hiding in Stasio's house, among them a little Jewish girl, Hana.

»Everybody, the whole street [...], neighbors, the entire town« participated in the crime; Pyton's grandfather was there too and took an active part (Rowicki 2015 [2008]: 124).³³

Pyton's possession by Hana's ghost acts as an incentive for him to delve into the past. Upon acquiring the desired parcel, he starts feeling unwell, »something cries« inside of him (Rowicki 2015 [2008]: 112). He behaves strangely, and his criminalist friends turn against him, as does his fiancé Żanet. In search of help, he turns to a local doctor, and then to a priest, before whom Hana makes her presence manifest when Pyton begins to speak Yiddish. Finally, he talks to a teacher, the only inhabitant of the town of Jewish descent, who does not even want to be recognized as such and who claims not to remember »anything« (ibid: 139). Pyton learns about the wartime crime, wants it exposed and commemorated, for the sake of justice and redress, for Hana and for himself. The possession transforms Pyton and his perspective on the town: »Maybe you have schizophrenia«, the doctor tells him, »maybe you are troubled by a nightmare, but thanks to this you see clearly, as if you had a laser turned on that illuminates this whole mossy

---

33 Rowicki recreates a scenario well known from historical research: a courageous individual, driven by empathy and genuine willingness to help, or to profit (cf. Grabowski 2008), decides to hide Jews. Polish residents of the town learn about this and, often quoting anticipated repercussions from the Germans, force the helper to eliminate the ›threat‹, and take over the fortune they have ostensibly amassed. The neighbors, claims the locksmith in Rowicki's play, »demanded that my father denounce the Jews, bring them to the police or to the forest [which, in this context, is synonymous with killing]. »He didn't want to. So they came and forcibly took them [...]. They stood around him with axes, it's either you or them [...].« (Rowicki 2015 [2008]: 124). It is fascinating to read how this story is being reconstructed in some reviews of Rowicki's play: »the Jewish children were killed out of fear of German retaliation« (Józefczuk 2008), writes one reviewer merely reproducing the perpetrators' perspective and constructing fear, and fear alone, as a legitimate justification for what was done to the Jews. Another reviewer, Agata Warzecha, asserts: »Hana and her mother were brutally murdered [...] by the Nazis. Also, Polish local residents contributed to the crime« (2008). It is not enough that she, contradicting Rowicki, relegates the responsibility for the murder to the Nazis; the reader does not learn either how or why the Poles »contributed« to the deaths.

swamp. Your eyes have been opened, you see through our backyard crimes […]« (Rowicki 2015 [2008]: 131). This new mode of vision, cutting through public secrets and entrenched »blindnesses«, renders Pyton vulnerable to exclusion and violence by other inhabitants of the town. And indeed, in the final scene, Pyton digs a grave for himself on the parcel where Hana's body lies. He is shot dead by one of his former friends, surrounded by a crowd resembling the one that was present at Hana's death. History comes full circle.

In critical reception, the framing of *Clinging* as a piece about memory of the Holocaust and wartime Polish anti-Jewish violence resulted in an interpretive foregrounding of the positionality of Pyton and his radical transformation arising as a result of possession, his quest for truth, acknowledgement of past crimes and redress. »It is a story about accountability, conversion, unwanted calling and its force which leaves no choice« (Warzecha 2008), proclaimed one reviewer. »The protagonist, willingly or not, makes a sacrifice for the past transgressions of the community of the town, including his own grandfather« (Zalewska 2008), asserted another. *Clinging* emerged, then, as a work about haunting that transforms, that broadens awareness and ethical horizons, that contributes to »Polish-Jewish reconciliation [sic!]« (Miłkowski 2008; cf. Zalewska 2008). The rhetoric of calling and sacrifice, deeply rooted in the Polish national imaginary's overt Christian symbolism of martyrdom and (heroic) victimhood, effectively prevailed over other aspects of the story: the question of the exclusion, murder and dispossession of the Jewish other seen through their implications for the present, of the structural continuity of violence, past and contemporary. Appropriated within the Polish narrative, the dybbuk again lost much of its disturbing force: in line with interpretations surrounding its previous renditions proposed by Wajda and Warlikowski, it came to represent a (self-congratulatory) readiness to embrace the ›Polish-Jewish past‹. Admitting this time to the violent legacy brought to light in the wake of the Jedwabne debate, the memory finally acquired content, but the ›haunting‹, pointing towards the past, was again invoked in order to absolve the Poles. But what if the story was about the present (and presence), and not about memory and the past?

In his adaptation of Rowicki's play, *Demon*'s director (intentionally or not) made some choices that allow for such an analytical shift, and which bring the plot closer to the traditional dybbuk story.[34] The film is set in the Polish countryside, where a Polish bride, Żaneta, and a foreign groom, Python/Peter, prepare for a traditional Polish wedding. It only subtly addresses specific historical events: there is a formerly Jewish house appropriated during the war by a Pole (the grandfather of the bride), and a Jewish corpse buried in the backyard. We do not learn about the particularities of the crime – in fact, much is left unsaid – but for the Polish viewer the message becomes clear immediately: the film tackles the wartime violence against Jews and the dispossession of their property. Yet the past constitutes merely a backdrop for a drama which unfolds in the present: upon discovering the bones of a Jewish woman, Hana, in the yard of the house in which he came to dwell with his fiancée, Python is not himself anymore, he is disturbed, haunted and, eventually, possessed; the wedding turns into a nightmarish spectacle of drunkenness, hypocrisy, embarrassment, and brutality; as in *Clinging*, Python ends up sharing a grave with his possessor.

The transformation of Rowicki's Pyton/Piotr into Python/Peter is of major consequence. Wrona skillfully plays with Python's unsettled and unsettling otherness. He comes from London, but can sing a Polish song his grandmother brought him up with; his attempt to speak the language of the Polish villagers often meets with dismissal and he is forced to resort to English instead. Żaneta's brother describes Python as »not ›made in Poland‹ but could be worse«, simultaneously disarming but also reinforcing his foreignness. Reviewers also remain undecided over how to attribute Python's identity. He is British, assumed one critic, condemning Wrona for constructing him as such, and for casting an Israeli actor, Itay Tiran, in the leading role. »For

---

34 Marcin Wrona did not participate in the debates unfolding after the release of *Demon*. Two days after the first projection of the movie at the Gdynia Film Festival, on September 19, 2015, Marcin Wrona hanged himself in a hotel room. Speculations about the connection between his unexpected suicide and the work on the movie abounded. I would also propose one: had he not taken his life, the perception of the movie might have significantly differed. In one of his last interviews, contradicting later declarations by Maślona, Wrona conceded that the plot of *Demon* revolves »around an attempt to reenact the mechanisms which lead people to a crime committed – in their view – in the name of group survival« (quoted in Teatr Dramatyczny 2015). Not memory, but the perpetuation of the order, at all costs, was the subject of the script.

›Pyton‹-Pole this [Polish-Jewish history and/or possession] was not a new thing, although entirely forgotten, ›Pyton‹-foreigner will not understand the context of events, will not comprehend [...] what is happening to him«, he claimed (Chosiński 2017).³⁵ Other reviewers speculated, instead, on the Polish descent of the possessed (Balana 2015).³⁶ And yet, Pyton's ›Jewishness‹ is indicated almost from the outset: during the wedding ceremony, he stomps on a glass, Żaneta, in turn, throws hers behind her back, reminding Python that, according to Polish tradition, this is how it is to be done. The film seems to suggest that it is Python's Jewishness that makes Hana's ghost materialize before his eyes only; all the other wedding guests remain blind and insensitive to her spectral presence. Python's erratic behavior, arising from the possession, only enhances his otherness, rendering him ill, awkward, or insane in the eyes of the Poles. This goes on until Hana begins speaking Yiddish through his mouth, at first softly and anxiously, and then,

---

35 Apparently, now the dybbuk belongs exclusively to the Poles.
36 And indeed, such an interpretation could also be legitimate. When in conversation with the Jewish teacher, the only person who speaks Yiddish, the Jewish ghost discloses her ›identity‹, the teacher recounts being in love with Hana (the phantasmatic ›beautiful Jewish girl‹). Hana, in turn, was madly in love with a Pole. But one day she suddenly disappeared. In the final scene, her former house is demolished and the ruins reveal a wedding photograph depicting Hana and Python in a historical setting. The time bends entangling the present and the past: is Python the Polish man Hana loved? Does Python know Jewish wedding customs because they married according to Jewish tradition? Did the Polish community exclude or even murder him (and her) as a punishment for violating the rules governing ›encounters‹ between Poles and Jews based on a strict politics of belonging and othering? Another scene which could substantiate this (but also a different) interpretation unfolds immediately before the wedding: from the window of the wedding car, Python gazes at Hana as she and another person, a man carrying a briefcase, talk to a priest at a Catholic cemetery. Is she arranging a burial for her Polish husband killed by his fellow citizens? Or, rather, is this an allusion to a scene which took place in Jedwabne (and other Polish towns) immediately before the massacre. Namely, Jewish residents of the town, bearing gifts, valuables and money, asked (in vain) the most important moral authority, the priest, for protection from the local populace, for an intervention on their behalf (Bikont 2015 [2004]).

suddenly, with anger and unexpected strength. (Such strength did not come through even once in Rowicki's play, his Hana is consequently childish, vulnerable, and powerless.) The scene represents, in fact, a crucial breakthrough in the plot, after which the action takes a violent turn: Python is beaten up, gagged and, finally, disappears. Hana's strong and angry words are not translated either in the Polish or in the subtitled version of the movie; neither the wedding guests nor the viewers are meant to understand what she says. But the meaning of her words is all but insignificant, they have the power to cause mayhem. She shouts »go away from my house!«: !גייט ארויס פֿון מײַן הויז

The foreignness/otherness of Python effectively prevents him from being framed as a carrier of the Polish transformative encounter with the Jewish past. Hana's words, in turn, critically intervene in the imageries of Jewish ›absence‹ underlying the Polish construction of the figure of the dybbuk. The presence of her corpse in the backyard of *her* house, ownership over which she powerfully reclaims, anchors Hana's ghost in material continuity in and with the present. It illuminates the violence but also the vulnerability of the dominant order, as much symbolic/political as economic. The implied ›Jewishness‹ of Python, who acts as a medium through which Hana's words and demands materialize, renders him, therefore, into an embodiment of her ›cause‹: he comes to incorporate the threat associated with the possibility of Jews returning to reclaim their property, which has been misappropriated by the Poles – a possibility which has haunted the country ever since the 1989 transition (and the beginning of the still unresolved reprivatization and restitution debates). In PRL, the property rights to »this parcel« could have remained unclear; since 1989, when the liberal economic order based on private property was (re)introduced in Poland, the situation has become more complex – claims to property and land could have been put forward by former (prewar) owners.[37] As the doctor in Rowicki's *Clinging* (2015 [2008]:

---

37 For a discussion on various Polish post-1989 reprivatization debates and the ongoing problems with introducing the countrywide law that would, in fact, enable the restitution of Jewish private property, see for instance Stola (2007); Krawczyk (2012). The first reprivatization bill from 2001, which granted the right to restitution exclusively to previous owners holding Polish citizenship before the war and in 1999 (effectively excluding the vast majority of Polish Jews), was vetoed by the president, Andrzej Kwaśniewski (under pressure from the European

130) says in passing: »The priest says that the Jews came to take what's theirs«. In fact, throughout the ›Jewish turn‹, the figure of a ›Jew‹ returning to reclaim their property constitutes a (haunting) double of the figure of the Jewish ghost (as memory), deprived of any haunting force. The violence that *Demon* evokes is thus hardly an articulation of the unwillingness to, or fear of having to confront the uncomfortable memory of past events already familiar to everybody. Instead, the violence is a response to unsettling questions about the status of the current reality, the status quo, about fragile ownership, and about a present predicated upon the exclusion, murder and dispossession of the Jewish other. In this context, the exorcism takes on a new, revised form. And so, the (untranslated) words are effectively silenced, the carrier(s) of the threat removed, the temporarily threatened order restored and reinforced; and the community can forget that anything has ever happened. The father of the bride proclaims: »There never was a wedding. You weren't here. I wasn't here… Neither is there a groom. And there never was.« Only the house and the corpse(s) remain; and the normative, symbolic, political, and material order founded upon them. Nothing has changed, history simply repeats itself. So much for the transformative power of the dybbuk.

In the introduction to *Ghostly Matters*, Gordon quotes from Zora Neale Hurston's *The Sanctified Church*: »Ghosts hate new things« (2008 [1997]: xix). At first, the sentence seems to contradict her theorization of haunting as a »transformative recognition« calling for a change, for revision of dominant social relations, cultural discourses, affects, and subject positions. But, in fact, the opposite is true: the presence of a ghost is, first and foremost, an indication that the conditions that called forth its presence continue to *live on*, that they are not at all of the past but of the present. »Ghosts are characteristically attached to the events, things, and places that produced them in the first place; by nature they are haunting reminders of lingering trouble«, observes Gordon (2008 [1997]: xix). And as long as the fact that the ›trouble‹ lingers on remains unacknowledged, invisibilized, or denied, ghosts will return, time and again, endowed with varying capabilities to affect, to change, disrupt, and unsettle. This is also true for Polish incarnations of the dybbuk – what they testify to is the unacknowledged continuity, the persistent presence of the frames and sensibilities, the lingering power structures between

---

Commission and NATO); the latest project of the bill on restitution of prewar properties, proposed in 2017, is equally exclusionary.

the Poles and Jews, both living and dead, which are based on othering, violence and exclusion. Wrona's *Demon* makes this abundantly clear, and as such it introduces a shift, if a subtle one, in the distribution of »insights and blindnesses« pertaining to the ›Polish-Jewish‹ past and present. But a dybbuk invested with the ability to instantiate a change is, apparently, still to come – if it ever really does.

Literature

Aleksiun, Natalia (2002): Dokąd dalej? Ruch syjonistyczny w Polsce 1944–1950, Warsaw: Trio.
Alexander, Tamar (2003): »Love and Death in Contemporary *Dybbuk* Story: Personal Narrative and the Female Voice.« In: Matt Goldish (ed.), Spirit Possession in Judaism: Cases and Contexts from the Middle Ages to the Present, Detroit: Wayne State University Press, pp. 307-345.
An-sky, S. (2000 [1914/1919]): »The Dybbuk, or Between Two Worlds: A Dramatic Legend in Four Acts.« In: David G. Roskies (ed.), S. Ansky: The Dybbuk and Other Writings, New Haven and London: Yale University Press.
Arves, Fabienne/Warlikowski, Krzysztof (2010): »The Path to *The Dybbuk*.« In: Polish Theatre Perspectives 1/1, pp. 88-92.
Baksik, Łukasz (2012): Macewy codziennego użytku/Matzevot for Everyday Use, Wołowiec: Wydawnictwo Czarne.
Balana, Ewa (2015): »Wieloznaczny i mroczny *Demon* Marcina Wrony.« In: kulturalnie.waw.pl (http://kulturalnie.waw.pl/artykuly/2084/wieloznaczny-i-mroczny-demon-marcina-wrony.html).
Bart, Andrzej (2008): Fabryka muchołapek, Warszawa: WAB.
Basara, Zbigniew (2004): »Teatr zaangażowany i teatr zmęczony.« In: Nowy Dziennik 9193, October 10 (http://encyklopediateatru.pl/artykuly/129669/teatr-zaangazowany-i-teatr-zmeczony).
Basara, Zbigniew/Warlikowski, Krzysztof (2004): »Teatr zaangażowany i teatr zmęczony. Rozmowa z reżyserem teatralnym Krzysztofem Warlikowskim.« In: Nowy Dziennik 9193, October 10 (http://encyklopediateatru.pl/artykuly/129669/teatr-zaangazowany-i-teatr-zmeczony).
Bator, Joanna (2012): Ciemno, prawie noc, Warszawa: WAB.

Bernstein, Michael André (1994): Foregone Conclusions: Against Apocalyptic History, Oakland: University of California Press.

Bikont, Anna (2015 [2004]): The Crime and the Silence: A Quest for Truth of a Wartime Massacre, London: William Heinemann.

Błoński, Jan (1990 [1987]): »The Poor Poles Look at the Ghetto.« In: Antony Polonsky (ed.), ›My brother's keeper?‹: Recent Polish Debates on the Holocaust, London: Routledge, pp. 34-48.

Bryll, Ernest (1988a): »Dybuk a« In: Dybuk: Program, Kraków: Teatr Stary, unnumbered pages.

Bryll, Ernest (1988b): »Dybuk b« In: Dybuk: Program, Kraków: Teatr Stary, unnumbered pages.

Bryś, Marta (2009): »›(D)ybuk‹ w ›(A)polonii‹. Między dwoma światami.« Didaskalia. Gazeta Teatralna 92/93, pp. 18-20.

Buzgan, Chewel (1970): »Słowo od inscenizatora i reżysera.« In: Dybuk: Program, Warszawa: Państwowy Teatr Żydowski im. E. R. Kamińskiej, unnumbered pages.

Cała, Alina (1995 [1992]): The Image of the Jew in Polish Folk Culture, Jerusalem: Magnes Press.

Cała, Alina (2012): Żyd – wróg odwieczny? Antysemityzm w Polsce i jego źródła, Warszawa: Wydawnictwo Nisza.

Chajes, J. H. (2003): Between Worlds: Dybbuks, Exorcists, and Early Modern Judaism, Philadelphia: University of Pennsylvania Press.

Chapetsky, Paddy (2017 [1960]): The Tenth Man, London: Forgotten Books.

Carlebach, Shlomo/Mesinai, Susan Yael (1996): Shlomo's Stories: Selected Tales, Oxford: Rowman & Littlefield Publishers.

Charnysh, Volha/Finkel, Evgeny (2017): »The Death Camp Eldorado: Political and Economic Effects of Mass Violence.« In: American Political Science Review 111/4, pp. 801-818.

Cheyfitz, Eric (1997 [1991]): The Poetics of Imperialism: Translation and Colonization from *The Tempest* to *Tarzan*, Philadelphia: University of Pennsylvania Press.

Chruściński, Sebastian (2017): »Między *Dybbukiem* a *Weselem*.« In: Esensja. Magazyn Kultury Popularnej, May 8 (https://esensja.pl/film/recenzje/tekst.html?id=24533).

Chutnik, Sylwia (2014): »Muranooo.« In: Sylwia Chutnik, W krainie czarów, Kraków: Znak, pp. 177-211.

Cichopek-Gajraj, Anna (2014): Beyond Violence: Jewish Survivors in Poland and Slovakia, 1944-1948, Cambridge: Cambridge University Press.
Cieślak, Jacek (2003): »Powrót sąsiadów.« In: Reczpospolita 257, November 4, p. 6.
Cieślak, Jan/ Krall, Hanna/Warlikowski, Krzysztof (2003): »›Bez dybuków będziemy gorsi i głupsi‹. Rozmowa z Hanną Krall i Krzysztofem Warlikowskim.« In: Rzeczpospolita no 232 (https://archiwum.rp.pl /artykul/458642-Bez-dybukow-bedziemy-gorsi-i-glupsi.html).
Cywiński, Piotr (2005): »Na bezludziu dybbuk nie zamieszka.« In: Więź 4/558, pp. 24-30.
Czapliński, Lesław (2015): »Dybuk i jego żywot w sztuce.« In: Strefa Blogeratury (https://bulanowski.wordpress.com/2015/10/02/dybuk-i-jego-zywot-w-sztuce/)
Drobnik-Rogers, Justyna (2009): »Krzysztof Warlikowski: Theatre as a Collective (Autho)Therapy.« In: TheatreForum 35, pp. 10-16.
Elior, Rachel (2008): Dybbuks and Jewish Women in Social History, Mysticism and Folklore, Jerusalem and New York: Urim Publications.
Engelking, Barbara (2003): ›Szanowny Panie gistapo.‹ Donosy do władz niemieckich w warszawie i okolicach w latach 1940-1941, Warszawa: Wydawnictwo IFiS PAN.
Engelking, Barbara (2011): Jest taki piękny słoneczny dzień… Losy Żydów szukających ratunku na wsi polskiej 1942-45, Warszawa: Stowarzyszenie Centrum Badań nad Zagładą Żydów.
Engelking, Barbara/Grabowski, Jan (eds.) (2011): Zarys krajobrazu. Wieś Polska wobec zagłady Żydów 1942-45, Warszawa: Stowarzyszenie Centrum Badań nad Zagładą Żydów.
Engelking, Barbara/Grabowski, Jan (eds.) (2018): Dalej jest noc. Losy Żydów w wybranych powiatach okupowanej Polski, Warszawa: Centrum Badań nad Zagładą Żydów.
Forecki, Piotr (2010): Od Shoah do Strachu: Spory o polsko-żydowską przeszłość i pamięć w debatach publicznych, Poznań: Wydawnictwo Poznańskie.
Fortuna, Grzegorz (2015): »*Demon*. Wesele w domu złym.« In: film.org.pl, December 1 (https://film.org.pl/r/recenzje/demon-wesele-w-domu-zlym-2-70709/).
Gary, Romain (1968 [1967]): The Dance of Genghis Cohn, New York: World Publishing Company.

Goldish, Matt (2003): Spirit Possession in Judaism: Cases and Contexts from the Middle Ages to the Present, Detroit: Wayne State University Press.
Goldman, Eric A. (2011); Visions, Images and Dreams: Yiddish Film – Past and Present, Teaneck: HM Publishers.
Gordon, Avery (2008 [1997]): Ghostly Matters: Haunting and the Sociological Imagination, Minneapolis: University of Minnesota Press.
Grabowski, Jan (2008): Rescue for Money: ›Paid Helpers‹ in Poland, 1939-1945, Jerusalem: Yad Vashem.
Grabowski, Jan (2013 [2011]): Hunt for the Jews: Betrayal and Murder in German-Occupied Poland, Bloomington: Indiana University Press.
Grabowski, Jan/Libionka, Dariusz (eds.) (2014a): Klucze i kasa. O mieniu żydowskim w Polsce pod okupacją niemiecką i we wczesnych latach powojennych 1939-1950, Warszawa: Stowarzyszenie Centrum Badań nad Zagładą Żydów.
Grabowski, Jan/Libionka, Dariusz (2014b): »Wstęp.« In: Jan Grabowski/Dariusz Libionka, Klucze i kasa. O mieniu żydowskim w Polsce pod okupacją niemiecką i we wczesnych latach powojennych 1939-1950, Warszawa: Stowarzyszenie Centrum Badań nad Zagładą Żydów, pp. 7-28.
Gross, Jan Tomasz (2001 [2000]): Neighbors: The Destruction of the Jewish Community in Jedwabne. Princeton and New York: Princeton University Press.
Gross, Jan Tomasz (2006): Fear: Antisemitism in Poland after Auschwitz, Princeton: Princeton University Press.
Gruber, Ruth Ellen (2002): Virtually Jewish: Reinventing Jewish Culture in Europe, Berkley, Los Angeles and London: University of California Press.
Gruszczyński, Piotr/Warlikowski, Krzysztof (2010): »Life in a Cemetery.« In: Polish Theatre Perspectives 1/1, pp. 93-108.
Grynberg, Henryk (2001): The Jewish War and the Victory, Evanston and Illinois: Northwestern University Press.
Grynberg, Henryk (2003): Monolog polsko-żydowski, Wołowiec: Czarne.
Haltof, Marek (2012): Polish Film and the Holocaust: Politics and Memory, New York and Oxford: Bergham.
Hernik-Sapińska, Jagoda (2008): »»Płacze od soboty.«« In: Piotr Rowicki, Przylgnięcie, Performance Programme, Warszawa: Laboratorium Dramatu.

Hirsch, Marianne (1997): Family Frames: Photography, Narrative, and Postmemory, Cambridge and London: Harvard University Press.
Hirsch, Marianne (2012): The Generation of Postmemory: Writing and Visual Culture after the Holocaust, New York: Columbia University Press.
Hurwic-Nowakowska, Irena (1996): Żydzi polscy (1947-1950). Analiza więzi społecznej ludności żydowskiej, Warszawa: Wydawnictwo IFiS PAN.
Janicka, Elżbieta (2014-15): »Pamięć przyswojona. Koncepcja polskiego doświadczenia zagłady Żydów jako traumy zbiorowej w świetle rewizji kategorii świadka.« In: Studia Litteraria et Historica 3/4, pp. 148-226.
Janicka, Elżbieta/Steinlauf, Michael (2014-15): »›To nie była Ameryka.‹« In: Studia Litteraria et Historica 3/4, pp. 364- 480.
Janion, Maria (2003 [2002]): »Świadkowie, niewyrażalność i tragedia.« In: Krzysztof Warlikowski, Dybuk: Programme, Warszawa: Teatr Rozmaitości, unnumbered pages.
Józefczuk, Grzegorz (2008): »Duch dziejów i polski strach.« In: Gazeta Wyborcza 240, October 13 (http://www.e-teatr.pl/pl/artykuly/60677.html).
Karpiński, Maciej (1991): Teatr Andrzeja Wajdy, Warszawa: Wydawnictwa Artystyczne i Filmowe.
Kącki, Marcin (2015): Białystok. Biała siła, czarna pamięć, Wołowiec: Wydawnictwo Czarne.
Konigsberg, Ira (1997): »›The Only ›I‹ in the World‹: Religion, Psychoanalysis, and *The Dybbuk*.« In: Cinema Journal 36/4, pp. 22-42.
Kopka, Krzysztof (1988): »Oni tu żyli.« In: Teatr 8, August 1 (http://encyklopediateatru.pl/artykuly/77584/oni-tu-zyli).
Krall, Hanna (2005a [1995]): »The Dybbuk.« In: Hanna Krall, The Woman from Hamburg and Other Stories, New York: Other Press, pp. 137-154.
Krawczyk, Monika (2012): »Status prawny własności żydowskiej i jego wpływ na stosunki polsko-żydowskie.« In: Feliks Tych/Monika Adamczyk-Grabowska (eds.), Następstwa zagłady Żydów, Polska 1944-2010, Lublin: Wydawnictwo UMCS and ŻIH, pp. 687-713.
LaCapra, Dominick (1998): History and Memory after Auschwitz, Ithaca and London: Cornell University Press.
LaCapra, Dominick (2001): Writing History, Writing Trauma, Baltimore: John Hopkins University Press.
Lease, Bryce (2016): After '98: Polish Theatre and the Political, Manchester: Manchester University Press.

Leder, Andrzej (2014): Prześniona rewolucja. Ćwiczenia z logiki historycznej, Warszawa: Wydawnictwo Krytyki Politycznej.

Legutko, Agnieszka (2012): Possessed by the Other: Dybbuk Possession and Modern Jewish Identity in Twentieth-Century Jewish Literature and Beyond. PhD Dissertation, Columbia University.

Machcewicz, Paweł/Persak, Krzysztof (eds.) (2002): Wokół Jedwabnego. Studia, Warszawa: Wydawnictwo IPN.

Majewski, Szymon/Rowicki, Piotr (2008): »Rozmowa z Piotrem Rowickim.« Teatr Dramatyczny m. st. Warszawy (http://teatrdramatyczny.pl/index.php?option=com_content&view=article&id=247:rozmowa-z-piotrem-rowickim&catid=70&Itemid=202).

Mamoń, Bronisław (1988): »Dybuk.« In: Tygodnik Powszechny 13, March 27 (http://encyklopediateatru.pl/artykuly/77559/dybuk).

Matyjaszek, Konrad (2013): Przestrzeń pożydowska. In: Studia Litteraria et Historica 3, pp. 130-147.

Matyjaszek, Konrad (2018): Produkcja przestrzeni żydowskiej w miastach dawnej i współczesnej Polski. Kraków: Universitas.

Mazur, Daria (2007): Dybuk, Poznań: Wydawnictwo Naukowe UAM.

Meng, Michael (2011): Shattered Spaces: Encountering Jewish Ruins in Postwar Germany and Poland, Cambridge and London: Harvard University Press.

Michlic, Joanna Beata (2006): Poland's Threatening Other: The Image of the Jew from 1880 to the Present, Lincoln and London: University of Nebraska Press.

Morewski, Abram (1957): »Od reżysera«. In: Dybuk: Program, Warszawa: Państwowy Teatr Żydowski im. E. R. Kamińskiej.

Neugroschel, Joachim (2000): The Dybbuk and the Yiddish Imagination: A Haunted Reader, New York: Syracuse University Press.

Niziołek, Grzegorz (2013): Polski teatr Zagłady, Warszawa: Wydawnictwo Krytyki Politycznej.

Ostachowicz, Igor (2012): Noc żywych Żydów, Warszawa: WAB.

Partga, Ewa (2004): »Trz w jednym.« In: Dekada Literacka 1, pp. 100-105.

Pascal, Julia (2009 [1992]): »The Dybbuk«. In: The Holocaust Trilogy, London: Oberon Books.

Peeren, Esther (2014): The Spectral Metaphor: Living Ghosts and the Agency of Invisibility, New York: Palgrave Macmillan.

Peñalosa, Fernando (2012): The Dybbuk: Text, Subtext, and Context, Palos Verdes: Tsiterboym Books.
Pysiak, Krzysztof (1988): »Między miłością a ortodoksją.« In: Życie Warszawy 72, March 27 (http://www.e-teatr.pl/pl/artykuly/77598,druk.html).
Romanowska, Dagmara (2015): »*Demon*: Gdy duchy znów przemawiają.« In: Onet film, September 14 (https://kultura.onet.pl/film/recenzje/demon-gdy-duchy-znowu-przemawiaja-recenzja/ptczx1y).
Rosenberg, Joel (2011): »The Soul of Catastrophe: On the 1937 Film of S. An-sky's *The* Dybbuk.« In: Jewish Social Studies 17/2, pp. 1-27.
Rowicki, Piotr (2015 [2008]): »Przylgnięcie.« In: Ikony, pseudoherosi i zwykli śmiertelnicy. Antologia najnowszego dramatu polskiego, Warszawa: Agencja Dramatu i Teatru.
Rudnicki, Adolf (1987): Teatr zawsze grany, Warszawa: Czytelnik.
Rudnicki, Adolf (1988a [1987]): Untitled. In: Dybuk: Program, Kraków: Teatr Stary, unnumbered pages.
Rudnicki, Adolf (1988b [1987]): Untitled. In: Dybuk: Program, Kraków: Teatr Stary, unnumbered pages.
Safran, Gabriella (2000): »Dancing with Death and Salvaging Jewish Culture in *Austeria* and *The Dybbuk*.« In: Slavic Review 59/4, pp. 761-781.
Safran, Gabriella (2010): Wondering Soul: *The Dybbuk*'s Creator, S. An-sky, Cambridge and London: Harvard University Press.
Sikorska-Miszczuk, Małgorzata (2014 [2011]): »The Mayor.« In: Krystyna Duniec/Joanna Klass/Joanna Krakowska (eds.), (A)pollonia: Twenty-First Century Polish Drama and Texts for the Stage, Calcutta: Seagull Books, pp. 58-121.
Skibell, Joseph (1997): A Blessing on the Moon, New York: Algonquin Books.
Słobodzianek, Tadeusz (2010 [2009]): Our Class, London: Oberon Books.
Sobolewski, Tadeusz (2003): »Narodziny dybuka.« In: Gazeta Wyborcza 235, October 8 (http://www.e-teatr.pl/pl/artykuly/77429,druk.html).
Sobolewski, Tadeusz/Krall, Hanna/Warlikowski, Krzysztof (2003): »Narodziny dybuka. Rozmowa z twórcami.« In: Gazeta Wyborcza 235, October 8 (http://www.e-teatr.pl/pl/artykuly/77429,druk.html).
Stańczyk, Ewa (2014): »The Absent Jewish Child: Photography and Holocaust Representation in Poland.« In: Journal of Modern Jewish Studies 13/3, pp. 360-380.

Steinlauf, Michael (2006): »›Fardibekt!‹: An-sky's Polish Legacy.« In: Gabriella Safran and Steven J. Zipperstein, The Worlds of S. An-sky: A Jewish Intellectual at the Turn of the Century, Stanford: Stanford University Press.
Steinlauf, Michael (2010): »Poland's Dybbuks: A Response to the Warlikowski Dialogues.« In: Polish Theatre Perspectives 1/1, pp. 109-114.
Stola, Dariusz (2007): »The Polish Debate on the Holocaust and the Restitution of Property.« In: Martin Dean/ Constantin Goschler/Philip Ther (eds.), Robbery and Restitution: The Conflict Over Jewish Property in Europe, New York and Oxford: Berghan Books, pp. 240-252.
Szczurek, Marian (1988): »Wśród popiołów.« In: Trybuna Opolska 181, August 6 (http://encyklopediateatru.pl/artykuly/77612/wsrod-popiolow).
Teatr Dramatyczny (2015): »Marcin Wrona nakręci film według *Przylgnięcia* Piotra Rowickiego.« In: Teatr Dramatyczny (http://teatrdramatyczny .pl/index.php?option=com_content&view=article&id=1825:marcin-wrona-nakrci-film-wedug-qprzylgniciaq-piotra-rowickiego&catid=81&Itemid=335).
Tokarska-Bakir, Joanna (2004): »Obsesja niewinności.« In: Joanna Tokarska-Bakir, Rzeczy mgliste. Eseje i studia, Sejny: Fundacja Pogranicze, pp. 13-22.
Trachtenberg, Joshua (2013): Jewish Magic and Superstition: A Study in Folk Religion, Mansfield: Martino Publishing.
Tuszyńska, Agata (1998): Lost Landscapes: In Search of Isaac Bashevis Singer and the Jews of Poland, New York: William Morrow and Company.
Unknown (1989): »Żydowskie *Dziady*.« In: Trybuna Opolska 77, April 3 (http://www.e-teatr.pl/pl/artykuly/77609.html).
Unterman, Alan (1991): Dictionary of Jewish Lore and Legend, London: Thames and Hudson.
Wach-Malicka, Henryka (1989): »Opowieść o świecie chasydów.« In: Dziennik Zachodni 78, April 4 (http://encyklopediateatru.pl /artykuly/77591/opowiesc-o-swiecie-chasydow).
Warzecha, Agata (2008): »Tu w środku coś płacze.« In: Dlastudenta.pl, October 21 (https://warszawa.dlastudenta.pl/teatr/artykul/tu-w-srodku-cos-placze,27277.html).
Wolitz, Seth L. (2006): »Inscribing An-sky's *Dybbuk* in Russian and Jewish Letters.« In: In: Gabriella Safran and Steven J. Zipperstein, The Worlds

of S. An-sky: A Jewish Intellectual at the Turn of the Century, Stanford: Stanford University Press.

Wyka, Kazimierz (1957): Życie na niby. Szkice z lat 1939—1945, Warszawa: Książka i Wiedza.

Zalewska, Kalina (2008): »Krajobraz po Grossie.« In: Dziennik Teatralny 12, December 15 (http://www.dziennikteatralny.pl/artykuly/krajobraz-po-grossie.html).

Zipperstein, Steven J. (2006): »Introduction: An-sky and the Guises of Modern Culture.« In: Gabriella Safran and Steven J. Zipperstein, The Worlds of S. An-sky: A Jewish Intellectual at the Turn of the Century, Stanford: Stanford University Press.

Żbikowski, Andrzej (2012): »Morderstwa popełniane na Żydach w pierwszych latach po wojnie.« In: Feliks Tych/Monika Adamczyk-Grabowska (eds.), Następstwa zagłady Żydów, Polska 1944-2010, Lublin: Wydawnictwo UMCS and ŻIH, pp. 71-93.

Not Your House, not Your Flat
Jewish Ghosts in Poland
and the Stolen Jewish Properties

Konrad Matyjaszek

Ghosts are real. And yet, most studies that analyze hauntings in literary texts, visual cultures, or (less often) in lived practice tend to depict ghosts as illusions, delusions, rhetorical figures, as figures of the imagination, of language, or art. Doesn't this approach leave us with a sense that our tendency to order and normalize things has deprived us of our knowledge of the specter's true identity; a sense that this unreflecting banishing of the ghost into the non-physical realms of psychology or literature might further conceal a substance hidden behind its non-materiality, a substance surprisingly solid, physical, and concrete?

This doubt refers strongly to the ghosts of Jews, particularly ghosts of Holocaust victims. In recent decades, Poles have reported sightings of such ghosts in their houses, in their public spaces, their cinemas, theatres and books.[1] This article attempts to track the history of a turn towards elusiveness

---

1   For an analysis of the absence of visual traces of Jewish history and the history of the Holocaust in the public spaces of Warsaw, see Janicka (2012). For Polish culture's visual vocabulary and iconography of ignoring Jewish history and the history of the Holocaust, see Janion (2009a, 2009b). For an analysis of Holocaust motifs in contemporary Polish theater, including an analysis of the categories of fear and trauma, see Niziołek (2019). Concepts of haunting Jewish ghosts are

and the uncanny that has been evident in the Polish Holocaust debate since 1989 in spite of the fact that unlike any other country Poland not only contains concrete material evidence of the mass murder and expropriation of European Jews, but in and of itself is evidence to these events. This chapter looks at contemporary Polish perceptions of Jews as bodiless non-subjects, transparent and mute, and at the relationship between contemporary Poles' sightings of Jewish ghosts and ideologies of collective identity developed within the Polish majority's culture during the last decades of the twentieth and the turn of the twenty-first century.

THE PHENOMENOLOGY OF GHOSTS

The doubt indicated above is a concern that the scholarly, analytical reduction of a ghost's non-material body to the sphere of psychology or literature carries a risk of further distancing this body's non-materiality from the matter it makes manifest. Philosopher Dylan Trigg attempts to counter this reduction by creating an analytical toolbox of a »phenomenology of ghosts«, and notes that »the phenomenon of the ghost risks being reduced to mental activity, which is taken as either an exercise in unreality or a blockage in a previously lived reality«. He adds: »Clearly, there is something unsatisfactory in the attempt to explain the experience of ghostly phenomenon in terms of either memory or imagination.« (Trigg 2012: 284) Trigg calls for equal attention to be paid to the embodiment of both sides of an instance of haunting, for »bridging a gulf that lies between conditions of haunting and being haunted«, between the seemingly separate subjects of these two actions (ibid: 287). His observation is largely in accord with an interpretation proposed by Maria Janion, a Polish literary theorist and analyst of culture who discusses ghostly apparitions in Polish Romantic drama, and asks:

Could ghosts be approached psychologically? Do they exist in the same way as humans? No, we instantly respond. But at the same time we pay little attention to the autonomy of ghosts in the drama of Polish Romanticism. And what is the nature of a represented relationship between ghosts and people [...]? Ghosts exist fully

---

discussed in Dziuban (2014), Waligórska (2014), and Sendyka (2016) [Editor's note: Waligórska's and Sendyka's articles are reprinted in this volume].

autonomously, are not emanations of the human psyche as it is claimed sometimes […], and even more – they interfere between themselves and with people. How to understand this? Certainly not with some specific ›ghost psychology‹, because there is no such theory, if it, indeed, would be a ›specific‹ psychology and not merely an imitation of the psychology of humans. What, however, does exist is a ›phenomenology of ghosts‹. (1991: 217)

What is this ghostly phenomenology? The classical phenomenological theorization of a living existence emphasizes one's topographical rooting, one's right to be in a body, to occupy a location and claim it for oneself. The phenomenology of human beings is a knowledge of modes in which a lived body occupies a space. Maurice Merleau-Ponty writes:

The word ›here‹ applied to my body does not refer to a determinate position in relation to other positions or to external coordinates, but the laying down of the first co-ordinates, the anchoring of the active body in an object, the situation of the body in face of its tasks. Bodily space can be distinguished from external space and envelop its parts instead of spreading them out, because it is the darkness needed in the theatre to show up the performance, the background of somnolence or reserve of vague power against which the gesture and its aim stand out, the zone of not being in front of which precise beings, figures and points can come to light. (2005 [1945]: 115)

The phenomenology of ghosts defines a parallel set of rules that apply to those without such a privilege. It allows an understanding of the embodiment of those who have no right to bodily space and no anchor in the external world. It attributes spatial rules to those who remain outside the scene, in the night's darkness, half-conscious; to those whose coordinates are set by someone else, who are refused even a vague power to perform basic gestures. The phenomenology of ghosts is a knowledge about the existence of those who have no place to exist, and yet are sensed or seen. To see a person who is not »here« is to see a space that is not occupied by this non-person's body, a space that was denied to them, a space they were forced to leave. The phenomenology of ghosts is, therefore, the knowledge of bodily and spatial repression. And the haunted person would know this: from their own deeds that exclude others from spaces in which to »situate the body« or from previous instances of gaze directed at a non-person that was deprived of such space. To quote Trigg again: »When we are shocked by things in the night, then it is only because we already have a relationship not only with the night, but also with the things that seek to commune with us from the beyond.« (2012: 289)

THE HAUNTED HAUNT THEMSELVES

»The gulf that lies between« the haunted and those who haunt is not necessarily a chasm of death. It is created by repression, by physical or symbolic violence. Repression may and would cause death, but death itself is not the primary reason for the existence of ghosts – it is a consequence. Repression, in this context, cannot be limited to a Freudian meaning of the term; it is not merely an act of delegating phenomena to the unconscious, but, rather, the prime consequence of a *hegemony*, of a socio-political situation described by Marxist philosopher Antonio Gramsci and further theorized by others, among them Henri Lefebvre. Lefebvre wrote that

Hegemony implies more than an influence, more even than the permanent use of repressive violence. It is exercised over society as a whole, culture and knowledge included, and generally via human mediation: policies, political leaders, parties, as also a good many intellectuals and experts. (1991 [1974]: 10)

From this point of view, It is neither a repressed memory nor the hiatus between the dead and the living that forces ghosts into and out of their dark non-spaces. Quite the opposite: it is the political and public rules of the phenomenology of the living and embodied that define, in reverse, the phenomenology of ghosts, their negative phenomenology. Zuzanna Dziuban observes that, in significant sections of critical theory, »ghosts [...] were either relegated to act merely as a subject of art or interpreted in terms of a projection of a troubled psyche or individual mind«. She argues that the publication of Jacques Derrida's *Specters of Marx* (1994 [1993]) initiated a shift »of the problem of haunting from the margins to the center of theoretical reflection«, leading to »a radical reconceptualization of the ghost as a philosophical problem« (2014: 114-115). For Derrida, central to the act of haunting is a return – not just the return of a ghost, but, most importantly, also of the socio-political context that forces a ghost to reappear; not just a return of the individual or collective unconscious, but yet another reappearance of repressive ideologies already known from previous stages of modernity.² The question of haunting is, for Derrida, »a question of repetition: a specter is always a revenant. One cannot control its comings and goings because it begins by coming back« (1994 [1993]: 11).

As for the specific repetition that haunts the text of *Specters of Marx*, Derrida was composing his essay during a significant historical moment. The book was written and published shortly after 1989, a year that was to mark the start of a new political era. It was then that the capitalist, liberal West announced the death of communism, of socialism, of left-wing ideologies epitomized by Marx's and Friedrich Engel's *Communist Manifesto* – a text that was to recede, and disappear, from the political landscape – and substituted these for a new theorization, that of »the end of history«. In 1989, history was coming to a close; ideologies were ending; no alternative was available. And, as Derrida points out, it was not the specter of Karl Marx that haunted Europe in 1989, or in the years that followed. What was (re)emerging was the cultural mechanism that holds the power to induce haunting, to produce ghosts. Derrida noted:

At a time when a new world disorder is attempting to install its neo-capitalism and neo-liberalism, no disavowal has managed to rid itself of all of Marx's ghosts. Hegemony still organizes the repression and thus the confirmation of a haunting. Haunting belongs to the structure of every hegemony.³ (1994 [1993]: 45-46)

---

2 Derrida writes about the scholarly reduction of ghosts: »What seems almost impossible is to speak always of the specter, to speak to the specter, to speak with it, therefore especially to make or to let a spirit speak. And the thing seems even more difficult for a reader, an expert, a professor, an interpreter, in short, for what [Shakespeare's] Marcellus calls a ›scholar‹. Perhaps for a spectator in general. Finally, the last one to whom a specter can appear, address itself, or pay attention is a spectator as such. At the theater or at school. The reasons for this are essential. As theoreticians or witnesses, spectators, observers, and intellectuals, scholars believe that looking is sufficient. Therefore, they are not always in the most competent position to do what is necessary: speak to the specter.« (1994 [1993]: 7).

3 In *Specters of Marx*, Derrida uses the term repression in both psychological and Marxist contexts, yet in a footnote to the quoted sentences discussing the relation between repression and hegemony he clarifies: »For a novel elaboration, in a ›deconstructive‹ style, of the concept of hegemony, I refer to Ernesto Laclau and

Derrida's observation holds a revolutionary importance both for understanding the »phenomenology of ghosts« in general and for grasping the mechanics of sightings of Holocaust victims' ghosts by contemporary Poles. If, as Derrida claims, haunting results from hegemonic structures, then it is not the ghost who causes the haunting but the haunted subject, and this subject is being haunted as a result of his or her own participation in hegemonic practices. Consequently, if the instance of haunting is structurally embedded in and resultant from the establishment of a hegemony, then it appears that the members of a hegemonic collective haunt themselves by means of a ghost; they are the ones who establish a ghost, shape it, (dis)place it, and produce it. In the light of Derrida's conceptualization, the act of haunting becomes less of an unexpected and shocking event, and more of a narcissistic action performed by those who own the means of hegemonic production, who »have a relationship not only with the night«, but also with the ghost itself. It transpires that the members of a hegemonic group hold the power to make a non-person a ghost, to alienate the ghost from the place where it shows itself, to cause an instance of haunting, and, finally, to be terrified by such an encounter. It is less surprising that a hegemonic influence will reach beyond the sphere of social, political and cultural visibility; what does surprise us is the idea of the ghost's insignificance, non-materiality, non-spatiality and muteness as essential parts of the dynamics of social, political and cultural power. In conditions of a »permanent use of repressive violence« exercised by »policies, political leaders, parties, as also a good many intellectuals and experts« (Lefebvre 1991 [1974]: 10), the ghost is as much invisible and absent as it is irreplaceable for legitimizing the haunted groups in their hegemonic status.

Chantal Mouffe, *Hegemony and Socialist Strategy: Toward a Radical Democratic Politics.*« (1994 [1993]: 46; Laclau/Mouffe 1985). Laclau's perspective on repression is discussed in *New Reflections on the Revolution of Our Time*, where he asserts that »all objectivity necessarily presupposes the repression of that which is excluded by its establishment. To talk of repression immediately suggests all kinds of violent images. But this is not necessarily the case. By ›repression‹ we simply mean the external suppression of a decision, conduct or belief, and the imposition of alternatives which are not in line with them.« (1990: 31)

THE TRAUMATIZED POLISH WITNESS

Importantly for the ghosts of Jews in Poland, and particularly for the ghosts of Holocaust victims, during the same political revolution of 1989, the hegemonic position was secured in Poland by the ›new‹ Polish nation, an imagined community established as the Polish communist political system ended. This group defined itself through values of anti-communism, capitalism, and Catholicism.[4] Its establishment certainly constituted yet another repetition, another return of a set of political ideologies developed by Poles in the course of the 19th century and during the years of the Polish Republic before the Second World War. Polish social life in the early 1990s was certainly not haunted by the specter of Marx but – precisely as Derrida argued – by the returning specters of neo-capitalism and neoliberalism, accompanied by revenants that only few observers in the West would recognize at this early stage: nationalism, Catholicism employed as a political ideology, and Romantic political messianism that placed special emphasis on territorial ›home‹ as the nation's seat,[5] as well as on collective suffering perceived as an act of community-making.[6] The hegemonic position of the newly established community was not – and could not have been – obvious: precisely because it was based on the Polish ideology of national suffering, infused with religious symbols, and intended to turn individual and collective victimhood into a political act, any claims that the Polish nation achieved a hegemonic position after 1989 would have been considered a sacrilege. It would have been even more blasphemous (partly even for international voices) to assert that the post-1989 Polish majority deployed »permanent repressive violence« in order to secure the imagined community's collective goals, or that such a violence was imposed »on society as a whole, including its culture and knowledge«. However, if seen through the prism of apparitions of Holocaust victims, the results of such violence exerted on society, culture and

---

4 For an analysis of the Polish revolution of 1989–1990, see Ost (1990; 2005). For a discussion of the nationalism that developed during that period, see Zubrzycki (2006).
5 For a discussion on the cultural structures of post-communist Eastern European concepts of home and domestication, see Leach (1999).
6 For a discussion of antisemitic mythologies of Polish Romanticism and Enlightenment, see Janion (2014).

knowledge become evident. Once we realize how suffering had become a core aspect of Polish political ideologies, it becomes clear that the Polish majority gained its power by exploiting narratives of real or imagined suffering, and that its ideologies were (and still are) constructed by appropriation of the Holocaust victims' suffering and collective trauma.

The concept of suffering as the basis of Polish collective identity is an old one, dating back at least to the 19th century. After 1989, it was expanded with an assertion that the Holocaust, the mass murder of Jews, was a psychological trauma experienced collectively by Poland's Catholic majority. Literary and cultural theorist Elżbieta Janicka argues that this assertion became the foundation of a Polish collective identity. As early as the 1990s, it translated into a morally charged concept of the Polish »witnessing« of the Holocaust, and finally took on the shape of a »traumatic paradigm« (2014-15: 150-152, 187-192).[7] This paradigm counterfactually separated non-Jewish Poles from the events of the genocide of Jews and the plundering of their properties.[8] It resulted in the creation of notions of a Polish »passivity« and »indifference« in the face of German Nazi atrocities, and as such was to supersede knowledge about Polish collaboration with the Nazi regime and

---

7 Janicka comments: »I perceive the concept of a traumatic Polish experience of the Holocaust as one of the strategies of internalizing this experience. It is a safe strategy, since it does not interfere with boundary conditions defined by the Polish dominant culture. What precisely happened is that the researchers working in Poland (or working on a Poland-originating material) – in their majority did not make an attempt to confront and to coordinate their research tools with the object of research. Acceptance of the toolset that defines the traumatic paradigm was largely uncritical. Also uncritical was their relation to the object of research – to the Holocaust narrative and to the absence of a Holocaust narrative. The shape of this narrative or its absence was explained as a result of a trauma, most often without an attempt to measure and problematize the gap between a representation of facts and knowledge about the facts derived from various sources. Absent was an awareness of their own location and of their own assumptions, which are especially necessary when a researcher speaks for one's own case.« (2014-15: 187)

8 For historical analyses of the participation of Poles in the Holocaust, see Gross/Grudzińska-Gross (2012 [2011]), Grabowski (2013 [2011]), Grabowski/Libionka (2014), Engelking/Grabowski (2018).

about Polish crimes against Jews perpetrated during and after the war (Janicka 2014-15: 163-165).

Janicka attributes the authorship of the concept of a »Polish trauma of the Holocaust« to American literary historian Michael C. Steinlauf, and notes that Steinlauf, firstly, »located reflection on the consequences of the Holocaust for the Poles in the field of posttraumatic culture [developed with an original purpose to describe the experiences of Jewish survivors – K.M.]« (ibid: 148; Steinlauf 1997).[9] Secondly, in Janicka's view, Steinlauf »assumed a structural relation between Jewish and Polish experience of the Holocaust«, allowing a situation to emerge where »the ›Polish Holocaust trauma‹ and the ›trauma of a witness‹ become accepted terms in the language of the [Polish] public debate« (Janicka 2014-15: 150, 148). Following this appropriation, the concept of a »trauma of the witness« became a reference point for Polish debates on the Holocaust, and has only occasionally been criticized and questioned.[10] A resultant situation was identified by literary historian Irena

---

9   Steinlauf proposed an analysis of the Holocaust as a shock that impacted on Polish Catholics and resulted in a »psychic numbing« that was to affect their worldview, and could have been a reason for Polish antisemitism and postwar Polish mass murders of Jews (Steinlauf 1997: 56-58). Critically engaging with this perspective, Janicka argues that Steinlauf »constructed his theory in relation to the Poles defined as witnesses of the Holocaust«, on the one hand approving of the Polish practice of translating the word »bystander« into the Polish *świadek*, which literally means »witness«, and on the other hand disregarding the critique of Raul Hilberg's theorization of the concept of the idle and inactive Holocaust »bystander« (Janicka 2014-15: 150).

10 A most influential critique of the »Polish witness« category was initiated by a »new approach to sources« proposed by Jan T. Gross. In *Neighbors*, an analysis of the history and background of the Jedwabne massacre, Gross commented that »it is simply not true that Jews were murdered in Poland during the war solely by the Germans, occasionally assisted in the execution of their gruesome task by some auxiliary police formations [...], not to mention the proverbial ›fall guys‹ whom everybody castigated because it was so easy not to take responsibility for what they had done – the so-called szmalcowniks, extortionists who made a profession of blackmailing Jews trying to pass and survive in hiding. By singling them out as culprits, historians and others have found it easy to bring closure to the matter by saying that there is ›scum‹ in every society, that these were a few

Grudzińska-Gross as a shift in the Polish self-image: a change from post-1989 self-identification as a society »›in transition‹, a ›normal‹ country, just like any other European country, returning to its usual, pre-Soviet-dominance way of being«, to a stage which »turned the politics of normalcy into the politics of trauma. [...] Poland was not a country just like any other anymore; it became a country of suffering« (Grudzińska-Gross 2016: 37)

A NORMAL COUNTRY

The appropriative concept of the Holocaust as the Poles' collective trauma has become a device of identity production across the entire political spectrum in Poland. Widely used by the overtly antisemitic nationalist right (as Grudzińska-Gross herself points out), it has also been deployed by authors with a liberal orientation, willing to see Poland as a ›normal European country‹. From such a non-nationalist perspective, the concept of a »trauma of the witness« is employed not so much to construct Poland's »exceptional« status as to further »normalize« the country's image by pointing out its connection to the public memory work performed in post-1968 West Germany and in other European Union member states. For authors representing this political position, the condition of being self-declaratively traumatized and haunted is

> ›socially marginal‹ individuals, and that they were dealt with by underground courts anyway. After Jedwabne the issue of Polish-Jewish relations during the war can no longer be put to rest with such ready-made formulas. Indeed, we have to rethink not only wartime but also postwar Polish history, as well as reevaluate certain important interpretive themes widely accepted as explanations accounting for outcomes, attitudes, and institutions of those years. To begin with, I suggest that we should modify our approach to sources for this period. When considering survivors' testimonies, we would be well advised to change the starting premise in appraisal of their evidentiary contribution from a priori critical to in principle affirmative. By accepting what we read in a particular account as fact until we find persuasive arguments to the contrary, we would avoid more mistakes than we are likely to commit by adopting the opposite approach, which calls for cautious skepticism toward any testimony until an independent confirmation of its content has been found. The greater the catastrophe the fewer the survivors.« (Gross 2001 [2000]: 138-140; italics in original)

a sufficient indicator that »memory work« is taking place in Poland, and that the country is adapting to the European postwar »memory culture«. At the same time these adherents of a »politics of normalcy« chose to overlook the general absence of Polish public education on the history of violence perpetrated by Poles on Jews, bypassing also the results of a fundamental change in European identity. In *Postwar,* Tony Judt noticed that what nowadays constitutes a »European entry ticket« is the recognition of the Holocaust as an »oppressive heritage«, a heritage that sees Christian Europeans as oppressors (2007 [2005]: 803). Commenting on the case of Poland, Judt wrote that such recognition would entail »officially acknowledging the war-time sufferings of Polish Jews, including their victimization at the hands of Poles themselves« (ibid.). Yet, with the exception of commemorations of the Jedwabne massacre (mentioned by Judt),[11] Polish public attempts to join the »memory culture« were focused not on allowing for victims' voices to be heard, but on appropriation of their position by spreading the »traumatic paradigm« over the contemporary Polish majority, the proprietor of the hegemonic tools of cultural production. Jewish ghosts were to become a means of Polish national identity-making.

In 2008, literary theorist Katarzyna Bojarska wrote in the context of Polish literature on the Holocaust that, »while in statements of Holocaust scholars the concept of ›postmemory‹[12] relates primarily to the children of

---

11 Judt writes that »In 2004 [it was, in fact, in 2001 – K.M], President Kwasniewski of Poland – seeking to close a painful chapter in his nation's past and bring Poland into line with its European Union partners – officially acknowledged the war-time sufferings of Polish Jews, including their victimization at the hands of Poles themselves« (2007 [2005]: 803).

12 Marianne Hirsh, who coined the term, writes: »Postmemory is the term I came to on the basis of my autobiographical readings of works by second generation writers and visual artists. The ›post‹ in ›postmemory‹ signals more than a temporal delay and more than a location in an aftermath. Postmodern, for example, inscribes both a critical distance and a profound interrelation with the modern; postcolonial does not mean the end of the colonial but its troubling continuity […]. Postmemory shares the layering of these other ›posts‹ and their belatedness, aligning itself with the practice of citation and mediation that characterize them, marking a particular end-of-century/turn-of-century moment of looking backward rather than ahead and of defining the present in relation to a troubled past rather

those saved from the Holocaust«, in her view »this concept can also accurately describe other, similar cases, and in the Polish context it achieves a particular importance, if we consider a specific ›haunting‹ of spaces by an uncanny character of events that took place in it« (2008: 90). Bojarska advocates the existence of a »Polish postmemory [of the Holocaust]«, and claims that »its sources are: works of culture, Holocaust sites, camps, memorials, and museums with the material remains of the Jewish world represented by them. And also numerous traces left by the Holocaust in the structure of cities and towns« (ibid.). Bojarska's argument is in accordance with an analysis by cultural anthropologist Magdalena Waligórska, who focuses on the cultural images of Holocaust victims' ghosts and argues:

[The] topos of the Jew as incorporeal, yet related to real historical events [...] suggests the emergence of a paradigm of memory, in which the medium of the fantastic is employed to deal with a collective trauma. In this case, however, the trauma is not that of Holocaust survivors, but one derived from what we could term a ›postmemory of witnesses‹, and is a specifically Polish one. (2014: 209)

Acknowledging that the concept of postmemory has been developed to describe experiences transmitted by the survivors, Waligórska nonetheless believes that »it is possible to use this category to investigate the way that images and narratives of trauma become transmitted not only among the descendants of victims, but also to children of bystanders, and even to perpetrators of the Holocaust« (ibid: 209-210).

Obviously, the possibility exists. Holding a hegemonic position in the field of culture and language makes much possible, but at what cost? The cost does not come up for discussion, because it is paid by the ghost. Waligórska does not specify the initial source of the trauma; in any case, the postmemory (a memory transmitted from previous generations) she describes does not seem to be connected to Jewish survivors. Instead, it is

---

than initiating new paradigms. Like them, it reflects an uneasy oscillation between continuity and rupture. And yet postmemory is not a movement, method, or idea; I see it, rather, as a structure of inter- and trans-generational transmission of traumatic knowledge and experience. It is a consequence of traumatic recall but (unlike posttraumatic stress disorder) at a generational remove.« (Hirsch 2008: 106)

expressed as a »memory of a [Polish] witness« which is »transmitted [...] to children of bystanders«. Consequently, the memory of violence perpetrated on Jews is attributed to the post-1989 phantasm of »Polish witnesses«, while the survivors' memory of the events is reduced to merely a comparable phenomenon, allowing for the bystanders' intergenerational processes to be recognized. Within this new »paradigm of memory« (undoubtedly identical with the Polish »traumatic paradigm« described by Janicka), the ghosts are assigned the duty of constructing the modern Polish self-image, while at the same time being dispossessed of their own memory and of its topographical, architectural and symbolic locations. This ›employment‹ of ghosts renders them into means of »dealing with a collective trauma«, a »specifically Polish« trauma for that matter. And to »deal with« means to »heal« (»healing by haunting«, as the title of Waligórska's text clarifies); to »deal with« is to cure the collective wounds allegedly inflicted on Poles by the act of helplessly or actively »witnessing« the Holocaust. Jewish ghosts are »employed« to restore wellbeing to the Polish national community, a community still »in transition«, still building its ›democratic‹, ›tolerant‹, ›European‹ and ›pluralistic‹ image. It is as if the alleged Polish Holocaust trauma was impeding the Polish nation's »normalizing«, and the ghost of a Holocaust victim, a »medium of the fantastic«, was here to help.

Bojarska's text adds more detail to the description of a position accorded to Jewish ghosts within Poland's »memory work«. A shift is also performed here, allowing the memory of a Jewish survivor to be appropriated as a »postmemory« of ethnic Poles. Bojarska posits that the category of postmemory »can also accurately describe other, similar cases« (2008: 90). Her assertion of »similarity« between otherwise sharply dissimilar war experiences of Jews and ethnic Poles is emphasized by a linguistic dis-positioning of the survivors, when, in the above-cited article, she replaces the Polish term *ocalali* (survivors) with its passive-voice equivalent *ocaleni* (literally, those who were saved or rescued). Bojarska suggests that establishing a collective postmemory has to occur in physical, topographical settings. »Polish postmemory« is sourced by means of haunting in spaces and material objects that formerly belonged to Jewish victims: among »Holocaust traces in cities and towns«; in between »material remains of the Jewish world«; and in Holocaust sites, i.e. the places where the victims met their death.

Posthumous Inclusion

These mechanisms cast a light on how and where the Jewish ghosts appear. It is not their own will, not some unfinished business they have among the living, and not the fact that wandering somehow lies in their nature, that brings the ghost into the open. The ghosts of Jewish victims are conjured up by members of the Polish majority with the clearly defined purpose of symbolic, material and spatial gains to be accrued from being haunted. These gains are made by displacement and dispossession of the ghosts. The first ownership that is taken from these ghosts is the right to knowledge of the circumstances, events, people and ideologies that took away their basic rights, that deprived them of their humanity and killed them. In the Polish context, summoning a Holocaust victim's ghost is conditional on establishing a false ›similarity‹ between the fate of Holocaust victims and the fate of ethnic Poles, the self-proclaimed ›witnesses‹, which results in a denial of knowledge of Polish collaboration in the Holocaust, an activity which can hardly be subsumed under the concept of ›witnessing‹. As a consequence of the production of an artificial, »specifically Polish postmemory of witnesses«, a ghost's memory is retrospectively altered, reshaped and remodeled to conform to the Polish postmemory's content. Ultimately, the ghost is deprived of the last structures that »anchor [it] in the external world« (Merleau-Ponty 2005 [1945]: 115), as the act of haunting exceeds the boundaries of memory discourse and allows the members of the Polish majority to gain symbolic ownership also of physical spaces and places. By using haunting as a device and in this manner, the Holocaust sites, former death camps, memorial sites, and Jewish museums all become »sources of Polish postmemory«. Following the appropriation of memory and identity, the »Polish postmemory« also occupies the »works of culture«, »material remains of the Jewish world«, and urban and architectural spaces whose structure carries »traces of the Holocaust«.

The act of summoning Jewish ghosts by contemporary Poles pertains to the Holocaust, but it is not a result of a critical collective memory of the Poles' participation in the mass murder of Jews. Quite the opposite, the conjuring up of Jewish ghosts originates from a set of historical mechanisms of symbolic, anti-Jewish violence, which has shaped Jewish history in Poland

and Europe for centuries.[13] Claiming that recognition of the Holocaust is now the »entry ticket« to Europe, Judt juxtaposed this situation to the pre-Holocaust European context: »For Jews, concluded the early 19th century German poet and satirist Heinrich Heine, baptism is their ›European entry ticket‹.« (2007 [2005]: 803) It appears that, in post-Holocaust Poland, a European identity is still somehow connected to the tradition of violently displacing Jewish identity to replace it with that of the majority group. The structural connection between the present appropriation of a non-corporeal ghost and the historical appropriation perpetrated on a Jewish victim of antisemitic repression *de facto* make the contemporary summoning of victims' ghosts an uncritical reenactment of mechanisms of violence present in former periods of Polish history, including the Holocaust itself. Elżbieta Janicka and Tomasz Żukowski identified such acts as the »posthumous inclusion« of victims in Polish culture and Polishness, arguing that such an operation »needs to be problematized«, as

[it] remains entwined with the question of whether it is possible to disregard the death of the object of inclusion, as well as causes and circumstances of that death. After all, we are dealing here with the inclusion which the living apply to the dead. Moreover, it is performed by the majority on the minority; by the group thus far excluding on the excluded group. (Janicka/Żukowski in this volume)

We cannot and should not disregard the circumstances of the victim's death because the encounter between those who haunt and those who are haunted is an interaction between those who were murdered and those whose community took part in, and profited from, murdering. Furthermore, such context cannot (and should not) be disregarded because the act of haunting takes place in architectural and urban environments that were objects of appropriation themselves: they were stolen from those who are now seen in these

---

13 For example, I am referring here to the prohibition of Jewish ownership of land or houses in Poland that lasted from the early medieval era until 1861-1864; the exclusion of Jews from citizen rights, which were first proclaimed in Polish lands in 1808 (Bartoszewicz 2006; Eisenbach 1961; Filipiak 2010); or interwar Poland's support of the economic boycott of Jews and their exclusion from universities and jobs in the state administration and army (Cała 2012: 325-418).

environments as ghosts. Describing how the Jews who remained in hiding in Nazi-occupied Poland were perceived by ethnic Poles who ›took care‹ of their possessions, Jan Tomasz Gross and Irena Grudzińska-Gross state: »While still alive Jews were treated as if they were temporary custodians of ›post-Jewish‹ property.« (Gross/Grudzińska-Gross 2012 [2011]: 75) The »post-Jewish property« is a key category here. It captures a set of material and symbolic goods that belonged to persons who held no right to own anything, including their identity and space to locate their body. It is a phrase that describes a category of goods that are free to be taken because their »custodian« is a non-physical individual, a ›ghost‹ with no rights to own, occupy space, or even exist.[14]

If the purpose of summoning is to »deal with« this history and to »heal« from its outcomes, then the very practice of conjuring up a Jewish ghost is an act of violence – of a »philosemitic violence«. It is in these terms that Janicka and Żukowski describe a violence (performed at times with good intentions) that is itself an act of revoking, a repetition of antisemitic patterns of culture. After all, an encounter between a living Pole and a dead, expropriated Jew is not just a return of the dead, but also a return of the violence that caused or facilitated the latter's death, a return of the hegemonic order where »one cannot control its comings and goings because it begins by coming back« (Derrida 1994 [1993]: 11). Taking place in »post-Jewish properties«, among »traces left by the Holocaust in the structure of cities and towns«, haunting by a Jewish ghost can be terrifying not because the ghost evokes terror, but because invoking a ghost brings forward and rehearses the violence and repression exerted on Jews and other minority groups by Polish society. The haunting may cause shock, because for a brief moment it casts light on the dark non-space to which Polish culture, unwilling to recognize its own hegemonic positionality, relegates those to whom it refuses citizen rights, the rights to settle and to exist.[15] The terror that this insight brings is real, and its reality does not diminish the reality of the ghosts. In fact, in this case the ghosts' reality lies in their very non-materiality and non-spatiality,

---

14 I discuss contemporary practices of appropriating »post-Jewish property« in Matyjaszek (2013).

15 For an analysis of connections between the history of Polish antisemitism and the hatred that became contemporary Poland's response to the post-2015 humanitarian crisis resultant from Syrian and Iraqi civil wars, see Gross (2015).

which are themselves the outcomes of violence. The spectrality of a Holocaust victim's ghost becomes all the more real the more it emphasizes the history of antisemitic exclusion, dispossession, and deprivation of bodily security and of a right to space. Consequently, if there is a »Polish memory« to be brought forward by the Jewish ghost, it is the memory of collectively sourcing »post-Jewish properties« and of the hegemonic repression that became Poland's concealed source of collective identity after 1989.

CONCLUSION: THE EXORCISM FORMULA

The forms of »Polish memory« described above can indeed cause terror, but only if they are seen from outside the hegemonic discourse. Such terror was first described in one of the best-known Polish literary texts about the Holocaust, Czesław Miłosz's »A Poor Christian Looks at the Ghetto«, written in Warsaw in early 1943. The poem was created shortly after the mass deportation of ghetto prisoners to the extermination camp at Treblinka, probably during the burning of the ghetto in the aftermath of the uprising. Since it is widely known, I shall only quote excerpts here. The first verses report:

Bees build around red liver,
Ants build around black bone.
It has begun: the tearing, the trampling on silks,
It has begun: the breaking of glass, wood, copper, nickel, silver, foam
Of gypsum, iron sheets, violin strings, trumpets, leaves, balls, crystals.
[…] (Miłosz 1990 [1943]: 51)

When reading these lines in the context of Polish culture, it may seem obvious that these verses describe the process of biological decomposition, or the process of burning down the ghetto; but they do not. In an interview given in 2011, Grudzińska-Gross related:

I've read [this poem] I don't know how many times, a dozen, tens of times, maybe more. […] I've always interpreted it metaphorically as a poem about the ghetto, about the period following its destruction, when nature did its thing, if you'll pardon the expression. That's actually how it starts, with bees and ants. But when I read it a few days ago, I suddenly realized that the first verse simply describes looting. I had never taken the poem literally. And yet that's literally what it's about. (Grudzińska-Gross/Szczęsna 2011)

The same had occurred earlier to writer and literary critic Artur Sandauer: »the Jewish district [i.e. the ghetto] is a pile of rubble plundered by scavengers whose activity the poet likens to the activity of ants and bees; here, man is not much different from an insect« (Sandauer 2005: 47).

»It has begun«. First, there appear images of plundering, of mass stealing of movable »post-Jewish property« left in the emptied flats and houses in the aftermath of *Grossaktion Warschau* (between July and September 1942) and before the ghetto uprising in April 1943. They are followed by images of the destroyed ghetto, of a burnt, »trodden down« space, and of non-spaces hidden under its surface. Sandauer comments on this part of Miłosz's text:

The vision of hideouts and burrows in which the remnants of the Jewish uprising perished conjures up the image of the underground guard, half-human and half-mole. The light attached to his forehead pierces the darkness [...] The poet links the guard with his headlight to the Jewish patriarch with the prayer box on his forehead, who bends over him as over one of the corpses. (Sandauer 2005: 47)

Slowly, boring a tunnel, a guardian mole makes his way,
With a small red lamp fastened to his forehead.
He touches buried bodies, counts them, pushes on,
He distinguishes human ashes by their luminous vapor,
The ashes of each man by a different part of the spectrum.
[...] (Miłosz 1990 [1943]: 51)

Here is the source of terror. »I am afraid, so afraid of the guardian mole«, writes Miłosz, haunted by this half-human Jewish figure, and the fear emerges from a place that was first plundered by looters searching for ›the Jewish riches‹, and later burned and dynamited, burying those trying to save themselves in the foundations. The fear emerges from this place, but the terrified person is less afraid of the presence of the victims' dead bodies or of the guardian mole's half-alive body than of his own. This is how the text ends:

My broken body will deliver me to his sight
And he will count me among the helpers of death:
The uncircumcised.
(Ibid.)

If Miłosz's narrator is haunted, he is haunted by himself. He is afraid of being seen in this place and being recognized as one of those good, poor Christians who got there just a few moments before to loot; he fears being identified as one of those »helpers«, allegedly ›passive‹ and ›indifferent‹, who came to the ghetto ›accidentally‹ after the deportations to ›take care‹ of »post-Jewish property«. It is a fear of being counted among these co-perpetrators, members of a group that profited from the Holocaust and facilitated its execution. If the mole is terrifying, it is because he, a Jewish non-person, witnessed the moment when the »Polish memory of the Holocaust« was created, and he knows what it contains.

Miłosz's poem is so immediate mainly because it was written »on site«, as the events unfolded, and before the first attempts were made to falsify the »Polish memory«. For this reason, it is probably one of few texts that depict the Jewish ghost not as an appropriated, non-material part of the »post-Jewish property«, but as a real phenomenon, real because it points at the materiality of events and spaces that might have been remembered. Half-ironically recognizing this immediacy, Sandauer wrote that Miłosz's Holocaust poetry »saved the honor of Polish literature« (2005 [1982]: 46). Subsequent interpreters of the poem tended to dilute this context. Particularly well-known is the 1987 interpretation of »A Poor Christian Looks at the Ghetto« developed by Jan Błoński. The literary critic used Miłosz's poem as a point of departure to construct the argument that a Polish co-responsibility for the Holocaust is a »responsibility for the crime without taking part in it, […] for holding back, for insufficient effort to resist« (Błoński 1990 [1987]: 46).[16] In order to substantiate this interpretation, Błoński baptized the guardian mole by asserting that, while it may look Jewish, in truth it only represents Miłosz's Catholic morality: »It is his [Miłosz's] own moral conscience which condemns (or may condemn) the poor Christian.«[17] (Ibid: 41) Błoński's attempt to employ

---

16 For a detailed discussion of Błoński's argument, see Żukowski (2013).
17 As Błoński argues: »It is a terrifying poem; it is full of fear. It is as if two fears coexist here. The first is the fear of death; more precisely, the fear of being buried

the ghost in a process of memory production can be considered one of the first instances of a posthumous inclusion that announced the Polish national revolution of 1989.

Today, with the »traumatic paradigm« widely functioning as a basis of Polish collective imagination, Muranów, the residential district located on the site of the Warsaw ghetto, is a well-known haunted spot. The local popular culture provides Jewish ghosts ready to be included in the Polish collective identity in lieu of historical knowledge. Among various contemporary equivalents of the specter baptized (and thus appropriated) by Błoński, one case of haunting is exceptionally informative as to the structure of hegemonic violence that stands behind the Polish society's preoccupation with Jewish ghosts. In December 2011, the national Polish television network TVN broadcasted an episode of its paranormal investigation documentary focusing on Jewish ghosts haunting Muranów. Besides local activists telling ghost stories and residents giving first-hand reports, the program featured an account by a professional psychic. The ghost specialist claimed that she had been asked for help by a family living close to the Ghetto Heroes and Martyrs Monument in the square bordered by Anielewicza Street in Muranów, in a

---

alive, which is what happened to many people who were trapped in the cellars and underground passages of the ghetto. But there is also a second fear: the fear of the guardian mole. This mole burrows underground but also underneath our consciousness. This is the feeling of guilt which we do not want to admit. Buried under the rubble, among the bodies of the Jews, the ›uncircumcised‹ fears that he may be counted among the murderers. So it is the fear of damnation, the fear of hell. The fear of a non-Jew who looks at the ghetto burning down. He imagines that he might accidentally die then and there, and in the eyes of the mole who can read the ashes, he may appear ›a helper of death‹. And so, indeed, the poem is entitled: ›A Poor Christian Looks at the Ghetto‹. This Christian feels fearful of the fate of the Jews but also – muffled, hidden even from himself – he feels the fear that he will be condemned. Condemned by whom? By people? No, people have disappeared. It is the mole who condemns him, or rather may condemn him, this mole who sees well and reads ›the book of the species‹. It is his own moral conscience which condemns (or may condemn) the poor Christian. And he would like to hide from his mole-conscience, as he does not know what to say to him.«
(1990 [1987]: 41)

flat where they had repeatedly seen three ghosts walking through rooms or gathering around a table. She recalled having to do some research before being able to give any advice, but in the end she provided effective instructions:

I advised that this woman communicate telepathically, so to speak, with these visiting persons, these figures, and tell them that it is not their house, not their flat, not their world, and that she ask them to wander back where they had come from, and to say their wishes or needs, if they had any. She did that, and it turned out that peace was restored. (TVN 2011)

LITERATURE

Bartoszewicz, Henryk (2006): »Projekty rewirów dla ludności żydowskiej w miastach mazowieckich 1807–1830.« In: Rocznik Mazowiecki 18, pp. 104-120.

Błoński, Jan (1990 [1987]): »The Poor Poles Look at the Ghetto.« In: Antony Polonsky (ed.), ›My brother's keeper?‹: Recent Polish Debates on the Holocaust, London: Routledge, pp. 34-48.

Bojarska, Katarzyna (2008): »Historia Zagłady i literatura (nie)piękna. ›Tworki‹ Marka Bieńczyka w kontekście kultury posttraumatycznej.« In: Pamiętnik Literacki 99/2, pp. 89-106.

Cała, Alina (2012): Żyd – wróg odwieczny? Antysemityzm w Polsce i jego źródła, Warszawa: ŻIH.

Derrida, Jacques (1994 [1993]): Specters of Marx: The State of the Debt, the Work of Mourning and the New International, London: Routledge.

Dziuban, Zuzanna (2014): »Memory as haunting.« In: Hagar: Studies in Culture, Polity and Identities 12 (Winter), pp. 111-135.

Eisenbach, Artur (1961): »Status prawny ludności żydowskiej w Warszawie w końcu XVIII i na początku XIX wieku.« In: Biuletyn Żydowskiego Instytutu Historycznego 3/39, pp. 3-16.

Engelking, Barbara (2011): Jest taki piękny słoneczny dzień. losy Żydów szukających ratunku na wsi polskiej, 1942-1945, Warszawa: Centrum Badań nad Zagładą Żydów.

Engelking, Barbara/Grabowski, Jan (eds.) (2018): Dalej jest noc. Losy Żydów w wybranych powiatach okupowanej Polski, Warszawa: Centrum Badań nad Zagładą Żydów.

Filipiak, Zbigniew (2010): »Ograniczenia praw politycznych i cywilnych ludności żydowskiej w Księstwie Warszawskim.« In: Studia Iuridica Toruniensia 4, pp. 5-30.

Grabowski, Jan (2013 [2011]): Hunt for the Jews: Betrayal and Murder in German-Occupied Poland, Bloomington: Indiana University Press.

Grabowski, Jan/Libionka, Dariusz (eds.) (2014): Klucze i kasa. O mieniu żydowskim w Polsce pod okupacją niemiecką i we wczesnych latach powojennych, 1939-1950, Warszawa: Centrum Badań nad Zagładą Żydów.

Gross, Jan Tomasz (2001 [2000]): Neighbors: The Destruction of the Jewish Community in Jedwabne, Poland, Princeton: Princeton University Press.

Gross, Jan Tomasz (2015): »Eastern Europe's Crisis of Shame.« In: Project Sindicate, May 13 (https://www.project-syndicate.org/commentary/eastern-europe-refugee-crisis-xenophobia-by-jan-gross-2015-09).

Gross, Jan Tomasz/Grudzińska-Gross, Irena (2012 [2011]): Golden Harvest: Events at the Periphery of the Holocaust, Oxford: Oxford University Press.

Grudzińska-Gross, Irena (2016): »Polishness in Practice.« In: Irena Grudzińska-Gross and Iwa Nawrocki (eds.), Poland and Polin: New Interpretations in Polish-Jewish Studies, Frankfurt am Main: Peter Lang, pp. 37-48.

Grudzińska-Gross, Irena/Szczęsna, Joanna (2011): »It's not about guilt: Talk with Irena Grudzińska-Gross.« In: Biweekly.pl 17/4 (http://www.biweekly.pl/article/2082-it%E2%80%99s-not-about-guilt.html).

Hirsch, Marianne (2008): »The Generation of Postmemory.« In: Poetics Today 29/1, pp. 103-128.

Janicka, Elżbieta (2012): Festung Warschau, Warszawa: Wydawnictwo Krytyki Politycznej.

Janicka, Elżbieta (2014-15): »Pamięć przyswojona. Koncepcja polskiego doświadczenia zagłady Żydów jako traumy zbiorowej w świetle rewizji kategorii świadka.« In: Studia Litteraria et Historica 3/4, pp. 148-227.

Janion, Maria (1991): Projekt krytyki fantazmatycznej. Szkice o egzystencjach ludzi i duchów, Warszawa: PEN.

Janion, Maria (2009a): Honor, Bóg, Ojczyzna, Warszawa: Dom Spotkań z Historią.

Janion, Maria (2009b): Żebro Mesjasza, Warszawa: Dom Spotkań z Historią.

Janion, Maria (2014): Hero, Conspiracy, and Death: The Jewish Lectures, Frankfurt am Main: Peter Lang.

Judt, Tony (2007 [2005]): Postwar: A History of Europe Since 1945, London: Pimlico.
Laclau, Ernesto (1990): New Reflections on the Revolution of Our Time, London: Routledge.
Laclau, Ernesto/Mouffe, Chantal (1985): Hegemony and Socialist Strategy: Toward a Radical Democratic Politics, London: Verso.
Leach, Neil (1999): »The Dark Side of the Domus: The Redomestication of Central and Eastern Europe.« In: Neil Leach (ed.), Architecture and Revolution: Contemporary Perspectives on Central and Eastern Europe, London: Routledge, pp. 150-162.
Lefebvre, Henri (1991 [1974]): The Production of Space, Hoboken: Wiley.
Matyjaszek, Konrad (2013): Przestrzeń pożydowska. In: Studia Litteraria et Historica 3, pp. 130-147.
Merleau-Ponty, Maurice (2005 [1945]): Phenomenology of Perception, London: Routledge.
Miłosz, Czesław (1990 [1943]): »A Poor Christian Looks at the Ghetto.« In: Antony Polonsky (ed.), ›My Brother's Keeper?‹: Recent Polish Debates on the Holocaust, London: Routledge, p. 51.
Niziołek, Grzegorz (2019): Polish Theatre of the Holocaust, New York: Bloomsbury
Ost, David (1990): Solidarity and the Politics of Anti-Politics: Opposition and Reform in Poland since 1968, Philadelphia: Temple University Press.
Ost, David (2005): The Defeat of Solidarity, Ithaca: Cornell University Press.
Sandauer, Artur (2005): On the Situation of the Polish Writer of Jewish Descent in the Twentieth Century: It is not I who Should Have Written this Study, Jerusalem: Magnes Press.
Sendyka, Roma (2016): »Sites that Haunt: Affects and the Non-Sites of Memory.« In: East European Politics & Societies 30/4, pp. 687-702.
Steinlauf, Michael C. (1997): Bondage to the Dead: Poland and the Memory of the Holocaust, Syracuse: Syracuse University Press.
Trigg, Dylan (2012): The Memory of Place: A Phenomenology of the Uncanny, Athens: Ohio University Press.
TVN (2011): Przeklęte Rewiry: Tajemnice Muranowa (https://www.youtube.com/watch?v=sWoKA-5W-2Y).

Waligórska, Magdalena (2014): »Healing by Haunting: Jewish Ghosts in Contemporary Polish Literature.« In: Prooftexts: A Journal of Jewish Literary History 34/2, pp. 207-231.

Zubrzycki, Genevieve (2006): The Crosses of Auschwitz: Nationalism and Religion in Post-Communist Poland, Chicago: Chicago University Press.

Żukowski, Tomasz (2013): »Wytwarzanie ›winy obojętności‹ oraz kategorii ›obojętnego świadka‹ na przykładzie artykułu Jana Błońskiego ›Biedni Polacy patrzą na getto‹.« In: Studia Litteraria et Historica 2, pp. 423-451.

Philosemitic Violence

Elżbieta Janicka and Tomasz Żukowski

Posthumous Inclusion?

»In some milieus«, writes Paul Zawadzki in *The History of Antisemitism* edited by Léon Poliakov,

The impression arises that there has been a change of sign in the value attributed to the Jews; antisemitism has been replaced by a kind of philosemitism. [...] All indications are that after the physical death during the Shoah, the symbolic at the moment of exile in 1968, and the metaphorical after the fall of communism, the Jews, or at least their ashes, will be incorporated into the pantheon of Polish culture. (2010 [1994]: 247)[1]

The concept of posthumous inclusion must be problematized. It remains entwined with the question of whether it is possible to disregard the death of the object of inclusion, as well as causes and circumstances of that death. After all, we are dealing here with the inclusion which the living apply to the dead. Moreover, it is performed by the majority on the minority; by the group thus far excluding on the excluded group.

We are interested in the conditions under which this posthumous inclusion takes place in Poland today and in analyzing the practices that constitute

---

1 What is striking in Zawadzki's statement is the uncritical – and *de facto* legitimizing – use of the antisemitic myth of »Jew-Communism« [żydokomuna]. For an analytical study, see Zawadzka (2007).

it. We find that, where there has been culturally consolidated and prolonged violence against minorities, reworking and rejecting the patterns that reproduce and perpetuate discrimination turns out to be extremely difficult. The old forms of subordination give way to new ones – sometimes despite the best intentions.

We examine this process through the example of Jolanta Dylewska's film *Po-lin. Okruchy Pamięci* [Po-lin: Scraps of Memory, 2008], considered here as evidence of inclusive intentions and practices that are also found elsewhere in contemporary Polish culture. The film was received enthusiastically.[2] Critics greeted it as both an antidote to anti-Semitism and an invitation to talk about the history of Polish Jews in an entirely new way. They emphasized with appreciation that Dylewska had chosen a point of view diametrically opposite to that of historian Jan Tomasz Gross, who exposed violence toward Jews committed specifically by Poles during and after World War II. Reviewers believed that the director was proposing a restorative language, »completely avoiding the issues of guilt, of mutual blame, antisemitism and anti-Polonism«, as Janusz Wróblewski wrote in the weekly *Polityka* (2008).[3]

Tadeusz Sobolewski called the film »an act of reconciliation« (2009/2010). »Dylewska has made a movie about life, not about the

---

2   The film received the following awards: Golden Teeth – Audience Award at the Polish Film Festival in Chicago (2008); Third Prize in the Feature-Length Film category at the Film and Art Festival *Dwa Brzegi* in Kazimierz Dolny (2008); the Krzysztof Kieślowski Beyond Borders Award at the Polish Film Festival in New York (2009); Golden Phoenix – Main Prize at the »Jewish Motifs« International Film Festival in Warsaw (2009); Golden Tape – Award of the Film Writing Circle of the Polish Filmmakers Association (2009).

3   The motif of »mutual guilt« of Poles and Jews before, during, and after the war is very common and requires a separate study. Katyń and Stalinism (or Communism in general) are quoted as instances of »Jewish guilt«. One of the most significant examples of the construction of symmetry of »mutual guilt« is a statement by the Primate of Poland commenting on revelations of the Jedwabne massacre. In a speech in March 2001, Cardinal Józef Glemp stated: »The case is somewhat reminiscent of the Katyń massacre«, and asked rhetorically about the reasons for the massacre (Glemp 2010: 570-573). For a critical stance on the construction of symmetry and reciprocity, see Żukowski (2001a: 26-27; 2001b: 40-42) and Janicka (2010: 190-201).

Holocaust«, he stated in a comprehensive review in *Gazeta Wyborcza* (2008: 13). The text indicates that, for Sobolewski, life is the area where the deep truth of Polish-Jewish relations is revealed, a forgotten one, and different from the picture that emerges from testimonies of the war.[4] *Po-lin* bares this truth and enables a return to it, acting as therapy for both groups mutilated by the Holocaust. »That Jewish world is assimilated by us only when it has ceased to exist,« wrote Sobolewski; and added, citing the authority supposed to represent the Jewish position: »Antoni Słonimski came to a similar conclusion in the poem ›Elegy for the Little Jewish Towns‹: he believed that that which is absent will allow for ›fraternally bring[ing] closer and reunit[ing] / two nations fed by the same suffering.‹ Is that not what happens between the closest people, that we begin to appreciate and to love someone, only when they are gone?« (Ibid.)[5]

Perhaps only the author of the *Po-lin* poster tried to convey the problematic nature of this »cinematic act of reconciliation«. The poster depicts two young, identical women facing each other, and so shown to the viewer in profile. Both wear earrings, one in the shape of a cross, the other in the shape of the Star of David. While the Polish woman is shown in color, the Jewish woman is portrayed in black and white. We understand that she belongs to the past. The figures' eyes are covered by the caption: »Before the Second World War 3.5 million Jews lived in Poland. Here they were born and died, prayed, loved and suffered. Here was their Fatherland. Po-lin.« The poster also exists in a parallel version, where the characters are placed back to back, suggesting the existence of at least two different versions of the story about

---

4 The director herself seems to support this vision. Answering the question of why her Polish characters do not resemble those in Gross's books, she said, »The difference is fundamental. Gross writes about what happened during the war and after the war, and my film is about what happened before. I went to those towns, found those Poles there and they talked to me like that. I did not ask them about what happened during the war and after the war, because I knew about it from a variety of accounts of the Jewish survivors of these towns, preserved in the archives of the Jewish Historical Institute.« (Dylewska/Bielas 2008: 14)

5 After 1989, the topos of a Polish-Jewish community of suffering was dominated by the theme of symmetry of suffering, equivalent but separate. This process began in the early 1980s.

the land of Po-lin. The image of sisterhood, partnership, and dialogue has thus been called into question; we do not know if this was intentional.[6]

For reviewers, the matter is much simpler: *Po-lin* refers to centuries-old coexistence, mutual relationships, respect, neighborliness, and benevolent memory. Constructed as a premise for contemporary tolerance, it takes a stand equally against antisemitism and so-called anti-Polonism.[7] Critics regarded the emphasis on positive aspects of tradition, and their incorporation into the cultural canon, as an attempt to overcome hateful stereotypes. We should look for what unites rather than what divides, the reviewers seemed to say. Though friction existed, the good and valuable prevailed throughout Polish-Jewish history; perhaps not an idyll, but at least everyday, neighborly life, which can and must oppose violence and hatred. »The director meticulously reconstructs the prewar world of Polish Jews, for whom the [Polish] Republic was the true and only home, a Fatherland, the Promised Land«, wrote Piotr Kletowski in *Tygodnik Powszechny*. »Contrary to the theses drawn up by fashionable historians, Dylewska shows that it was possible for Jews and Poles to live in harmony even when the shadow lay over their relations – real, but not unique or exceptional – of Polish antisemitism.« (Kletowski 2008)[8]

Let us now examine this cinematographic image of harmonious coexistence.

---

6   To see the poster, visit http://www.filmweb.pl/film/Po-lin.+Okruchy+pamięci-2008-480047/posters.

7   »Anti-Polonism« as a construct and phantasm, and its very persistent inclusion in the antisemitic ›package‹, deserve a separate monograph.

8   »Fashionable historians« are – as we can guess – Jan Tomasz Gross and the team led by Barbara Engelking in the Centre for Holocaust Research at the Institute of Philosophy and Sociology in the Polish Academy of Sciences. We should add that the purpose of the director was not a polemic against the researchers: »My intention was not to have a discussion with Gross, because you don't discuss facts.« (Dylewska/Bielas 2008: 14)

THE COMMUNICATION SITUATION: *QUID PRO QUO*

Po-lin is composed of accounts belonging to two universes: the Jewish and the Polish. The same text and images convey different meanings in each. Dylewska achieves the effect of harmony through the obliteration of these differences. The viewers' attention is effectively drawn away from the significance of the context in which messages are received, and from the consequences of the information imparted. Distortion is the price: the gestures and words spoken by Jews to Jews come across as messages intended by the Jews for the Polish audience – as a message from which to draw conclusions about the relationships between Polish and Jewish neighbors.

Dylewska uses documentary films shot by Jewish emigrants who travelled from the United States to visit relatives in Poland in the 1930s. The films are family mementoes, created by amateur filmmakers for relatives and friends abroad. The residents of Jewish towns knew the people behind the camera and the audience for whom the recorded images were intended. This purpose governed the behavior of both the amateur photographers and their protagonists. The convention of commemorative photography determined the subject: the films recorded not so much everyday life as the festive atmosphere that accompanied visits of long-unseen relatives and friends, usually perceived as successful. Hence the bearing of those filmed: they are sympathetic, interested in the camera and well-disposed to those filming. They are cheerful. Smiling, they greet those who will watch them overseas. They want to make a good impression. The holiday atmosphere is not conducive to thinking about problems and concerns. This can be seen even in the scenes depicting the poor, beggars, and local madmen.

A smile for a cameraman from one's own community is one thing; in Dylewska's work, however, this smile becomes a greeting that the minority directs towards members of the dominant group. Moreover, the director seems to strengthen this communicative misunderstanding. At the beginning of the film, an announcement about the origin of the archival footage appears: »Due to the course of history«, we read, »the amateur materials filmed by an unskilled hand, often by unknown authors, preserve *for us* scraps of the non-existent world of the Polish Jews« [italics added].[9] The »us« pertains to the Polish film crew, Polish viewers, and – most likely – Poles in general.

Thus, the message becomes an important voice in the discussion that has been underway in Poland since the publication of Gross's book *Neighbors: The Destruction of the Jewish Community in Jedwabne, Poland* (2001 [2000]), and, initially, inspired by Jan Błoński's article *Poor Poles Look at the Ghetto* (1990 [1987]). The filmmakers joined the public debate, calling as their witnesses the Jews from the archival footage.

This has profound consequences. The »cinematic act of reconciliation«, so often written about by the reviewers, turns out to be grounded in an absence of intergroup communication. The original context of transmission and reception altogether excludes the problem of relations with Christians. The dominant group deals, therefore, with a voice that does not address the matter it wants to discuss. From the films used by Dylewska, we learn nothing about what the inhabitants of the shtetl had to say about their Polish neighbors.

Furthermore, by condensing the Jewish archival footage, the contemporary material allows the Jews to say only what is put into their mouths by the Polish director. It thus distorts the meaning of the original Jewish messages and creates the illusion of a conversation, based, in fact, on denying the members of the minority group a voice. The film images of the shtetls and the messages contained in them become part of a whole, over which the Polish narrator has absolute control. The Jews are rendered the instrument of a Polish narrative about themselves and about how the Christian majority treated them.

---

9   The theme returns in the *Gazeta Wyborcza* interview: »Katarzyna Bielas: The protagonists of the amateur *home movies* filmed before the war [...] approach the camera, smile, and look us in the eyes [italics added]. The friendly, cheerful atmosphere is striking. Jolanta Dylewska: I felt the same thing when I watched these films in various archives around the world for the first time, and it's exactly this feeling that I wanted to preserve for future viewers.« (Dylewska/Bielas 2008: 11)

THE HARMONY OF MEMORIES AND THEIR CURATOR/CONTROLLER

The falsification goes deeper, beyond the context of reception. The superior perspective of the dominant group is constitutive of the structure of *Po-lin*. The film does not begin with Jewish archival footage. Instead, we see the Jewish world through the eyes of »witnesses«: Poles recalling their former neighbors. The story takes as its vantage point the accounts of people who remember the Jews and speak of their »disappearance« and the void they left behind.

Dylewska introduces the archival material through a contemporary sequence. It features two Polish women. One says that she no longer dreams of the Jews, although there was a time when she did. Then she asks her companion about her dreams. The camera zooms into the other woman's face. Her eyes are empty, focused on something distant, as though not of this world. The film image follows this look. In a close-up, architectural details emerge, blurred at first, but soon becoming sharper. We see doors, house gates, walls. Only people are missing, but outside the frame we can hear Jewish-style music, murmurs imitating the sounds of the Jewish street and the voice of Piotr Fronczewski, who reads accounts about the Jewish residents of the town from Jewish memorial books.[10] The actor's deep voice, timbre, and intonation are reminiscent of the bass of the famous hypnotist and healer-celebrity, Anatoly Kaszpirowski. And finally, they appear: the Jews, summoned from nothingness through archival photographs. They move closer to the camera – and thus to »us«. They come up from the depths of the frame. They have bashful smiles on their faces.

The »witnesses« – the Poles – are filmed according to two conventions. Dylewska resorts primarily to the documentary style: she shows the Polish protagonists in the places where they live and work, in casual conversation with the interviewer standing behind the camera. She records their memories

---

10 This is an outcome of conformist influence on the director: »In the first version, the commentary was to be read by a woman. I was thinking about Maja Komorowska, but, unfortunately, it turned out that at that time she was busy. Then the producer suggested Piotr Fronczewski. He said: ›Jola, you realize that the most important texts in the history of mankind have always been read by men?‹ I didn't know what to say...« (Dębogórska/Dylewska 2008)

and emotions. In the decisive moments of the narrative, however, she switches to the convention of the psychological drama, using close-ups that fill the entire frame, the camera capturing the speakers' eyes as if they were sunk in the past. In an interview for the online magazine *Stopklatka*, the director maintained, »After the conversations, the cameraman Józek Romasz would put the camera in front of them, and I would ask them to look into the lens and think about a close Jewish neighbor from that period. I believe that the lens conveys also the unseen...« (Dębogórska/Dylewska 2008) Dylewska consciously summons an image of ›spiritual depth‹ and elevates her Polish interlocutors.

In addition, the director assumes – or to be more precise, produces – congruence between Polish and Jewish memories, because the archival films shot by Jewish amateurs both materialize the Poles' memories and substantiate their authenticity. The past lives on in the »witnesses«, who are symbolically located on the same side as the victims. As noted above, the encouraging smiles of the Jews captured in the 1930s footage are not addressed to »us«. But the Polish curator/controller knows better.

When, in the interview for *Stopklatka*, Dylewska was asked about anti-semitism, she responded that it was not – and is not – a marginal problem. She pointed out, however, that in the Polish accounts »there was more about good things«, and added:

Of course, there were also pogroms. But above all I made the film to bring the Jews back into collective memory. On the other hand, I created it also for those who survived the Holocaust. I thought it might be nice for them, if someone were to say, like Józefa in the film – that without them it had become somehow empty and sad. I thought it was important to let them hear these words. (Dębogórska/Dylewska 2008)

We are dealing here with a conscious directorial choice. Dylewska chooses to show »what is good«. Simultaneously, she asserts that what she shows, in fact, conveys the main attribute of Polish-Jewish towns. »The bringing back of the Jews into collective memory« unfolds, therefore, on very specific terms.

The impression of harmony between Polish and Jewish memories is reinforced by the juxtaposition of two kinds of nostalgia. The Polish nostalgia is constructed through Dylewska's filming technique: the picturesque shots of traces of the former Jewish presence, the psychologizing portraits of her interlocutors, and the erasure of any reminders of antisemitism. The Polish nostalgia is all the easier to create because it does not require any action, any revision of habits or attachments. Dylewska's interlocutors know that they are safe in this respect; the Polish majority has taken care to avoid the possibility of real encounters and real communication. The few Jews who survived did so by escaping. Those who were murdered are long gone, they want nothing from the Poles, they say nothing, they are merely a projection of those remembering[11] – a projection which brings them back to the times of their youth, and these are always melancholic. At the end of the film, one of the Polish protagonists repeats melancholically: »Everything passes...«. This universal wisdom is absolutely true. One can only agree: *Panta rhei. Tempus fugit. Où sont les neiges d'antan*!

The Jewish nostalgia is primarily the nostalgia of the memorial books, published by the communities of Jews who left Poland. Survivors created them for other survivors, offering each other accounts of the murdered Jewish world, in which their Polish neighbors are rarely mentioned.[12] From among these stories, Dylewska selects fragments written almost in the style of a fairy tale, further accentuated by the anointed, hieratic interpretation of Piotr Fronczewski. The fairy tale speaks of the good old days. What it omits is the fact that the times were good not because of the kindness of the Polish majority and decent living conditions, but because everyone was still alive.

---

11 The *Gazeta Wyborcza* reviewer writes truthfully, yet he fails to grasp the double meaning of his own words: »They smile. They're not blaming anyone, they don't need anything from us. They are something we need.« (Sobolewski 2008: 13)

12 »Although in the sections pertaining to the interwar period, we find relatively few details about relations with the Christian population, in the parts on the wartime and postwar period there is much more information on various attitudes of the Poles. [...] Reading the Jewish memorial books can be very instructive for the Polish reader whom the texts might surprise with their different perspective or, indeed, with the sharpness of formulated opinions. It should be remembered, however, that most of the books were written shortly after the war, when the Jewish community in Poland, which went through so much during the Holocaust, was additionally affected by the wave of antisemitism whose crowning despicableness was the Kielce pogrom in July 1946.« (Adamczyk-Garbowska 2009; cf. Adamczyk-Garbowska/Kopciowski/Trzciński 2009)

In *Po-lin* both nostalgias are placed side by side, creating an impression that they resonate with one another. Yet none of the speakers traverse the boundaries of their own community. No encounter takes place at all. Of pivotal importance is what happens on the Polish side; as the dominant group speaks of the minority, it also creates an image of itself. It transpires that what is at stake in this Polish documentary about the Jews is the image of the Poles themselves.

FAMILY ALBUM: VIDEO AND AUDIO

Dylewska inscribes the Jewish archival footage into a Polish narrative about the Polish community. As noted above, these materials appear on the screen to visualize the content of the recollections of Polish »witnesses«. In this way, the Jewish amateur films are granted a special status. The film's first sequence consists of 1930s photos of Jews coming up from the depths of the frame towards the camera. This gesture of openness and friendship is repeated six times, involving different people each time.[13] The next four shots show family photographs. Elders and children line up, posing for a souvenir photo. The narrative of *Po-lin* suggests that these photographs have been offered to »us«. They become part of the collection of family memorabilia belonging to these »witnesses«, who then share them with the film crew and audience. It is because ownership determines the meaning of a collection of photographs – as is the case with any family album.

The album seems to be a record *par excellence*; after all, the pictures it contains are a mechanical recording of reality. The situation is not so simple, however. A collection of photos is a cultural fact, a story that cannot be told without guidance and, sometimes, manipulation.[14] In the case of the

---

13 The gesture of approaching the lens – a gesture of trust and devotion – additionally exposes the Jewish protagonists to violence exercised by those who will take possession of the films and use them for their own purposes. Dylewska did not notice this danger. The images that belong to the minority were surrendered to the mercies of the majority's violence.

14 Photographs define the circle of family and friends, and, more importantly, determine the status of the owner of the album, who uses the images to create a narrative about themselves – one that suits them best and which they aspire to. It is

collection presented by Dylewska, three interconnected aspects of the presentation are crucial. Firstly, archival photographs are taken over and framed within a dominant narrative. Secondly, they become part of the identity clichés constitutive of that narrative. Thirdly, they are doctored in a way that renders them unable to resist the curators/controllers.

In *Po-lin*, the neighbors' commemorative family photo album seals the friendly covenant. Regardless of their own intentions, the Jews in *Po-lin* are inscribed in the Polish family saga of Polish genealogy, identity, and uniqueness against the backdrop of Europe – the saga of the *Paradisus Judeorum*.[15] And so emerges the fundamental status of the 1930s archival photographs as framed by the Polish story in Dylewska's *Po-lin*: that of subordination and availability. The director – the new owner of the archive – takes control of the images, in an act that could rightly be labelled an appropriation, if not theft.

As a result, the majority gets what it likes the most: agreeable, satisfied Jews, who obligingly welcome the Polish version of events. This comes at a cost: the elimination of any opportunity to see in the mute material a silent void arising from extermination. The shock that forces us to recognize the

---

constructed of building blocks of variously culturally constructed clichés about status and attitudes, be it a view of a white mansion, of shots of a holiday in Nice at the beginning of the century, or photos with celebrities. A family album may consist of images of real family and friends, but it need not be the case. The slogan »Buy yourself ancestors!« renders the archives of old photographs available to ever new owners. Regardless of the authenticity, the principle remains the same: those who own the images author their meaning, construct a genealogy and identity from them (cf. Sekula 1984).

15 In the self-representation of the majority, the figure of *Paradisus Judeorum* serves important functions. This can be seen on the website of a Polish foundation of this name (www.paradisusjudeorum.org). A psychologist and psychotherapist interprets it as follows: »Poles want to see their country as a haven of tolerance, with centuries-long traditions – a country without burning stakes. (The fact that it was a country with a significantly lower number of burning stakes is not enough – it has to be ›without stakes‹, as we were taught in school.) The combination of the name with antisemitic content on the foundation website provides a clear message: Poland was a haven for the ungrateful Jews, and Poles acted in the roles of angels.« (Biedka 2008)

mechanisms of crime and to confront its social embodiment, in order to – as Adorno wrote – »arrange [...] thoughts and actions so that Auschwitz shall not repeat itself, so that nothing similar shall happen« (2005 [1966]: 365), vanishes as the Polish community engages in trouble-free self-affirmation. The scenes in which pre-Holocaust reality is contrasted with contemporary images of the same, deserted places are immediately seized upon by the dominant narrative of harmonious coexistence, a mood aided by impressive formal techniques.

To make this appropriation work, the audience cannot for a moment be left alone with the material in the form in which its Jewish authors and owners produced it. The viewer's intellect and senses are therefore constantly governed and formatted. Silent images are supplemented with a soundtrack, which consists of all the possible sounds corresponding to particular frames. When looking at a street, we hear footsteps and the hum of a distant conversation. When a horse moves across the screen, we hear a clatter of hooves and neighing. When a railway station appears, the soundtrack provides a train whistle and the sound of an accelerating train off-screen. The black-and-white photographs have all the characteristics of amateur archival materials – they are blurred, scratched, grainy. In comparison with the archival footage, the sound is striking in its technical perfection. It is hyperreal: hyperclean and hyper-polished. Through this contrast, the soundtrack stands out, autonomizes itself, and attracts attention as a separate work – an authorial construction.

The sound makes the images come alive. Reviewers pointed out that Dylewska »meticulously recreates« the world of pre-war Jewish towns.[16]

---

16 This formulation comes from the already quoted review by Piotr Kletowski (2008). There are more similar voices. Piotr Śmiałowski wrote, for instance, that Dylewska »decided on the technique, which is probably the best idea in *Po-lin*: the old tapes are somewhat slowed down. They are underscored by sounds that to some extent interact with what is happening on the screen. However, these sounds are not ordinary. They are reverberant and are also slightly distorted. [...] All these elements create the impression that we are listening to a kind of folk tale, and the image itself becomes what we might imagine at that moment, if our eyes were closed.« (2008: 91). In Barbara Hollender's view: »On the black and white tapes, the world that we know today mostly from Kawalerowicz's *Austeria* is revived. [...] And if someone bandies around slogans of Polish antisemitism, they should

The added sounds become part of the operation of »recovering« the past, as is the slow motion of the archival footage and close-ups of individual characters. All this highlights the great care and effort put into the making of the film, and the dedication of the people who created it. This technique binds the filmmakers themselves, as well as the audience, to the Polish »witnesses«. The »we« for whom the archival materials were saved, together »revive« the Jewish world, extracting it from nothingness and passing it on to future generations. Here, the majority group directs itself.

In addition, the problem of the silence of the people watched on the screen disappears. The sense of communing with the Jewish voice is strengthened by the commentary read by Fronczewski. At the beginning of *Po-lin*, the message appears: »Those who survived wrote MEMORIAL BOOKS – SIFREI ZIKARON. Thanks to these books, the commentary for this movie was created.« The impression is irresistible: the Jewish victims are being given the opportunity to speak and, together with the Polish »witnesses«, they convey information about the land of Polin.

The commentary is consistently maintained in the present tense. Dylewska says of this choice of grammatical form:

Hanna Krall [...] made a brilliant and fundamental correction to the film. She said: ›How come? Why in the past tense? After all, they're all still alive.‹ Because of this change, the viewer may feel that this world lives on. Preserving the present tense renders these people more alive. Maybe someone in the audience will have the impression that this world can still be saved. From my point of view, this could be an important emotional investment of the viewer into the movie. (Dębogórska/Dylewska 2008)

definitely watch this film. [...] The images stored on the tapes, the painstakingly recreated sounds, the mood music of Michał Lorenc. This wise film, full of longing and tolerance, should enter the school canon.« (2008: 20) »Her touching film consists almost entirely of carefully restored fragments of amateur recordings registering the most ordinary behavior, carefree and fleeting moments of happiness«, wrote Janusz Wróblewski (2008). Tadeusz Sobolewski stated, in turn: »This nonexistent life – recorded on amateur, coarse, scratched film, filmed with a shaky camera – gains an incredible intensity. Precisely because of the technical imperfections of the tapes, we have the feeling of direct contact with a living reality.« (2008: 13)

The director's statement reveals some problems with considering memory as presentification. Memory (the subjective) is to be substantiated here by the mechanical image (the objective). Dylewska seems to think that such a procedure allows her to become objective: the past is brought back in its real shape. In fact, recollection comprises a creation of the past, a creation whose rules are always dictated by the authors of the historical narrative.[17] In the case of the relationship between the dominant group and the minority, the problem gets more complicated, especially when the reconstruction takes place after the extermination, against the backdrop of the Holocaust and its long shadow.[18]

The »re-enactment« of the past in *Po-lin* transpires, in this way, as an attempt to put the Holocaust in parentheses. Because the memory concludes in the time prior to the extermination, framed through a belief that it can be revived, the extermination ceases to be a crucial turning point. The emphasis shifts from the need to rethink the mechanisms of genocide and the behavior of the dominant group vis-à-vis those exterminated, towards a cultivation of the memory of the Jews from before the disaster – or, indeed, of their image constructed by the majority, which precludes any need for revision of its belief and behaviors.

Dylewska is aware that she herself partakes in the »recovery« of the annihilated world and invites the audience to play a similar role, but she does not problematize this process. As a result, nothing protects the protagonists of the footage from the curator/controller's authority. The memory summons images of those absent, which conceal their absence and distances the audience from reality. The sense of communing with the dead is false, yet all the easier and more reassuring because the dead are subject to the majority narrative and do not question it in any way. As the story takes place in the present tense, the protagonists may appear to be »more alive«,[19] but, in fact, they

---

17 This phenomenon was subject to exhaustive analysis by Hayden White, who foregrounded the decisive role of narrative conventions through which culture, community, and, finally, historians perceive and organize facts. For White, historical narrative is not so much a simple reflection of the past as a production of its image (White 1975).
18 It is in these terms that Feliks Tych referred to postwar antisemitism (1999).
19 It is, indeed, difficult to understand what this phrase is supposed to mean in relation to the victims of the Holocaust.

are permanently put to death. Memory turns into a fetish, around which the false consciousness of the dominant group organizes itself.

CREATING »WITNESSES« AND »GUARDIANS OF MEMORY«: *PERPETUUM MOBILE*

At first glance, it may seem that *Po-lin* introduces traces of Jewishness. But in fact, the emphasis is on the *relationship* between living Poles and those traces of Jews. Dylewska frames it in one of the opening sequences pertaining to a post-Jewish home. It begins with close-ups of windows, doors, and walls. The lens pauses at door handles and locks. It moves into the interior. It captures a room with a painting on the wall. Though the camera focus draws the viewer's attention to a doorframe and a mezuzah nailed to it, we can discern that the painting depicts the Blessed Virgin Mary. The owner's voice is heard in the form of a voiceover: »In this house a Jewish blessing remained. There was one on every door, but only this one has survived. This is a token of this house, and so it must be.« We hear a ticking clock; it emerges in the scene in close-up. In the background, emphasized by a change in the depth of field, an image of the Black Madonna of Częstochowa, placed on a family altar, comes into view. The frame consists of warm colors. The Madonna's face is hidden behind the blurry shapes of flowers – the essence of a Polish home. Fronczewski's voice, which had just been reading from a Jewish memorial book, now proclaims solemnly, »These are the last of dozens of generations of Poles who lived for hundreds of years alongside Polish Jews. The last witnesses who connect us with their lives. The last.« The intent faces of the Poles appear on the screen in closeups. Clocks tick. And now, the »witnesses« begin to recount their memories.[20]

---

20 This construction has not left reviewers indifferent: »Avoiding pathos, we must nevertheless conclude that *Po-lin* enchants and attracts because it attempts to show a way of life that once existed. [...] On the other hand, the film is a tribute to the character of the witness themselves. [...] Dylewska's Polish witnesses are living examples of the past, the eponymous ›scraps of collective memory‹, who, thanks to the director and the archival footage, return to their childhood in order to testify.« (Ostrowska 2009: 72)

Dylewska plays with icons of identity. The trace of the murdered Jewish residents of the house – the mezuzah on the doorframe – coexists harmoniously with the archetypal sign of Polishness: the family shrine and the image of the Black Madonna of Częstochowa. The filming technique only serves to emphasize this harmony. The transition is smooth, the image remains in an undisturbed, intimate, and homely atmosphere. The Polish attitude is presented as caretaking of the traces left behind. Yet the poetics of the statement (»There was one on every door, only this one survived«) brings to mind the expertise of specialists on prehistory (»Until our times only fragments have been preserved of the skeleton of *Archaeopteryx*«); one that effectively invalidates the question of what happened to the Jews and their property. It is as if they had been consumed by a cataclysm in which these witnesses played no part.[21] It is to the Poles' credit, by this reasoning, that they look after the remnants.[22]

This care seems to be accepted and consecrated by the Jewish dead. The sentence »In this house, a Jewish blessing remained« is ambiguous. It can refer to the parchment scroll with verses of the Torah, but it can also be understood to mean that the blessing of the former owners – or the Jewish community in general – still protects the house and its new residents. The latter interpretation seems to be confirmed by the soundtrack. Fronczewski, who lends his voice to the Jewish community, announces – as though on their behalf – that we are dealing with the »last witnesses«. What is more, we are talking about the »guardians of memory« of the murdered Jews. »This is a token of this house, and so it must be«, says the resident of the post-Jewish property, symbolically establishing all Poles featured in the film as those who have accepted the task of saving the memory of their Jewish neighbors and are fully aware of their mission.

The introduction of categories such as »guardian of memory« and »witness« might evoke a Polish-Jewish community, and construct Poles as those who were granted implicit permission by the Jews to guard their mementoes

---

21 Dylewska does not mention that, even in poor families, mezuzahs were usually silver and thus a welcome loot for people who were looting Jewish homes.

22 The subject of our analysis is the construction of the film *Po-lin*. We know people who are marginalized in their own communities because they have taken upon themselves the task of guarding Jewish traces and traces of traces. Their stories are not particularly soothing.

carefully, and thus to show loyalty to their former neighbors. The Poles prove to be worthy heirs of the Jewish heritage. Now we understand why that which is Polish coexists in harmony with that which is Jewish. Both communities – despite all differences – are unified in the same mission: to preserve the memory threatened by the passing of time. The clocks tick. The Blessed Virgin Mary looks at the mezuzah with care.

This flattering image of the Polish community and of Polish-Jewish relations hinges on silencing basic facts and questions. Although we are looking at a post-Jewish house, we learn nothing about the circumstances under which it passed into the hands of its new owners. Yet, even if Dylewska's interlocutors are thoroughly honest people, these circumstances matter a great deal. In order to relate a complete story about the prewar Jewish world, one cannot leave out the Holocaust, the attitudes of the »Aryan side« towards exterminated Jews, and Polish attitudes towards Jews after the war. This is all the more important because the people called the »guardians of memory« live in former Jewish homes.

Dylewska circumvents this problem by addressing antisemitic violence obliquely and reassuringly.[23] While she avoids talking about the Holocaust, she does in fact address it. In contemporary Polish language, the word »witness« is a fundamental concept in describing the extermination of the Jews.[24]

---

23 The issue of Polish violence against the Jews appears on the margins of the story and is not developed. First, in the section of the movie devoted to Jewish social organizations and self-organized communities, the Zionists are mentioned: »Antisemitism is on the rise and Zionist Scout organizations are preparing young people to emigrate to Palestine.« The next sequence takes the audience to Kolbuszowa. One of the residents of the town assures the audience, »Coexistence between Poles and Jews before the war was completely normal. Just look at Kolbuszowa's coat of arms – it shows two hands clasped, Polish and Jewish, the Star of David and a cross.« The theme of antisemitism appears again in the description of a market. Fronczewski declares, »Sometimes Polish nationalist squads turn up and start knocking over and beating people.« For a moment, the music changes to a minor key. We see contemporary close-ups of bread, garlic, and carrots, over which a shadow falls. That is all. After a while, the lively, cheerful music returns and the story goes on.

24 The term »witness« [świadek] is the Polish translation of the category of »bystander« introduced in Raul Hillberg's *Perpetrators, Victims, Bystanders: The*

For Dylewska, it pertains to the time before the Holocaust. At the same time, she evokes signs of the Shoah – the things left behind by the exterminated Jews – to suggest that, if in the post-Jewish home the mezuzah coexists with the Jasna Góra icon, then during the war nothing disturbing happened between the Jews and their Polish neighbors. Yet the appropriation of Jewish objects by Poles – to frame the activity euphemistically – was a mass phenomenon. It unfolded in a context in which, on a social plane, there was no room for being a passive witness. This fact makes it impossible to label the Polish community a »guardian of memory« without further explanation. A witness is someone who looks on, who does not participate in the situation, and who has no bearing on what happens. There are three reasons why this word does not fit the reality.

First, during the war, the life or death of the Jews depended on the attitude of the Aryan side – on active support, without which it was impossible to survive, or on passivity, which would allow the Jews to vanish in the midst of the Polish community.[25] In fact, Jews could count on neither of these.

Jewish Catastrophe, 1933-1945 (1992). The shift of emphasis, if not of meaning, which results from this translational decision, deserves a separate discussion. [Translators' note: the authors do not refer here to the second connotation of the word, also fundamental in relation to the Holocaust, that of actively bearing witness, commemorating the genocide; this meaning, as it pertains to Jewish survivors of the Holocaust, can hardly be extended onto Poles. In fact, in her writings, Elżbieta Janicka demonstrates that the appropriation of the concept of witnessing to describe the Polish experience of the Holocaust has served to invisibilize Polish involvement in the Holocaust. She proposes, therefore, another term to capture the positionality of Poles during the Holocaust, that of »initiated participating observer« (obserwator uczestniczący wtajemniczony) (2008: 238; 2014/2015: 160-165)].

25 »Those Jews who got out from the ghetto, who obtained ›Aryan‹ documents, and who had somewhere to live should have saved themselves. They could and should have lived afterwards as peacefully as non-Jewish Poles, as Polish Christians did. […] Why couldn't those Poles who did not intend to denounce or blackmail a Jew they had seen, keep it a secret? […] After all, nothing was asked of them so much as silence, as not whispering to others who were as friendly toward Jews, who carried on with their whispering until the Gestapo got wind of it. If they had simply remained silent, almost all fugitives from the ghetto would have saved

Polish streets and countryside were deadly dangerous for Jews in hiding. Poles did not hesitate to expose them. Blackmail and theft were common practices, as was escorting Jews to Polish or German police stations. Jews also ran the risk of being hunted in battue or being murdered.[26] Those who decided to hide Jews hid them first and foremost from their neighbors. The courage of the Righteous consisted primarily of their opposition to the standards in force in their own Polish Catholic community. The prevailing attitudes of the Polish majority contributed to the execution of the Final Solution. A community that did not allow the Jews to hide on the Aryan side, and that greatly benefited from their slaughter, cannot define itself as a »witness«, still less a »guardian of memory«.

Second, wartime attitudes towards the Jews did not come out of nowhere. They merely reflected the already well-established code of Polish culture. The annihilation of the Jews was contained, as a potentiality, in the structure of antisemitism, both pre-modern and modern (cf. Tokarska-Bakir 2004: 66-67). The dominant religion of the majority morally sanctioned antisemitism. The phantasms of liquidation were articulated in Poland before the war, and prepared the social imagination for what was to happen in the 1940s (cf. Janion 2000: 144-145). Even children knew about them. Critically engaging with the conceptual triad of perpetrators, victims, and bystanders/witnesses, Elżbieta Janicka observes that the alleged »witnesses« of the Holocaust were deeply involved in the ›Jewish question‹, as instantiated by the antisemitic discourse:[27]

> In this context, the third link in Hilberg's triad does not work. […] I would propose, instead, the term ›initiated participating observer‹, because ›active observation‹ is not enough. [The former] would unfold in the mode of thought, word, deed, and

---

themselves… After all, no German did at first distinguish between a Jew and a Pole, Slav…«, observed Maria Nowakowska (quoted in Żbikowski 2008 [1986]: 297-298).

26 For a stance on the tacit agreement between the Germans as the »editor responsible« for the Holocaust and the Polish community, which contributed to it and profited from its outcomes, see Calek Perechodnik (1996 [1995]; 2004); cf. also Tomasz Żukowski (2013 [2010]).

27 Adorno qualifies the category of the »Jewish question« (*die Judenfrage*) as a sign of antisemitic attitudes and consciousness (1950: 691).

negligence. In this category – it seems to me – there is space for plurality and nuance of manifestations. And perhaps it also helps to comprehend that it was the majority – decisive and, above all, deciding: that ›all of Poland was a ghetto‹. (2008: 238)[28]

In light of the available historical knowledge, and of prevalent attitudes transmitted to this day in Polish society, the category of »witness« loses its meaning in relation to the Polish community as represented by Dylewska.

Third, antisemitic violence – again, exercised by Poles – was one reason for the mass exodus of Polish Jews *after* the war.[29] In 1968, violence perpetrated in the name of law and order resulted in the expulsion of ten to twenty thousand citizens. It was sufficient to construct them as Jews. *Po-lin* completely ignores the fact that it was not the Holocaust but its extension – carried out by Poles – that ended the Jewish presence in Poland. Postwar pogroms, train actions, and widespread killing of people trying to return home and ascertain the fate of loved ones, demonstrated that the Jews were not wanted in Poland. The Holocaust was generally accepted (cf. Libionka 2006: 15-139), as were its tangible effects. Those who took over Jewish property did not want the former owners to return. This is another reason against the residents of formerly Jewish homes being called »witnesses« and made into »guardians of memory«.

Po-lin effectively silences the exterminated Jews. The movie is a self-representation of a group, nostalgically gazing at the traces of their former neighbors, not a tale of the Polish Jews. We are dealing here with a *perpetuum mobile*: the melancholic poetics produces innocent »witnesses« and »heirs« – the innocent »witnesses« and »heirs«, a melancholic poetics. We move endlessly in a circle of images of ourselves, without having to confront reality.

---

28 The last formulation comes from Jan Karski: »It wasn't so hard to go out and come back. It was difficult for the Jews for other reasons. […] Let's say that a Jew escaped from the ghetto, and then what? […] All of Warsaw was a ghetto. All of Poland was a ghetto.« (Karski/Cichy1999: 15)

29 Joanna Tokarska-Bakir frames this phenomenon as ethnic cleansing (2011:803).

PROCESSING THE HOLOCAUST

Beyond History (Mythologization)

Dylewska consistently overlooks the Shoah. Indeed, she does so with every concrete social fact. The film commences with an explanation:

The Jews, fleeing pogroms and pestilence in Germany, arrived in Poland. They met with hospitality and a warm reception. They said PO-LIN in Hebrew – here we shall dwell – thus giving Poland a Jewish name. This is what the thirteenth-century legend says.

On the following screen, we read: »At the outbreak of the Second World War, 3.5 million Jews lived in Poland, accounting for 10 per cent of the population of the Republic.«

The history of the »sudden disappearance« of the Jews – as the reviewer in the daily *Rzeczpospolita* calls it (Hollender 2008: 20) – is presented from a particular, mythologizing perspective. And so, in the thirteenth century, the Jews flee from cruel Europe and find hospitality in Poland. We recognize this image and ourselves in it. It is the well-known and popular topos of *Paradisus Judeorum*. Nothing interferes with it, because we learn nothing about the 700 years of Jewish life in Poland. The use of the paternalistic formula of »hospitality«[30] – otherwise completely ahistorical – might suggest that

---

30 This formula belongs to the nationalist and, in fact, xenophobic discourse, which constructs the state as belonging to the dominant ethnic group. Katarzyna Chmielewska analyzes this motif using the example of secondary school social studies textbooks (Report on the *School of Openness* program of the Open Republic – Association Against Antisemitism and Xenophobia, 2004). The word »hospitality«, with regard to Polish-Jewish relations, also performs an ironic function in publications of otherwise reserved historians. We quote from Jan Grabowski's *Hunt for the Jews: Betrayal and Murder in German-Occupied Poland*: »Much worse, [...] [the] list of ›helpful Poles‹ includes even one Michał Kozik who [...] was said to have saved ten Jews. In fact, Kozik sheltered three Jews, whom he killed with an axe, in the late fall of 1944, when they ran out of money to pay for hospitality.« (Grabowski 2011: 55) [Translators' note: In the

something is not quite right. Yet, in the dominant Polish discourse, it is bundled with the topos of *Paradisus Judeorum* and, as such, is not considered suspicious. The film's narrative leads us to believe that the archival footage and the memories of »witnesses« reflect centuries of harmonious coexistence between »guests« and »hosts«. It was Europe – whose violence manifests itself from the beginning in the form of Germany – that destroyed the idyll.

Somewhere Far Away (Extraterritorialization)

The two screens of introductory text convey hidden assumptions essential to Dylewska's story: Violence against the Jews in Poland is external. Poland and the Poles bear no responsibility for it and, in this sense, do not belong to Europe. They are the exception to the antisemitic norm epitomized by Germany, which has been hostile to the Jews since the time of the Crusades. One can, therefore, draw the conclusion that what happened after 1939 was an undue interference in the world of neighborly coexistence – a foreign violence not corresponding with local reality.

But this is still not enough. Fronczewski reads a text that mentions the legend of Rabbi Elimelech:

In the 1760s, a young Elimelech and his brother Zusha wandered from city to city as beggars to learn the Hasidic custom of humility. They came to a small town. Although they were hungry, they could not eat. Although they were exhausted, they could not sleep. They were overcome by a feeling of indescribable fear. Deepest sorrow engulfed them. In the middle of the night they left the city and never returned. This town was called [dramatic pause] Auschwitz.

Jews were deported from all the shtetls we see in *Po-lin*; in some cases, they were killed on the spot. Meanwhile, the Polish community perpetrated terrible crimes, known from survivors' testimonies and from the accounts of some Poles. Yet Dylewska reduces the Holocaust to just one symbol – Auschwitz. The extermination is placed within extraterritorial limits. Since the holy men did not feel fear in other places, could eat and sleep elsewhere, it seems that nothing really disturbing happened anywhere else. Monstrosity

---

2013 English translation of Grabowski's book, this irony is lost, as the sentence ends, »when they run out of money to pay for their shelter.« (2013 [2011]: 50)]

is limited to a strictly German place; even the German-sounding name shows that this also extended to the cultural sense. In addition, the site is geographically separated from the other places mentioned in the film. The odium does not concern Poles in the least. In this story, after all, they play the role only of »witnesses« – of those physically and symbolically separated from the crime. The viewers, as well as the present inhabitants of the former Jewish towns, can sleep peacefully at night.

The »Sudden Disappearance« (Predestination)

The tale of Elimelech and Zusha is a part of a larger whole. Dylewska integrates her story into the rhythm of nature (day, week, season) and the natural cycle of human life. The narrative of the shtetls – framed through the Poles' memories of their Jewish friends and neighbors – starts with the beginning of the day. The towns come to life, we observe many manifestations of their everyday existence. Then comes the end of the week, the Sabbath. Work ceases. We follow the rhythm of holy days – Hanukkah, Passover, Rosh Hashanah, and Yom Kippur. The story of the two Hasidim in Auschwitz forms the transition to images of dusk, winter, death, cemeteries, and eternal life.

Harbingers of the Holocaust emerge earlier, however. The first example is in the story of Moishe Fuksman, a man »surrounded by an aura of holiness«, »an ardent follower of the tzaddik of Lubavitch«, to whom all the »Jews and Orthodox Christians, and Catholics«, would come for a blessing. His story ends with the sentence, »Ten years and ten months remains«. In the background, we hear the sound of gusting wind. This auditory motif repeats three times subsequently. The *memento mori* is repeated in an identical form when the film mentions misfits. Finally, at the end of a section about feasts, just before the story of Elimelech and Zusha, we see archival footage of children walking one after another in single file. The narrator talks about their futures, lists their names, and concludes, »They have still ten years ahead of them«.

The threefold forewarning of impending catastrophe creates a sense of predestination for the people in the archival images. The sound of the wind, reminiscent of Gothic poetics of uncanniness and horror, makes viewers feel an involuntary chill. At the same time, it places the Holocaust within the field of meanings associated with nature, with natural disasters such as whirlwinds, or with winter as a time of death. The Shoah is placed on a par with events whose causes lie outside the human world, in the realm of forces on which neither the individual nor the community have any impact.

In the Divine Order (Trivialization)

To this, Dylewska adds yet another context – a religious, specifically Hasidic one.[31] Death, including the Holocaust, becomes part of the divine order, and thus moves even further away from social actuality. In the story of Rabbi Elimelech, both circles of meaning overlap. We hear the howl of the wind, see stumps of dug-up bushes in the dilapidated cemetery, focus in on the ashes of an extinguished bonfire. Elimelech and Zusha metaphysically foresee the Shoah as an excess of supernatural evil inscribed in the divine plan.

The next sequence is about cemeteries. The Jewish understanding of death is summarized in these words:

On hearing the news of someone's death, they evoke a special blessing: ›Blessed be the righteous judge!‹ Of the dead, they say: ›He resides in the world of truth.‹ They call the cemetery ›the house of life‹ – ›a good place‹ – and consider it a sacred place. Aside from people, they bury old torn books and leaves from the holy writ.

The narrator talks about Esther Chaja, who spoke with the dead. Contemporary shots of Jewish cemeteries appear on the screen, captured in a tasteful, picturesque style. We hear the howl of the wind.

The cemeteries we see refer to two distinct symbolic orders. First, they evoke the natural deaths of those who died before the Holocaust. Second, they are signs of extermination, traces of the community that no longer exists. Dylewska's film blurs this distinction. Since the parable of Elimelech inscribes the genocide into the supernatural order, the religious understanding

---

31 The parable of Elimelech was evoked as a part of the story about the great tzaddiks and cemeteries. The Hasidic world is a world of communion with God and with the dead. The holy tzaddiks are intermediaries: halfway between God and women and men. Death only increases their power, as it brings them closer to heaven, but at the same time not too far away from the people. We see the *ohels* built over their graves and cards with requests and intentions left there. The voice-over assures us that »no one left the tzaddik unheard«.

of death also extends to the Shoah. Since the dead »live in a world of truth«, and since Jews call the cemetery the »house of life« and »a good place«, the Holocaust can be embraced and accepted. Yet, in the context of the gas chambers, it is extremely difficult to accept the words, »Blessed be the righteous judge!« It is equally impossible to agree with a perspective that establishes death as a path leading to a better life or as a stage in the sequence of generations. This trivialization of catastrophe is all the more problematic when a Polish voice prevails in the narrative – the voice of the dominant group, which does not want to talk about its own involvement in the extermination.

Out of Context (Universalization)

The religious and supernatural context ultimately unlinks the Holocaust from any social actuality. The imagery of melancholically beautiful and picturesquely abandoned cemeteries locates the Shoah in the realm of universal transience. One of the Polish »witnesses« makes this explicit: »It is as if one had fallen asleep, woken up, and there was nothing left. Those years, it seems, as if it were a year ago, and it is already... Everything passes terribly and irrevocably. [The camera films a faint, restlessly moving hand.] Everything... Irretrievably...«

This is hard to deny. But the Jews in Poland ›passed‹ differently than »everything passes«. The gap between the dominant group – even if only as bystanders – and those exterminated is so radical that the Jewish deaths cannot be reduced to the common denominator of universal transience. The Polish community needs to forget this difference in order to avoid confronting their own behavior. Instead of investigating what actually happened on the border between the ghetto and the Aryan side, and what this means for »us« today, *Po-lin* offers a false and superficial confrontation, shrouded in mystery.

Let us analyze the mechanism of universalization through the story of Rachel Szemesz. One of the Polish women says, »During the occupation, I was working at the post office... in Kolbuszowa. I remember once I was going to work and saw a... a handicapped Jewish woman being led by Twardoń, I mean the county governor of Kolbuszowa. [...] And I just felt that he was leading her to her death.« In short, this is a canonical scene of the ritual of catching the Jews and handing them over to die, in broad daylight, in public view.[32] Dylewska's interviewee is very moved. It is clear that she is touching upon her most painful memories. But she does not finish her story. We move instead to footage from the 1930s. Fronczewski's cavernous voice asks, »Will it be Rachel Szemesz? Rachel Sun?« He ends with one of three *memento mori* appearing in *Po-lin*: »She is still standing here.« A close-up of the archival footage is accompanied by the sound of howling wind. Dylewska does not delve into who Twardoń was; the executioner's Polish-sounding name does not raise her suspicions. The film's narrative immediately drops this fragment, which would otherwise shatter the harmonious story, by showing the event from the perspective of prior fate, not that of a history of human activity.[33]

»We Dream about Them Smiling«: Friendship Until Death, Friendship After Death

In the section on winter and death, Dylewska once again puts the Polish »witnesses« in direct proximity to the victims. A montage alternates between the faces of »witnesses« and archival photographs, giving the impression that vivid images are being summoned from memory. The description of Yom Kippur ends with the image of a rabbi blessing men and women. »And they«, preaches the narrator, »aware that the Book of Life and the Book of Death have just been opened in heaven, repent, ask God to forgive their weaknesses and failings, to list their names in the Book of Life for a new, good year.« The archival photos disappear; the camera shows a contemporary window, its glass reflecting trees. Cut. People from archival photos gaze, as if at the window just shown, waiting for something. The last phrase about the Book of Life is accompanied by a shot of a headstone (*matzevah*) with the design of an open book. The camera closes in on it; we can see scratches on the

---

32 In Jan Grabowski's book devoted to the subject, the following terms are used: *ritual*, *scheme*, *scenario*, and *routine* of murders and executions (2013 [2011]).

33 Dylewska consistently avoids the topic of Polish antisemitic violence as a phenomenon or, in fact, a social ritual, dressed up in numerous rationalizations and justifications. The excerpt about Twardoń is by no means related to the theme of prewar antisemitism. Dylewska does not question whether there is any connection between Polish-Jewish relations in the times her film addresses and the later death of Rachel Szemesz. Instead, she shows us the Kolbuszowa coat of arms.

stone and a finger of the hand holding the book. The next scene shows a Polish woman recalling her Jewish friend, and, after her, more »witnesses« in a similar role. One speaks about a friend he dreamed about: »He was smiling, content... Well, I'm saying, maybe he is smiling.« A Polish woman recounts her memories of a poor Jewish girl. A poor Jewish girl – most probably a different one – waves to the audience from the archival footage. As does another remembered friend, a talented violinist. Thus the Polish »witnesses« are to be the Book of Life. This sequence, on the one hand, confirms their role as »guardians of memory«, and on the other, presents them as those over whom the Jewish dead watch.

The »witnesses« in *Po-lin* indicate that their dreams about the victims of the Shoah retain an optimistic aura, which is further strengthened by the structure of Dylewska's film. Dreams about the dead are rarely serene. The Poles, therefore, enjoy a rare privilege. First, Polish and Jewish neighbors were on such good terms that the »sudden disappearance« of the Jews has changed nothing. Since the »witnesses« were friends – and continue to maintain their friendship as »guardians of memory« – the dead show them gratitude. Second, from the religious point of view, framed through the story of the Hasidic travelers and thus constructed as Jewish, death is not so terrible an event. This is why we can suppose of the murdered friend that »maybe he is smiling« on the other side. This view is expressed directly by another »witness«: »I know that these souls know about us, see us, remember us. And they live on, but in a better world.« This language absolves the sins of this world. Up against eternity, everything that happened here – during the victims' lifetimes, in the moments before their deaths, and in the Holocaust's aftermath – loses its gravity.

From the perspective of *Po-lin*, and of the narrative constructed by the dominant group, the dead Jews give their Polish neighbors the best possible reference. It is for this reason that contemporary photographs of Jewish cemeteries can – or even must – be impeccably composed and filled with warm light.[34] Such depictions convey the image of the dominant group, not that of

---

34 At one point in *Po-lin*, we see the disturbing picture of a *tzaddik's ohel* (a structure built over the burial place of a holy man) standing on a car park of sorts. Only the trained eye will recognize it as a Jewish cemetery or, in fact, as an actual cemetery (because dead bodies are still there), but unmarked by external signs. The uninitiated – or skillfully anesthetized – eye will not understand or even register this

Jewish tragedy. In Dylewska's film we see *matzevot* blending into trees, bearing a striking resemblance to the crosses grown into trees in Krzysztof Hejke's album *Polesie* [Polesia, 2009]. We receive an image of the Polish soil embracing the Jewish dead – our own image, as we would like to see ourselves.[35]

JEWS AS THE MYTHICAL »JEW«

Relocation to the Reservation (Separation and Folklorization)

Who are these Jews so fondly remembered by the Poles? *Po-lin* begins its construction of Jewishness with music. The composer, Michał Lorenc, draws from motifs culturally recognizable as traditional markers of Jewishness: the klezmer fiddle and cimbalom. The music in *Po-lin* is evocative and emotional. It puts the audience in a specific mood, favoring affirmative reception over a critical stance. The soundtrack also places the film images in the realm of folklore, constructed as an icon of identity, thereby enclosing »Jewishness« in a field of cultural otherness. The »Jewishness« is, at the same time, domesticated and relegated to a separate space; a clear border is established between the Polish and the Jewish. Recognition of difference goes hand in hand with division.

The main feature of the images curated in *Po-lin* is a life revolving around religion and traditional occupations, a world of trade, crafts, and services that do not traverse the boundaries of the shtetl's minority subculture. Thus folklore – intrinsically entwined with religion – becomes the basis for understanding the Jewish world, social rules, and, above all, identity. Jewishness emerges as an unchanging essence of sorts, and the Jewish community is

---

view. We use the medical category of anesthesia purposefully here. In his work devoted to old synagogues in Poland, Wojciech Wilczyk demonstrates that, in Polish culture and history, the category of the innocent eye is a misunderstanding (2010).

35 This idea allows us to disregard the postwar devastation of Jewish cemeteries, accompanied by the ingenious utilization of stolen *matzevot* (cf. Baksik 2012).

placed outside history. The Jews constitute a separate universe, which has little in common with the rest of society and the changes it undergoes. This is accomplished at a heavy cost, as historical and sociological realities disappear. The image of the Jewish community proves uniform and stereotyped. Most phenomena associated with modernization, and thus with the position of Jews within a modern society, are missing. As members of a homogeneous and separate community, the Jews do not place any demands on the Polish majority. They do not intervene in a public sphere, where questions about equality are unavoidable. The conviction that the majority is tolerant can remain intact, because there is no room for discussion about granting equal rights to a minority that stays outside the space recognized by the dominant culture as its own.

In reality, the end of the nineteenth century was marked by the birth of Jewish political parties and emancipatory movements. The 1905 Revolution, the October Revolution, and the Polish-Bolshevik war of 1920 shook the Old World and its social imaginary. The Jews and other minorities in the Second Polish Republic were particularly affected by the assassination of Gabriel Narutowicz and the death of Józef Piłsudski.[36] The 1930s marked the end of shtetls in their traditional form, characteristic of an estate-based society. The modern market and the nation-state created a space in which business entities and citizens were, at least formally, equal. This fueled aspirations that extended beyond the boundaries of traditional communities. Jews in increasing numbers saw no reason not to participate in a shared space on an equal footing, and they did so as professionals, political activists, party members, workers, scientists, participants in culture and sports. At the same time, in the 1920s and 1930s, antisemitic acts of violence were commonplace and increasingly aggressive. The Polish state plunged the Jews into the position of, at best, second-class citizens. It employed increasingly overt methods to

---

36 [Translators' note: Gabriel Narutowicz was the first president of independent Poland, assassinated five days after taking office on December 16, 1922. He was supported by the Block of National Minorities, opposed by right-wing parties, and labelled »Jewish president« by antisemites. Józef Piłsudski, the Minister of Military Affairs and, since the 1926 coup d'état, *de facto* leader of Poland, died in 1935. After his death, the political scene changed, the prevalent antisemitism was embraced by those in power, and the situation of minorities, especially Jews, worsened significantly.]

remove them from politics, economy, and culture. The emergence of Jews in any realm of public life was commonly considered »over-representation«. These are the historical developments that Dylewska does not want to address.[37]

Dylewska remains blind to the realm where actual encounters between Poles and Polish Jews took place, and in which Polish culture revealed its attitude towards Jewish citizens. The director creates an image that sanctions the boundaries marked out for the minority by the dominant group: the Jews remain picturesque inhabitants of an exotic world and do not appear in spaces reserved by the Poles for the Poles. This is the case despite the fact that, in the archival footage, modernity is clearly present. The emigrants who created the pictures evince this; they left the country seeking social advance, which was impossible in Poland because of antisemitism.[38] The recorded reactions of shtetl residents testify to their new ambitions: They enjoy the prosperity of the visitors, gaze at their fashionable outfits with surprise and admiration, and imitate their lifestyles. The pictures capture the difference between the grandparents in their traditional clothes, the men bearded, the women in wigs, and their children and grandchildren, who clearly aspire to new cultural patterns and to the equality promised by modernity.

---

37 Political parties are mentioned in *Po-lin* only once, when addressing Jewish self-government institutions. In the passage about Kałuszyn, young Communists are depicted as »apostates of the faith« who »once a month meet under the Warsaw bridge, where the thin Comrade Eidel from Warsaw reads from a brochure summarizing Marx's *Das Kapital*.« In contrast with this single mention, the narrative returns again and again to religion and folklore as constitutive of the image of the Jews.

38 One man, who internalized the point of view of the majority (in this case, the »Aryan« Polish intelligentsia), discovered, after being expelled from Poland, an entirely different world: »I had contact with many professors at American universities and much to my surprise found out that many of them were Jews, in whose case either they themselves or their parents were born in Pińsk, Białystok, Rymanów, Włocławek or other similar Polish towns or cities. This shows how much completely unrealized intellectual potential was hidden in the provincial masses of Polish Jews.« (Hurwic 1996: 171)

A ›Sympathetic‹ Reverse of an Antisemitic Cliché

But it is not enough to sequester the Jews. In addition, the Polish collective memory, recorded and perpetuated in *Po-lin*, deploys a specific image of the »Jew«, one that is a function of the majority's own beliefs, that allows the majority to maintain a high opinion of itself and that, if necessary, justifies and legitimizes violence. We are speaking, of course, of negative stereotypes, very rarely invoked in the film, but also of positive stereotypes, which Dylewska treats as manifestations of benevolent memory. What Dylewska's interlocutors appreciate about the Jews is their piety and solidarity, as well as their boundless tolerance for all the forms of discrimination that they encounter when dealing with Poles.

»Here, in the land of Po-lin, lie those who departed this world in glory. Admors,[39] teachers and masters, supports of our world, holy and pure, learned and pious, princes of the Torah. Many have followed and still follow them« – *Po-lin* is full of similar descriptions. We see people walking out of synagogues. Men and boys in traditional clothing sport beards and sidelocks. The homogenous image of the »Jew« is complemented here by a series of explanations of Jewish religion – preferably in its Hasidic variant.

Jewish piety may be admirable, but this is a special kind of admiration. Dylewska's interlocutors appreciate those characteristics of Jews that, in their view, the Polish community lacks. Jews respected their religion more than Poles respected theirs – meaning that Poles should respect their own more. The underlying premise is that each group must ensure its cohesion. The image of the pious Jew strengthens the Poles in their belief that there exists a fundamental difference between the two worlds, and that the Polish Catholic community needs to consolidate against the other. Piety – perceived as a guarantee of tight group affiliation – serves as an essential, distinguishing feature. At the same time, Jewish piety remains ambivalent. For the Polish majority, this piety also constitutes one of the reasons for the stigma against Jews and a potential source of their ominous power.

---

39 Admor is a word that belongs to Hasidic tradition. It is an acronym for »Adonainu, Morainu, VeRabbeinu« (our master, teacher, and rabbi), and refers to a founder of a Hasidic dynasty and/or an outstanding spiritual leader, a great *tzaddik*.

Perceptions of Jewish solidarity function in a similar way. One of Dylewska's interlocutors, evidently drawing from collective myths about the Jews, recounts:

There was one, you know, who used to drive to the station, well, to the train, to pick up guests. They called him Męczyje [Tormentor]. Męczyje, because he overworked the horses. So they, you know, gathered in the synagogue and bought him a horse [smacks], splendid! And he'd ride it for a month and overwork it again, because he didn't feed it. Do you think they condemned him?! They bought him another one! And he overworked that one too! Would ours do that? The hell they would! That's what it's like here! There was solidarity among them!

Alongside this story, we see archival footage of good-looking, bearded Jews, perhaps the community elders. We can guess that they oversee solidarity among the Jews.

We are dealing here with an antisemitic cliché. The example – absurd, exaggerated, and bearing all the characteristics of colloquial imagination – conveys a common stereotype of the Jews: they are loyal to each other, sometimes beyond the limits of common sense. This intragroup solidarity guarantees prosperity and – implicitly – serves as the basis of the Jews' strength vis-à-vis the outside world. In this reasoning, Jewish solidarity becomes an argument for similar solidarity among Poles – a solidarity whose absence Dylewska's interlocutor grieves. Any competent user of the Polish language recognizes the phantasm of Jewish solidarity as an excuse for the majority to ally against the Jews. Strangely, Dylewska takes the story at face value and adds no critical commentary. More than this, she disingenuously substantiates it with images. The phantasm is objectified and viewers can see with their own eyes that what the Polish »witness« says is true.

The seemingly positive image of the »Jew«, produced by the dominant group and presented by Dylewska as a benevolent memory is the reverse of the antisemitic cliché and, simultaneously, its element. Here, admiration does not translate into affirmation of otherness, but serves rather as a handy justification for defense – it is, *de facto*, an excuse for violence against the Jews as others and for their exclusion from the space reserved for the Poles. It is an image that overpowers and isolates them, and does not offer any grounds for hope for a change of status accepted by the majority. Folklore, robes, beards, and sidelocks relegates the Jews to the reservation, separate from the present and from real life. Their otherness is revealed, perhaps worthy of admiration, but also dangerous to the majority. In *Po-lin*, the Jews – in a frighteningly anachronistic form – are sent to the museum. It is, however, not a museum that preserves the memory of their real life; it hosts, rather, the majority's fear-ridden misconceptions about their power and the threats it potentially represents.

Sacralization of Exclusion

Because of the sanctity attributed to the Jews, the image of them produced by the majority turns out to be infrangible. In *Po-lin*, the commentary often takes on a biblical tone. The narrator speaks of »God-fearing men, learned and righteous«, of »gentle and humble women, dedicated to their families with all their hearts«, of »women humble, pious, and brave«.[40] The mythical register renders any criticism of the Polish memory virtually impossible; it holds, after all, so sublime an image for posterity. But the sanctification of the Jews' image also entails sanctification of its underlying logics. It seals the beliefs of the majority, the distribution of roles and spaces. The respect for the *sacrum* enshrined in memory cannot be separated from the sacralization of practices of the dominant group, which, in this way, only further reinforces its power over the minority.

The *de facto* separation of the two communities coincides with sham encounters. Culinary philosemitism perfectly serves this role. Dylewska's interlocutors talk at length about the flavors of Jewish dishes and their own attempts to prepare them. Regarding this as a compliment, they emphasize that their Jewish specialties never tasted as good as those served by their former neighbors. A sentiment for *cholent* or *kugel*, and the insinuation of a shared table, constitute a proof of friendship. Yet, judging by other elements of the description, the friendship never really existed. Basic knowledge of recipes is no indication of understanding. Again, it is difference and otherness that are being underscored.

---

40 Dylewska complements the patriarchal language about humble Jewish women with a scene featuring laughing girls. We see them giggle, talk, birds twitter in the background. The narration about respectable mothers is coupled with an image of charming, nubile young women. Both elements match without discord; in fact, they are two sides of the same stereotype.

Po-lin inspires melancholy, feeding on the most stereotypical representations of Jews. They bolster the convenient, unproblematic self-image of the Polish majority – an image of its own creation, one in which it can recognize itself contentedly.

THE »GOOD JEW« AND THEIR USES

The »Jew« Will Forgive You Anything

In Polish memories, the Jews come across as being exceedingly polite, compliant, and friendly to Poles. Let us examine first an account given by a cultured lady from Słonim:

> 1936 or 1937 marked the beginning of mobilization among the Poles, who thought that the borderland towns must be a little de-Jewed [odżydzone] in terms of trade. And, indeed, in Słonim there was a big commotion. The Jews were very upset by this. The Kosmowski family came with capital, with decent goods, and opened a huge craft store. I know that my parents used to shop in Mr. Meszel's semi-warehouse store. He would give us some discounts. My mom wanted to support Polish trade. So, with real regret and a shame of sorts, mom went and said, ›Mrs. Meszel, I have to go.‹ The latter wept bitter tears, but said that she understood.

There is no doubt that we are dealing here with the description of an antisemitic act. The »Do Not Buy from Jews!« campaign, launched by Poles, was a boycott intended to deprive Jews of all means of livelihood, and thus to destroy the economic basis of their existence. Without work and wages there was no way to live. The only alternatives were misery, starvation, or emigration, which itself required resources. In *Po-lin*, however, the event is related in language that conceals the brutality of the situation. The categories underpinning the antisemitic worldview seem to be rooted in the very nature of things. Poles are Poles, Jews are Jews, and both are bound by commitment to group solidarity. The Jews constitute a problem – »the Jewish question«. It cannot be tolerated, so something has to be done. The rules of conduct are dictated for the Poles by *force majeure* in the form of categorical imperative:

if trading is »in the hands of the Jews«,[41] the town »must« be »de-Jewed«. There is no other choice.

In this context, the Polish language, with its power to form new words and its vast store of diminutives, comes to the aid of the cultured antisemite. »De-Jewing« was a »must«. »A little« [troszkę]. Though we do not really learn how much. This »a little«, one can gather, does not refer to the scale of the economic boycott, and, therefore, does not describe reality – in fact, the violence went on unstopped – but serves, instead, as a euphemism. »And, indeed, in Słonim there was a big commotion«, says the cultured lady. »A big commotion« to »de-Jew a little«? This situation »upset« the Jews – another euphemism – not »a little«, but »very«. Maybe they should have been only »a little« upset – in proportion to the size of the »de-Jewing« planned by Poles? The juxtaposition of the terrifying »de-Jewing« with the diminishing, and even belittling and infantilizing, »a little« allows the perpetrator to feel comfortable, while the victim of violence is seized by terror.[42]

Force majeure, however, remains *force majeure*. »De-Jewing« has nothing to do with antisemitism, obviously. It is all about patriotism – understandable in itself – and about the measurable quality of goods. Polish competition is basically unrivalled. The Polish Kosmowski family's shop is huge. It has capital and »decent goods«, which differentiates it from the Jewish Meszel family's »semi-warehouse«, described with a note of contempt, whose owner gave »some discounts«. An economic boycott – as the antisemitic stereotype suggests – puts an end to the proverbial »Jewish rubbish« [żydowska tandeta]. In terms of images, we move from the squalid alleys captured in the archival photographs to an elegant shopping street. In the foreground, a group of workers hangs telephone cables on poles. We see shop windows: H. Brański sells textiles [towary łokciowe], Wł. Szejkierc – a Pole, judging from his first name – trades in wines and vodkas.

---

41 The motif of small-town trade being »controlled« by Jews appears several times in *Po-lin*.

42 Similar logic governed the speech of Władysław Gomułka's at the Sixth Trade Union Congress in June 1967, in which Gomułka explicitly stated that not all Jews have a reason to be concerned. It was clear to both the minority and the majority that he actually had all Jews in mind. Yet, from the point of view of the Poles' self-image, Gomułka's wording sounded better than speaking about the matter openly.

There is no language in Polish memory in which the persecution of the Jews could be addressed from outside the antisemitic stereotype, from a position of distance that would enable us to grasp what is really happening. In the account of the lady from Słonim, it is not violence that is at stake but a fair and cultured treatment of the Jewish neighbors. The price one has to pay for this fair and cultured behavior is discomfort. »Real regret and shame of sorts« testify to the mother's high moral sensitivity and emotional delicacy, because, after all, she could just as well have done without all that courtesy towards Mrs. Meszel, given the objective necessity of the boycott. The mother of the lady from Słonim is therefore more than fair. The moral is clear. Poles may be sorry about the suffering of the Jews, but still, they have no choice. To paraphrase Roman Dmowski's words of wisdom: They are Poles, so they have Polish duties.[43]

The reasons behind the Polish »Do Not Buy from Jews!« campaign are obvious to both parties in *Po-lin* and require no commentary. As a rule of coexistence, they are also respected by the minority. The Polish woman »must«. The Jewish woman understands, lending psychological support to the Polish woman in a difficult situation. The Polish woman feels »real regret«. The Jewish woman weeps. Clearly, not only the majority suffered. For Dylewska, there is absolutely no doubt that the discriminated minority understood and respected the principles established by the dominant group, approving of them as if there were no alternative. The director illustrates this account with an archival image of an elderly Jewish woman, standing in a doorway and smiling warmly at the camera. Light radiates from her white blouse. The »good Jew« summoned from Polish memory embraces the Poles' antisemitism with no grievance.

That would be it when it comes to Polish phantasms. In reality, the Jews – victims of injustice and violence – were well aware that they were being denied the right to live in Poland, more and more openly and frequently. They realized that they were defenseless and, at all costs, needed to stay on good terms with the members of the majority, because, when violence escalated, their lives would depend on their relationships with their neighbors. They

---

43 [Translators' note: Roman Dmowski was a Polish politician, co-founder and chief ideologue of the right-wing and openly antisemitic National Democracy. He died in 1939.]

practiced mimicry not to annoy their persecutors and, if possible at all, to somehow win them over.[44]

»When Poor, Ask a Jew«[45]

Similar forms of mimicry and compliance appear in other accounts. The sequence that ends with the story from Słonim introduces the topic of Jews in trade. A Polish »witness« complains, »They would call a Pole *goy*. [...] What is this *goy*? It is an insult to Poles!«[46] His tone of voice and behavior attest to his ferocity and his satisfaction at revealing the truth about the Jews to those who wish to whitewash their memory. His companion soothes him: »But you could go to them, they gave you credit, and they waited, and so on, and they always helped.«

The subsequent stories about Jewish kindness act as a response to the accusation of »the insult to the Poles!« There is no more mention of aggression, clearly heard in the grievance over the allegedly insulting »goy«. Thus Dylewska treats this grievance as a description of reality and responds with counterexamples, such as this story, narrated by a man from Kurów:

---

44 A picture from Kałuszyn: »The Jews claimed that they could easily elect a mayor of their nationality, but my father later explained to me that the administrative authorities would never approve of a mayor of the Jewish faith anyway. From my parents I learned about a custom (a rather peculiar one from the contemporary point of view) that prevailed, probably not only in Kałuszyn. According to the custom, a newlywed policeman introduced his wife to all Jewish traders. From then on, she could take whatever she needed from them for free, but only if it was for her own use. For the traders, it was still a better deal than paying fines for dirt in their shops and especially for repeatedly trading on Sundays (customers were then let in through the back entrance).« (Tazbir 2005: 13) What draws attention in the quoted excerpt is the rationalization and downplaying of antisemitic violence. For categories and criteria of dirt, see Mary Douglas (1966).

45 The entire proverb goes like this: »When poor, ask a Jew. When it gets nice, ask the Jew to kiss your ass« [Jak bida, to do Żyda, a jak po bidzie, pocałuj mnie w dupę Żydzie] (quoted in Markiel 2011: 47).

46 *Goy* is a Hebrew word that literally means »nation«, and describes a non-Jewish person.

When my father was building a barn, and he ran out of sheets of ten square meters for the roof, he went to the *Społem* cooperative. Well, the cooperative wanted him to pay. So he went to the Jew: ›Mosiek or Yosek [in diminutive], I need ten square meters of sheeting, but I have no money now, well, can you help me?‹ ›Mr. Wójcicki, I will always help you. You are a responsible man. I know you, we know you, take it. Once you've done it and you have the money, you will give it back.‹ Ha!

And again, *Po-lin* conveys the same misunderstanding. What the majority considers proof of friendship and neighborliness is, in fact, an indication of a veiled but constantly present threat of violence against the minority. The lack of symmetry in the exchange of courtesies is in itself reason for concern. The Jew treats the Pole with clear respect, addressing him as »Mr.«, while the Pole calls the Jew by his first name in the diminutive form. Moreover, »Mosiek« is not necessarily the name of this particular person. In Polish it serves as an offensive term to denote a Jew (singular: Mosiek, plural: Mośki), and as one of the most identifiable signs of antisemitic discourse.

Everybody knows, moreover, that trade is not a domain of sentiments. Since the *Społem* cooperative refused to give Mr. Wójcicki a loan, there was evidently a reason for it. We might assume that in a small town like Kurów, the co-operative employees knew their customers as well as did the sympathetic »Mosiek or Yosek«. There are, therefore, reasons to suspect that, from the economic point of view, the Jewish merchant acted recklessly. Dylewska's narrative, however, conceals both the seeming irrationality of the Jew's action and the rationale behind it.

Meanwhile, the reasons for »Mosiek or Yosek's« behavior – friendly, as the Pole remembers it – are clearly evident. What we learn from *Po-lin* about the reality of the 1930s is enough to comprehend that the generous merchant did not want to expose himself to the hostility, potentially dangerous if acts of open hatred were to take place. Better to give the Pole goods for free than risk his revenge during a pogrom. This strategy has been known in the Diaspora for centuries. But the reasons might have been deeper. Facing the boycott and a decrease in customers, the Jewish merchant had to take a risk that the *Społem* cooperative would not accept. The Jews had access only to the least lucrative parts of the market. Uncertain credit is the last and least secure opportunity to earn money. The majority's violence thus forced the minority into subordination to most unfavorable rules. Instead of friendship, as

Dylewska would want it, we are dealing here with enforcement resulting from the majority's antisemitic behavior.

In the narrative of *Po-lin*, reality gives way to the myth of harmonious coexistence, rendering discrimination effectively invisible. Dylewska presents violence in a way that makes it look like good neighborly relations. Even when wronged, the minority must put on a brave face – just like Mrs. Meszel, the store owner from Słonim. Against the Polish tales of friendly neighborliness, any demand for equal rights put forward by the Jews would be received as an expression of the mythical Jewish ingratitude and impudence – in short, as aggression. The majority – and, unthinkingly, also the creators of *Po-lin* – put a false alternative before the Jews: antisemitism or ›friendship‹, a friendship conditioned on consent to antisemitic violence.

The Patriot Jew Versus the Communist Jew

All this makes the music of the cimbalom, which runs throughout the film and discreetly evokes a concert performed by Jankiel, the Jew in Adam Mickiewicz's *Pan Tadeusz*, echo with a false note.[47] The majority requires Polish patriotism from the Jews, but, as *Po-lin* indicates, this is tantamount to a demand for subordination to majority norms. The Poles and certain well-remembered Jews reach understanding in specific, symbolically marked moments over their shared hostility to Communists. The cultured lady from Słonim recounts:

> That last year I lived on Berka Joselewicza Street, with the Jews, the Łęcewiccy. We had two small rooms, and the third one, behind the kitchen, was occupied by Mr. Łęcewicki's mother. She was an old lady, and there was a conflict. The young people were already sympathizing with Communism. And the grandmother, blind and deaf, would tell me, ›Listen, see, whether the Sabbath has begun.‹ Whether the rabbi has already lit the candles. [...] So I considered it to be my sacred duty. I would go to her and say, ›Mrs. Łęcewicka, the candles are already lit at the rabbi's.‹ ›Oh, thank you‹.

---

47 [Translators' note: Adam Mickiewicz's *Pan Tadeusz* [Sir Thaddeus, 1834] is a national epic of Poland. Jankiel is one of its protagonists: an old Jew, innkeeper of a leased tavern, cymbalist, and a great Polish patriot – a feature which is reflected also in his music performed for the Polish protagonists.]

She would pinch my cheek and quickly light the candles at home. And the young were already [Communists]... She would say, ›They're Communists! They're Bolsheviks!‹

The actual conflict between the older, religious generation and the young is layered over and reframed by the stereotype of »Jew-Communism« [żydokomuna]. For Dylewska's interlocutor, Communism is a Jewish destiny of sorts. The young people were »already« sympathizing with Communism, she says. Their choice only confirms what was already inevitable. The stereotype posits Jews as the others who brought an alien and hostile ideology to the Poles. The phantasm of »Jew-Communism« has served primarily to legitimize the nationalist concept that the nation and the right wing that represents it are the only legitimate authority in the Polish state.[48] The encounter between Poles and Jews, at least those deserving of benevolent memory, in the context of animosity toward Communist Jews, seems at least suspicious.

In the majority narrative, the »good Jew« can occupy only one place: that of someone who reaffirms the dominant group's ideas – and, in this case, also its fears and phobias – about the minority. Jews who accepted the »Jew-Communism« stereotype agreed to a division into »us« and »them«, in which the right to decide on common matters belonged exclusively to Poles, and in which Jews were never to be fully trusted. Dylewska accepts this state of affairs and does nothing to reinscribe into the collective memory the Jewish Communists nor, in fact, any Jews who attempted to enter the majority community on equal terms. There is no place for them in the narrative of *Po-lin*. And, consequently, there is no incentive to reconsider the prejudices and practices of the dominant group.

Instead, Dylewska's interlocutors praise the Jews' patriotism. »Mr. Tau taught me history«, recalls with sentiment a resident of Kolbuszowa. »He was a Jew. He was a great historian, and he really taught me to love my Fatherland. He taught us history very beautifully«. But Jewish and Polish love of country mean totally different things. For the Polish majority, patriotism means acceptance of the *status quo*. It entails solidarity limited to ethnic Catholic Poles, a boycott of Jewish trade, the figure of the »good Jew«

---

48 Cf. August Grabski's statement in Anna Zawadzka's documentary *Żydokomuna* [Jew-Communism, 2010].

who gives credit when a Polish shop refuses it, hatred of »Jew-Communism« and the like. All this is unthinkingly received as obvious.

But for the Jewish minority, patriotism required identification with an idealized image of Poland, produced and sustained at the expense of complete blindness to reality. It could also denote an act of faith and a hope that everything would eventually work out, that it would be possible finally to be at home in their own country. In extreme cases, it could mean consent to the *status quo* and internalization of antisemitism as justifiable and deserved. Especially the representatives of Jewish intelligentsia, to which Mr. Tau belonged, exhibited this ›patriotic syndrome‹. Nevertheless, in whatever form it took, Polish Jewish patriotism contained a dream of equality. The possibility of such a fundamentally altered relationship was not envisioned by the Poles praising Jewish patriots. And so the tale of Mr. Tau rings a false note. It ignores discrimination; it serves, rather, to perpetuate it. Just in case, we learn nothing about the wartime fate of this Polish patriot from Kolbuszowa.

The Jews who are so positively remembered by Dylewska's interviewees make no demands. They show no trace of protest, discontent, resentment, bitterness, irony, anger or aggression against the dominant population. They feel comfortable in the Polish culture, which does not constitute a source of serious problems for them. In this beautiful Polish story, antisemitism ceases to be a social practice that organizes the life of the minority. It appears merely as an incident that changes nothing in the substantially good relations between the Poles and the Jews.

The role of the figure of the »good Jew« (as the culmination or the supporting structure of the Polish narrative) requires separate study. Philosemitism could not, however, exist without the »good Jew«, a figure whose function is to issue certificates of morality for Poles, to absolve them, to deny accusations of antisemitism, to express consent to antisemitic behavior, to condemn »bad Jews«, and, finally, to legitimize the majority's version of history.

ZVI KAMIONKA

Problematic is also the role in which Dylewska cast the only Polish Jew to speak in the film. Zvi Kamionka appears at the end of *Po-lin*. He says surprisingly little. Let us analyze how the director introduces and develops this figure.[49] The sequence on cemeteries and death ends with a sentence that summarizes the image of Jews presented in the film. Fronczewski declaims, »In the Jewish cemeteries in the land of Po-lin, only stones bear witness that modest, pious, brave women, and God-fearing, learned, and righteous men are buried here.« We are within the field of majority fantasy: the Jews are religiously Orthodox, safely locked in their own world, and dead. The shtetls are gone. The Holocaust puts an end to the story about the land of Po-lin.

We have already analyzed how the director presents the Shoah. The words of Polish »witnesses« about the irreversible passage of time are echoed in images of abandoned cemeteries. In the distance, we hear the wind – the same sound that accompanied all previous mentions of the Holocaust. This is when Zvi Kamionka appears, and says,

In 1942, when the Germans liquidated the ghetto in Kałuszyn, they would systematically transport hundreds of Jews to this spot and shoot them; then they would bring new ones, and those new Jews would dig mass graves, bury the dead. They killed two thousand Jews this way. My relatives lie here, eighty people, paternal and maternal family. My father's name was Kamionka, and my mother's name was Hepner. [Pause] Yes, those two families. They are lying here [Tutaj są zakopani].

That's all he says. Dylewska asks no further questions. All we have learned from this scene is the victims' ›resting place‹, and that the Germans were responsible for the crime. Kamionka stands on a big, deserted piece of land. Nearby, we see houses, outbuildings, a greenhouse. We guess that he is standing on the ›grave‹ of his relatives, but no trace of those murdered is to be seen: neither a stone nor a monument nor commemorative plaque. This goes entirely unnoticed. The director does not ask the survivor, a living man, what he thinks about this situation. She does not inquire about his prewar or wartime memories. She poses no question about why he left Poland after the war. The film narrative focuses on something else: on the unity of Polish and Jewish memory.[50]

---

49 It needs to be stressed that we are looking here at the figure of Zvi Kamionka that the director creates, as distinct from the real person.

50 We can see the panorama of Kałuszyn right before the appearance of Zvi Kamionka's silhouette. It resembles a shot from the beginning of the film, in which the camera moves towards the ground, symbolically descending to the graves in order

Serene archival images appear on the screen: Kałuszyn 1936. Let us digress a bit. In June 1936, a pogrom took place in the neighboring town of Mińsk Mazowiecki.[51] Over the next few years, the tragedy of the Jews unfolded here and in other places, ceaseless in its schematic repetition:

> Those who planned to save themselves knew that it was not going to be easy; they were aware of what lay in store for them. Adam Kamienny from Kałuszyn wrote in his diary in 1944: ›We will be hunted and pursued day and night. No one will let us under his roof or offer us a piece of bread. Even if someone wanted to do it, he refrained out of fear that a neighbor would notice and inform on him. We will have to hide in the woods like wild animals, exposed to murder by bandits, who seemed to be teeming everywhere.‹ (Engelking 2016 [2011]: 35)

In Barbara Engelking's book ›*Such a Beautiful Sunny Day…*‹ *Jews Seeking Refuge in the Polish Countryside, 1942-1945* (2016 [2011]), one can find many stories from

---

to summon the spirits of the dead and trigger the memories of the Polish »witnesses«. In that shot, the camera stops precisely at the level from which the same place was filmed by an amateur filmmaker in the 1930s. We see a flash of light, as if the film had jammed for a moment, and then we are suddenly in that world. Right before the shot in which Zvi Kamionka appears, the camera travels down until, in a close-up, we see grass covering the spot where those murdered lie. The signal indicating descending into the graves and awakening the memories of the living is the same, and identical archival footage illustrates the Polish and the Jewish memory.

51 »A motionless crowd looks at burning houses. No one comes to help. Where is the fire brigade? Jewish houses and shops are burning. It is the ›Mińsk pogrom‹. Judka Lejb Chaskielewicz shot Jan Bujak, his former superior from the 7th Regiment of Lublin Uhlans stationed in Mińsk. Why? For some personal reasons. But the rumor was circulating in town that Bujak died when he was walking out of the church and that it was a revenge for his participation in activities undertaken to retake trade from the Jews (he was running a non-commissioned officers' mess). It is a miracle that no one died, even though there were several dozen people beaten and several dozen burnt, plundered and vandalized houses too. A miracle or… a training Because if the 7th Regiment was not on the training ground but in the town instead…« (Goźliński 2011) The pogrom in Mińsk lasted one week.

here – of Jews in hiding, handed over, executed on the spot or sent to the gendarmerie or blue police [...]. (Goźliński 2011)[52]

End of digression.

Po-lin. Kałuszyn 1936. We hear the wind howling. We see the faces of people smiling for the camera. Large families, like Zvi Kamionka's, 80 people. The sequence of images is interrupted by a close-up of Zvi Kamionka's face. Cut. Then, instead of the face of an athletic man in a short jacket, who is facing the camera here and now, we see a face equipped with all the attributes of an Orthodox Jew recorded on the black-and-white tape back then. The living man with a name is reduced to the mythical »Jew«, as if translated and converted into an anonymous icon in which the majority encapsulated the dead victims of the Shoah. But this is not all, ladies and gentlemen. Next comes the black-and-white image of a girl – »a little Jewess« – waving from the screen to »us« Poles. In the film credits, the name »Zvi Kamionka« has been placed after the names of the Polish »witnesses«; separated but, at the same time, connected through the conjunction »and«.

In the closing sequence, we see exactly the same panorama of Kałuszyn as at the beginning of the film, except that now the camera moves upwards. The narrative has come full circle. The beginning and end are arranged in a visually impressive bracket. The vanished world cited in the memories of »witnesses« falls back into oblivion. The last shot, a long one, which lasts almost a minute, starts with Kamionka's profile and bears the caption, »Zvi Kamionka, Israel. One of the saved [ocalony] Jews of Kałuszyn« The passive form – »saved« – should give us pause in relation to a man who owes his survival only to himself.[53]

The camera looks from on high and moves farther upwards. Kamionka turns and walks away. We see him on the paved cobblestones of a square, then he becomes smaller and smaller, and finally disappears in the general outline of the town. The panorama of Kałuszyn expands. Among the houses, at the center of the screen, rises the church tower – yet another Freudian slip.

---

52 In the very same text, the author considers *Po-lin* a »perfect documentary«.

53 [Translators' note: The authors address here the consequential semantic difference between the passive form of the transitive verb *ocalić* [to rescue / to survive] as opposed to *ocalały* [survivor], which does not imply, as the word *ocalony* [saved] does, that survival was thanks owed to the help of gentiles.]

The film crew begins to read the names of Holocaust victims. First, each of them is pronounced separately, then the voices overlap and merge. The image darkens to black. Emotions escalate.

A living man from the prewar shtetl appears in *Po-lin*. His memory is excellent. He can recount everything – of his own accord, personally, in Polish, without an interpreter. But he is not allowed to speak on the topic that constitutes the subject of the film. He talks, instead, about something else: about war and death – even though the director has declared that she was not interested in war and death, but in the prewar period and life. This astonishing choice can be neither understood nor justified, not even by the filmmakers' good intentions.

It is hard to resist the impression that the way Zvi Kamionka is deployed constitutes a strategic element – a *pièce de résistance* – of the story Dylewska constructs. This character's role is to legitimize the essential elements of the majority's narrative. The way the figure is cast, including the spaces in which it appears, confirms that there is no difference between Polish and Jewish memories. This reinforces the message of the commentary, which encloses Jews within a traditional, religious category of difference. This is the case despite the fact that Zvi Kamionka is not a Hasid. He is a man with a secular higher education and a former soldier in the Israeli army, where he moved in 1950.[54]

The way Dylewska constructs Zvi Kamionka's figure further legitimizes the film's representation of the Holocaust. Dylewska does not ask her protagonist about issues that cannot be ignored in this story about Polish and Jewish memory. It is not enough to say that the Jews of Kałuszyn were murdered by the Germans. Transporting and murdering 2000 people is not an easy task. It requires the cooperation of many individuals, if only to prevent the victims from escaping. What were the Polish townspeople doing at the time? It is known that the local Volunteer Fire Brigade – an institution that during the Shoah gained terrible notoriety elsewhere – took part in liquidating the ghetto in Kałuszyn.[55] Was the deportation of Kałuszyn's Jews accompanied by looting, as in other Polish towns? What happened to the property

---

54 Email from Zvi Kamionka to Elżbieta Janicka, August 16, 2011.
55 Chróścicki (2008: 248). In the same issue of *Kałuszyn Yearly*, we read: »The members of the Voluntary Fire Brigade passed yet another test of patriotism during the Second World War.« (Charczuk 2008: 301)

of the eighty members of the Hepner and Kamionka families? Did anyone escape and survive? Did anyone escape and get caught? Was there somewhere to hide and, if not, why not? Were those in hiding denounced? What did the local parish priest have to say? What happened in Kałuszyn after the war? What does Zvi Kamionka think and feel about all this?

Since none of these questions is posed, we can assume that the creators of the film, and with them the majority of Poles, are not interested in what their Jewish neighbors experienced, what they felt and thought – neither those who died nor those who are still alive. Polish memory of the Holocaust is to be the memory of ethnic Catholic Poles. The Holocaust is to be remembered as the end of the Jewish presence in Poland, caused by external violence. If the Jews' memory differs from this dominant version of events, it has no place in the consciousness of the majority. It remains external, alien, and unnecessary.

Zvi Kamionka, our contemporary, is presented in *Po-lin* as an envoy of the actual and symbolic abyss to which the Polish majority has driven Polish Jews. After playing the role assigned to him, he is to return to that place. The caption at the bottom of the screen identifies him as a visitor from afar – a foreign guest who has come only to visit a cemetery. The film character walks away, leaving the blame and responsibility to the Germans, and to the Poles the role of »witnesses« and »guardians of memory« – along with the good mood this engenders. The Polish majority does not need the real Zvi Kamionka. It is better that he disappears quietly and without protest.[56] His silhouette fading into oblivion reaffirms the pleasant melancholy *Po-lin*

---

56 It is impossible not to quote here an excerpt from Calel Perechodnik's *Spowiedź* [Confession, 2004]: »Indeed, every Pole had at least one Jewish friend, who begged them, with tears in his eyes, to take things for safekeeping. Poles would generously agree, and if the Jew was obliging and went to Treblinka, the matter was solved. Possessions increased, the conscience clear, *tout va très bien*. It was worse when a Jew appeared to be ›bothersome‹, wanted to live and reclaim their things. It was clear that there was no point in giving them their possessions back, the Jew would not survive the war anyway; they would not be able to repay the favor after the war, to lodge charges [against Poles] before a court, or cast a shadow on their unblemished name. So people, say for yourselves, there is no point in returning anything, it is simply a sin before God – we give them possessions back and others will come and take them for themselves.« (2004: 125)

evokes for the Polish audience. And this melancholy is all the easier to embrace because the film character does not want anything from the majority: neither to reclaim property, nor to bring thieves and murderers to justice, nor to revise the collective imaginary.

CONCLUSION: BLACKMAIL WITH SWEETNESS

Where dispute is open, the path to negotiation also remains open. The outcry of protest or anger gives hope for an articulation of problems in which the parties might set the rules of coexistence on an equal footing. The *Po-lin* narrative, however, leaves no room for criticism, as it does not provide space for a Jewish voice. Even worse, the image of sweet, harmonious neighborly relations between Poles and Jews acts as the most effective gag – and as blackmail.

Dylewska's film was greeted as a work of good will, driven by solicitude towards the archival materials, attentiveness to the traces of Polish Jews, sympathy to the voices of Polish »witnesses«. Kindness obliges; those who receive it should respond in the same way, take the outstretched hand. We know this situation from the famous play every Pole reads in school, titled *Wesele* [The Wedding, 2012 (1901)]. It is 1900. A Pole addresses a Jew as Mosiek (name in diminutive),[57] calling him to witness their good neighborly relations: »But aren't we friends?« The cornered Jew does not want to lie but

---

57 In Polish, the exchange reads as follows: »No, my jesteśmy przyjaciele« (the Pole), »No, tylko że my jesteśmy / tacy przyjaciele, co się za bardzo nie lubią« (the Jew). In Stanisław Wyspiański's canonical play, the Jew calls the Poles »Mister«, regardless of their social position. Poles, in turn, address him using a derogatory generic name »Mosiek« or other insulting formulations, such as, »you dog shit«. [Translators' note: Wyspiański's play was inspired by an actual wedding reception which took place in the village of Bronowice near Kraków in 1900. Wyspiański's friend, the poet Julian Rydel was marrying Jadwiga Mikołajczyk. The name of the Jewish tavern keeper, who at that time rented the tavern from the local parser, was, in fact, Hirsz Singer.]

cannot tell the truth. His answer is »It's just that we're the kind of friends / who don't much care for one another« (Wyspiański 2012 [1991]: 39).[58]

Once again, we are dealing with a set-up hinting at violence: the Polish outstretched hand versus the proverbial Jewish clenched fist. If the Jews do not shake the outstretched hand, they expose themselves to the accusation of ingratitude, and today – after the Holocaust – they also confirm the view that they did not deserve to be treated well, let alone saved – which would explain why, during the war, so few Poles were willing to assist or even to remain indifferent towards the Jews, who craved for nothing but indifference. Dylewska's film might come across as a friendly gesture, but it offers neither equality nor room for an unconstrained articulation of the Jewish experience.

Contemporary Polish Jews, real people, who will have to do something with this friendly gesture, will find themselves in trouble. Refusal is not polite. But shaking the outstretched hand? If they accept the film's proposed conditions, the only role left for them to play is that of the »good Jew« who understands everything, forgives everything, and maintains the *status quo*. But if they refuse? The authorities, who always know where the golden mean is to be set, will talk about a lack of objectivity, of exaggeration, of seeing only the dark side of Polish-Jewish history. Meanwhile, the rules of the so-called Polish-Jewish dialogue request: »to look for what unites, not exaggerate what divides«. Now, at least, the ungrateful, insolent, and, God forbid, vindictive »bad Jews« will face the hard and definite dismissal they deserve.

Translated from Polish by Robin Gill and Zuzanna Dziuban

---

58 The Jewish protagonist of *Wesele* adds, »A Jew, I'm used to being reviled.« (Wyspiański 2012 [1901]: 42) The situation would be completely different if the interlocutors were equal. An American author whose family came from Drohobych says, »I recently, during a seminar, met a Ukrainian officer. When I told him that my family was originally from Ukraine, he threw his arms around me, saying: ›So we're family!‹ I thought about it for a few days and finally explained to him why no descendant of the Jews who fled pogroms in Ukraine, could say that we are a family.« (Lankosz/Waldman 2011)

LITERATURE

Adamczyk-Garbowska, Monika (2009):»Macewy ze słów. Księgi pamięci gmin żydowskich.« In: Kultura Enter February (http://kulturaenter.pl /0/07sn01.html).

Adamczyk-Garbowska, Monika/Kopciowski, Adam/Trzciński, Andrzej (eds.) (2009): ›Tam był kiedyś mój dom...‹ Księgi pamięci gmin żydowskich, Lublin: Wydawnictwo UMCS.

Adorno, Theodor W. (1950):»Anti-Semitism for What?« In: Theodor W. Adorno et al., The Authoritarian Personality, New York: Harper & Brothers, pp. 617-621.

Adorno, Theodor W. (2005 [1966]): Negative Dialectics, London and New York: Routledge.

Baksik, Łukasz (2012): Macewy codziennego użytku/Matzevot for Everyday Use, Wołowiec: Wydawnictwo Czarne.

Biedka, Łukasz (2008):»Pomiędzy poczuciem wstydu a poczuciem dumy – psychologiczne zabiegi wokół narodowego wizerunku w debacie historycznej.« Paper presented at the 9th conference of the Israeli-Polish Mental Health Association, Nazareth, 6-8 November 2008.

Błoński, Jan (1990 [1987]):»The Poor Poles Look at the Ghetto.« In: Antony Polonsky (ed.), ›My brother's keeper?‹: Recent Polish Debates on the Holocaust, London: Routledge, pp. 34-48.

Bułhak, Jan (1939): Polska fotografia ojczysta. Poradnik fotograficzny, Poznań: Ossolineum.

Cała, Alina (2003): Ostatnie pokolenie. Autobiografie polskiej młodzież żydowskiej okresu międzywojennego ze zbiorów YIVO Institute for Jewish Research w Nowym Jorku, Warszawa: Sic!

Charczuk, Wiesław (2008):»Ochotnicze Straże Pożarne południowego Podlasia i wschodniego Mazowsza – dzieje i teraźniejszość.« In: Rocznik Kałuszyński 8, pp. 301-306.

Chmielewska, Katarzyna (2004):»Sprawozdanie z badania gimnazjalnych podręczników do wychowania obywatelskiego.« In: Tomasz Żukowski (ed.), Wyniki monitoringu podręczników gimnazjalnych do języka polskiego, historii, i wiedzy o społeczeństwie (wychowanie obywatelskie i wychowanie do życia w rodzinie), Warszawa: Stowarzyszenie Otwarta Rzeczpospolita, pp. 30-53.

Chróścicki, Władysław (2008): »O ratuszu miasta Kałuszyn, jego budowie i ponad 100-letniej siedzibie Władz Miasta, o budynkach publicznych i urzędnikach.« In: Rocznik Kałuszyński 8, pp. 243-262.

Dębogórska, Agnieszka/Dylewska, Jolanta (2008): »Historia polsko-żydowska. Rozmowa z Jolantą Dylewską, autorką Po-lin. Okruchy pamięci.« In: Stopklatka, November 7 (https://archiwum.stopklatka.pl/news/historia-polsko-zydowska-rozmowa-z-jolanta-dylewska-autorka-po-lin-okruchy-pamieci-150170).

Douglas, Mary (1966): Purity and Danger: An Analysis of Concepts of Pollution and Taboo, London and New York: Routledge.

Dylewska, Jolanta/Bielas, Katarzyna (2008): »Plunięcie w wieczność.« In: Wysokie Obcasy November 9, pp. 10-18.

Engelking, Barbara (2016 [2011]): ›Such a Beautiful Sunny Day...‹ Jews Seeking Refuge in the Polish Countryside, 1942-1945, Jerusalem: Yad Vashem.

Glemp, Józef (2010): »Jedwabne – wina sprawiedliwie uznana.« In: Adam Michnik (ed.), Przeciw antysemityzmowi, Kraków: Universitas, pp. 570–573.

Goźliński, Paweł (2011): »Ostatni seans w Kałuszynie.« In: Gazeta Wyborcza April 1, p 21.

Grabowski, Jan (2011): Judenjagd: Polowanie na Żydów 1942-1945: Studium pewnego powiatu, Warszawa: Stowarzyszenie Centrum Badań nad Zagładą Żydów

Grabowski, Jan (2013 [2011]): Hunt for the Jews: Betrayal and Murder in German-Occupied Poland, Bloomington: Indiana University Press.

Gross, Jan Tomasz (2001 [2000]): Neighbors: The Destruction of the Jewish Community in Jedwabne, Poland, Princeton: Princeton University Press.

Hejke, Krzysztof (2009): Polesie, Poznań: Wydawnictwo Zyski S-ka.

Hilberg, Raul (1992): Perpetrators, Victims, Bystanders: The Jewish Catastrophe, 1933–1945, New York: Lime Tree.

Hollender, Barbara (2008): »O sąsiadach, którzy nagle zniknęli.« In: Rzeczpospolita November 5, p. A20.

Hurwic, Józef (1996): Wspomnienia i refleksje. Szkic autobiograficzny, Toruń: Wydawnictwo Comer.

Janicka, Elżbieta (2008): »Mord rytualny z aryjskiego paragrafu. O książce Jana Tomasza Grossa ›Strach. Antysemityzm w Polsce tuż po wojnie. Historia moralnej zapaści‹.« In: Kultura i Społeczeństwo 2, pp. 229-252.

Janicka, Elżbieta (2010): »Pamięć nieprzyswojona?« In: Kultura Współczesna 1/63, pp. 190–201.
Janion, Maria (2000): »Spór o antysemityzm. Sprzeczności, wątpliwości i pytania.« In: Maria Janion, Do Europy – tak, ale razem z naszymi umarłymi, Warszawa: Sic!, pp. 144–145.
Karski, Jan/Cichy, Michał (1995): »Widziałem.« In: Gazeta Wyborcza October 2-3, pp. 14-16.
Kletowski, Piotr (2008): »Do ciebie, człowieku!« In: Tygodnik Powszechny June 15 (https://www.tygodnikpowszechny.pl/do-ciebie-czlowieku-131007).
Lankosz, Magdalena/Waldman, Aylet (2011): »Zagonimy was batem do domu. Z Ayelet Waldman rozmawia Magdalena Lankosz«. In: Wysokie Obcasy August 27 (http://www.wysokieobcasy.pl/wysokie-obcasy/1,96856,10173372,Zagonimy_was_batem_do_domu.html).
Libionka, Dariusz (2006): »ZWZ-AK i Delegatura Rządu RP wobec eksterminacji Żydów polskich.« In: Andrzej Żbikowski, Polacy i Żydzi pod okupacją niemiecką 1939–1945. Studia i materiały, Warszawa: Wydawnictwo IPN, pp. 15–139.
Markiel, Tadeusz (2011): »Gniewczyna w czas wojny«. In: Tadeusz Markiel and Alina Skibińska, ›Jakie to ma znaczenie, czy zrobili to z chciwości?‹ Zagłada domu Trynczerów, Warszawa: Stowarzyszenie Centrum Badań nad Zagładą Żydów, pp. 21-133.
Ostrowska, Joanna (2009): »Polsko-żydowskie okruchy pamięci. Po-lin Jolanty Dylewskiej jako świadectwo zapomnianego świata«. In: Res Publica Nowa 5, pp. 68-72.
Perechodnik, Calek (1996 [1995]): Am I a Murderer? Testament of a Jewish Ghetto Policeman, Boulder: Westview Press.
Perechodnik, Calek (2004): Spowiedź. Dzieje rodziny żydowskiej podczas okupacji hitlerowskiej w Polsce, Warszawa: Ośrodek KARTA.
Sekula, Allan (1984): Photography Against the Grain: Essays and Photo Works, 1973-1983, Halifax: Press of Nova Scotia College of Art and Design.
Śmiałowski, Piotr (2008): »Po-lin. Okruchy pamięci«. In: Kino 10, pp: 90-91.
Sobolewski, Tadeusz (2008): »Film z tamtego świata«. In: Gazeta Wyborcza November 8-9, p. 13.

Sobolewski, Tadeusz (2009/2010): »Polskie kino dojrzewa«. In: Gazeta Wyborcza, December 31/January 1 (ttp://wyborcza.pl/1,75410,7410028, Polskie_kino_dojrzewa.html).

Tazbir, Janusz (2005): »O Kałuszynie i – sitarzach«. In: Rocznik Kałuszyński 5, pp. 9-17.

Tokarska-Bakir, Joanna (2004): »Żydzi u Kolberga.« In Joanna Tokarska-Bakir, Rzeczy mgliste. Eseje i studia, Sejny: Fundacja Pogranicze, pp. 66–67.

Tokarska-Bakir, Joanna (2011): »Następstwa Holocaustu w relacjach żydowskich i w pamięci polskiej prowincji w świetle badań etnograficznych.« In: Feliks Tych and Monika Adamczyk-Grabowska (eds.), Następstwa zagłady Żydów. Polska 1944–2010, Lublin: Wydawnictwo UMCS, pp. 775-811.

Tych, Feliks (1999): Długi cień Zagłady. Szkice historyczne, Warszawa: Żydowski Instytut Historyczny.

White, Hayden (1975): Metahistory: The Historical Imagination in Nineteenth-Century Europe, Baltimore and London: The John Hopkins University Press.

Wilczyk, Wojciech (2010): Niewinne oko nie istnieje/There's No Such Thing as an Innocent Eye, Łódź: Atlas Sztuki.

Wróblewski, Janusz (2008): »›Po-lin. Okruchy pamięci.‹ Świadectwa koegzystencji Żydów i Polaków na Kresach Wschodnich«. In: Polityka November 10 (http://www.polityka.pl/kultura/film/273316,1,recenzja-filmu-po-lin-rez-jolanta-dylewska.read).

Wyspiański, Stanisław (2012 [1901]): The Wedding, London: Oberon Classics.

Zawadzka, Anna (2009): »Żydokomuna. Szkic do socjologicznej analizy źródeł historycznych.« In: Societas/Communitas 2, pp. 199–243.

Zawadzki, Paul (2010): »Polska«. In: Léon Poliakov (ed.), Historia antysemityzmu 1945–1993, Kraków: Universitas, pp. 215-247.

Żbikowski, Andrzej (2008 [1986]): »Epilogue.« In: Samuel Willenberg, Revolt in Treblinka, Warszawa: Żydowski Instytut Historyczny, pp. 290-310.

Żukowski, Tomasz (2001a): »Mówić, nie mówiąc za wiele. O dyskusji w sprawie Jedwabnego.« In: Bez Dogmatu 47, 26–27.

Żukowski, Tomasz (2001b): »Panu Bogu świeczkę i diabłu ogarek.« In: Midrasz 6/50, pp. 40–42.

Żukowski, Tomasz (2013 [2010]): »Savoir-vivre: Ironic Strategies in Calek Perechodnik's ›Confession‹.« In: Teksty Drugie 2, pp. 166-181.

Authors

Dziuban, Zuzanna, is a postdoctoral researcher and lecturer at the University of Amsterdam and Freie University of Berlin. Her research focus is on memory studies, dead body studies, and the afterlives of the Holocaust. She is the author of *Obcość, bezdomność, utrata. Wymiary atopii współczesnego doświadczenia kulturowego* [Foreignness, Homelessness, Loss: Dimensions of Atopia of Contemporary Cultural Experience, 2009] and editor of *Mapping the 'Forensic Turn': Engagements with Materialities of Mass Death in Holocaust Studies and Beyond* (2017).

Janicka, Elżbieta, is a literary historian and visual artist. She is an Associate Professor at the Institute of Slavic Studies of the Polish Academy of Science in Warsaw. Her research interests lie with the socio-cultural legitimacy of violence and exclusion, with a special focus on Polish antisemitism. She is the author of the monographs *Sztuka czy naród? Monografia pisarska Andrzeja Trzebińskiego* [The Art or the Nation? On Andrzej Trzebinski's Literary Output, 2006], and *Festung Warschau* [Fortress Warsaw, 2011], and coauthor of *Przemoc filosemicka? Nowe polskie narracje o Żydach po roku 2000* [Philosemitic Violence? New Polish Narratives on Jews after 2000, 2016, with Tomasz Żukowski].

Matyjaszek, Konrad, is an architect and cultural studies researcher. He is an Assistant Professor at the Institute of Slavic Studies of the Polish Academy of Sciences in Warsaw. His work focuses on architecture and urban public spaces as devices of collective identity production, on Polish discourses of antisemitism and racism, and on Eastern European narratives of modernity and modernization. He is the author of the forthcoming monograph

Produkcja przestrzeni żydowskiej w dawnej i współczesnej Polsce [The Production of Jewish Space in the Cities of Premodern and Contemporary Poland, 2019].
ORCID 0000-0002-0236-4524

Molisak, Alina, is an Associate Professor at the Institute of Polish Literature of the Faculty of Polish Studies at the University of Warsaw. She was a lecturer at the Humboldt University of Berlin and University of Hamburg. She is the author of monographs *Judaizm jako los. Rzecz o Bogdanie Wojdowskim* [Judaism as a Fate: On Bogdan Wojdowski, 2004] and *Żydowska Warszawa – żydowski Berlin. Literacki portret miasta w pierwszej połowie XX wieku* [Jewish Warsaw – Jewish Berlin: Literary Portrait of the City at the Beginning of the Twentieth Century, 2016].
ORCID 0000-0002-1862-8782

Sendyka, Roma, is a Director of the Research Center for Memory Cultures, and Associate Professor at the Department of Anthropology of Literature and Cultural Studies of the Jagiellonian University in Krakow. Her areas of expertise cover cultural theory, visual culture studies, and memory studies. She focuses on relations between images, sites and memory, and, currently, is working on a project on non-sites of memory in Central and Eastern Europe. She is the author of the monographs *Nowoczesny esej. Studium historycznej świadomości gatunku* [The Modern Essay: Study of the 20th Century Critical Approach to the Genre, 2006] and *Od kultury ›ja‹ do kultury ›siebie‹. O zwrotnych formach w projektach tożsamościowych* [From the I-Culture to the Culture of the Self: On Reflexive Forms in Identity Projects, 2015].

Ubertowska, Aleksandra, is a Professor of Modern Polish Studies at the University of Gdańsk. Her area of expertise covers Holocaust literature and art, memory studies, and ecocriticism. She is the author of numerous journal articles and books, including the monographs *Świadectwo, trauma, głos. Literackie reprezentacje Holokaustu* [Testimony, Trauma, Voice: Literary Representations of the Holocaust, 2007] and *Holokaust. Auto(tanato)grafie* [Holocaust Auto(thanato)graphies, 2014].

Waligórska, Magdalena, is an Assistant Professor for East European History and Culture at the University of Bremen. Her fields of interest include the revival of Jewish heritage in post-Holocaust Europe, representations of Jews in Polish and German popular culture, as well as Holocaust commemoration and nationalism studies. She is the author of *Klezmer's Afterlife: An Ethnography of the Jewish Music Revival in Poland and Germany* (2013) and co-editor of *Jewish Translation – Translating Jewishness* (2018).

Żukowski, Tomasz, is a literary historian and Associate Professor at the Department of Contemporary Literature and Social Communication, and at the Institute of Literary Research of the Polish Academy of Sciences in Warsaw. His interests focus on the problematics of identity at the point of convergence between minorities and the dominant group, on discursive mechanisms pertaining to the Shoah in Poland, and discourses around the Polish People's Republic. He is the author of *Obrazy Chrystusa w twórczości Aleksandra Wata i Tadeusza Różewicza* [Images of Christ in the Works of Aleksander Wat and Tadeusz Różewicz, 2014], and coauthor of *Przemoc filosemicka? Nowe polskie narracje o Żydach po roku 2000* [Philo-Semitic Violence? New Polish Narratives on Jews after 2000, 2016, with Elżbieta Janicka].